The Only Book I'll Ever Write

Dr Paul Coffey

In loving memory of my husband, Paul

•

Thank you

Laura, Patrick and Duncan, our wonderful children who encouraged Paul to write in the first place and then helped by reading drafts, giving suggestions and editing.

Lucia, for doing the lovely artwork on the cover of this book.

Family and friends who read the text and gave feedback which helped to shape this book.

The medical and nursing teams in Oxford and London; you were so helpful, kind and supportive.

The biggest thank you goes to my wonderful husband who wrote this memoir for us and for others. He worked hard and lived life to the full. He was just amazing and I miss him so much.

•

The names of patients, colleagues and the people treating Paul have been changed to protect their identities.

Contents

Preface

In 2012 at the age of 60 Dr. Paul Coffey ran his first marathon. In late 2016 he entered the ballot in the hope of getting a place again. That was not to be.

Towards the end of his working life, in late 2016, Paul was diagnosed with stage four stomach cancer. He was given a very short life expectancy which forced him to abruptly retire from the work he loved. The news was received with disbelief and caused emotional turmoil. In a twist of fate, two weeks later the diagnosis was revised to a rarer neuroendocrine cancer with a longer life expectancy. It was still cancer. It had still spread widely but from despair emerged a glimmer of hope. Paul's family encouraged him to write about his experiences.

Paul was born in 1952, the youngest of four siblings and both his parents were GPs. He followed in their footsteps qualifying as a doctor in 1975 and he discusses the many changes that took place in general practice from the 1950s to the present day.

Paul enjoyed the process of creative writing enormously and this memoir is peppered with anecdotes from his professional life. He had a wonderful way with words writing about even the most mundane events in a humorous way.

Sadly, Paul died in 2021. His wife Jane completed the last chapter describing how stoic and brave he was throughout his illness. Never 'why me?' only 'why not me?'.

Chapter 1

You Learn a Lot From Your Patients

'I'm very sorry' I said, after telling Peter that his barium meal had revealed stomach cancer.

I was, indeed, very sorry to have to break the news to him, as I would have been to anyone. But Peter wasn't just anyone. There was something about him that made him a bit different. In his fifties, with a craggy face and steel grey hair, there was a physical robustness about him that spoke of his time as a paratrooper. He looked a pretty tough customer and the fact that he was Scottish seemed to accentuate the effect – at least to my eye. In contrast to his rugged appearance, he spoke with an educated, soft Edinburgh burr and, on the few occasions I'd seen him in the surgery, had been impressively polite, measured and considerate. He'd been very supportive and non-judgmental of his brother, Archie, who had developed alcholic cirrhosis, brought on, Peter explained, by the stress of working on oil rigs. Peter had shown great tenderness and love towards him, caring for him in his own home for the final few months. There was, I suppose, a sort of nobility about Peter.

And now this admirable man was, in all likelihood, going to die. And probably very soon. It wouldn't be an easy death either, judging from the patients of mine who had developed stomach cancer. None had lived for even a year, but this was almost three decades ago and things may be a little better now.

I paused deliberately to let the words 'stomach' and 'cancer' sink in. I knew he'd be reeling from the shock, trying to take in the enormity of what he'd just heard. He'd probably be speechless initially and a little emotional, maybe even tearful and ask me if there was any doubt about the diagnosis. He'd want to know what would happen now and what treatments might help. And how quickly he could see a specialist. He might ask what he should tell his wife and family. I hoped he wouldn't ask me how long he would have. At least not yet.

The pause was short-lived.

Maybe my face had betrayed too much. Maybe my voice had faltered a little or I'd looked distressed as I spoke to him. Though I doubt it. Even then, in the early nineties, I was pretty experienced. Attending boarding school from a young age had made me develop a pretty tough outer shell and usually able to break bad news, without betraying any emotion.

'Oh, please don't feel sorry for me doctor,' he said calmly, 'I've got a good wife and a great family and I know that when I die they will definitely miss me, which means in my book that I've had a successful life – that my life has been worth living. So, I'm OK about it. Really.'

He was comforting me. Reassuring me that he could accept and deal with what was ahead of him.

My pause was not intentional this time. I was unprepared for such a selfless response and was in awe of his reaction. I had seen people in similar straits react with quiet dignity, but for his first thought to make the moment easier for his doctor, was extraordinary. It was humbling. I felt very privileged to be his GP.

Peter's simple explanation of what counts in life had a profound effect on me. Over subsequent decades I've repeated his philosophy many times to patients and friends in similar situations. I hope it provides a measure of reassurance and comfort that, although their lives may be ending, they have similarly been worthwhile.

You learn a lot from your patients.

It might not be possible for many of us to deal with a terminal diagnosis with quite as much dignity and fortitude as Peter did, whose story I shall continue later, but I have had him in mind a lot and have tried to emulate him as best I can.

Despite the lessons I learnt from patients like Peter over the thirty-six years I was a GP, I was unprepared for the vagaries of becoming one. It still feels shocking years later to be on the receiving end of medical advice rather than dispensing it and to have to rely on colleagues for, in effect, my very existence. The unfamiliarity of not being in charge in a consulting room and the loss of control that comes with being a patient are alien to all doctors. It's far from easy treating doctors but, having been in both positions, it's definitely harder for a doctor to be a patient.

My patient experience started in October 2016, when I was diagnosed with advanced inoperable (or stage four) stomach cancer and told I would in all likelihood not be alive for more than a few months. That diagnosis was later changed to a different, rare form of cancer with much less certainty about its outcome.

No medical training can prepare you for the feelings of despair and uncertainty this entailed, but Peter's lesson made it a lot easier than it otherwise would have been. His simple, beautiful philosophy has come to mind on many occasions, particularly when someone called round or accompanied me on a walk, wrote a note offering to help or sent flowers. Each time it was literally life-affirming.

How do I feel about having cancer? In truth, just unlucky. My view, in common with most of the medical profession, is that all of us have a chance of getting any cancer and it is a lottery whether your number comes up or that of your neighbour. You can increase your risks of certain cancers by, for example, smoking, being obese, drinking excessively and having a poor diet, and you may have an increased risk with some cancers that run in families, but you can't really do anything to remove the inherent risk. So 'Why me?' becomes simply 'Why not me?' That awful randomness means any of us can get just about anything. There are really no known risk factors for my cancer other than occasionally it can run in families, although it doesn't in mine, so there is no way I can properly beat myself up for getting it. Not that that has stopped me though.

I feel that generally I've had a pretty reasonable share of good luck in life and, on the occasion of our fortieth wedding anniversary celebration a few years ago, expressed this in the toast to my wife Jane:

'Forty years have gone so fast that I've been asking myself what has happened to time since 1976. My theory is that if you have the great good fortune to be married to someone as fantastic as Jane and then are blessed with three amazing children, the Gods determine that you have been given far too many blessings and riches for one person and so make forty years disappear in the blink of an eye'.

My nephew, who records with the band 'Laish', turned those words into a beautiful song 'The Blink of an Eye' which was a wonderful gift.

Looking back on that toast, I think I was aware at the time, that my good luck might well run out sometime, though I couldn't have expected it to happen so quickly. With hindsight, it almost seems as if, in speaking of my good fortune, I was indeed tempting the Gods to decide that enough was enough.

Tempting the Gods is not listed in the medical books as a cancer risk factor.

Chapter 2

Life Before General Practice

I was born in a small village in rural Lincolnshire in 1952. My parents, Patrick and Mary, were both GPs who had come over from Ireland and met in England, marrying in 1945. It's a bit of a cliché, but still absolutely true, that an Irish mother then, above all else, wanted a son, who, if things went well, might become a priest and if the family was very blessed, perhaps even a bishop. Maybe this is no longer yearned for quite as much in the light of subsequent revelations about the clergy, but it was indisputably the case then. Nonetheless, when my sister Máire was born in 1947 there was great rejoicing at her birth. Hopefully the next baby would be a boy. Catherine came along in 1948. Then Helen in 1950. Trusting in the science of medical statistics – which as a discipline had not yet been dreamt up – my dogged parents persisted until in 1952 they were finally blessed with a boy. Yours truly was born at home and had the requisite number of toes and other bits and pieces and didn't look much odder than any other new-born baby does.

Christened 'Paul', after an Aunt who, perhaps a little surprisingly, had taken the name of 'Paul' as her religious name when she became a nun, and 'Patrick', after my Dad and millions of other Irish first-born sons, I was inevitably, the apple of my mother's eye and spoilt rotten, much to the chagrin of my sisters. Doubtless a degree of overprotectiveness on her part was understandable, as one night, whilst being bathed in the kitchen, my Dad noticed a slight bend in my spine – a scoliosis. This necessitated a period in hospital in a plaster of Paris straightjacket and later a steel and leather contraption that I had to wear until I reached my teens. This was to try to straighten me up, the legacy of which is a stiff back. One result of this was that no matter how annoying I was being, my sisters were absolutely forbidden from fighting with me. All my character failings I blame on having three older sisters and a doting Irish mother. However, over half a century later, any sense of resentment among my sisters seems to have gone, which is pretty magnanimous of them, all things considered.

I vaguely remember feeling a bit self-conscious about putting the steel and leather jacket on, but it had some advantages. At the age of about eleven, after a playground fight, my vanquished opponent tearfully protested that it had been an unfair fight as he had hurt his fist thumping the steel spine on my back.

He would have lost anyway.

My father ran the village General Practice with support from my mother who also did public health clinics. They had a three-roomed surgery across the drive from our house. My father did most of the consulting in the middle room whilst my mother was in a small dispensary in the next room, with the door ajar, so that she could hear what was being discussed and thereby anticipate the medication that would be needed, which was then ready before the patient left the consulting room. There wasn't an appointment system, so patients just waited and were seen in the order they arrived in. There were no receptionists, secretaries, nurses or dispensers and the morning and evening surgeries only lasted about an hour but there were lots of home visits. All rather different from today's general practice. To enable my parents to do their work, they employed someone to answer the phone when they were out or to answer the door to patients who called round if they didn't have a phone and also, to look after us. They also employed a daily cleaner and a gardener/odd job man who also drove us to and from our school six miles away in my Dad's pride and joy, his Morse-type Jaguar. I really loved that car.

My Dad had a half-day on a Thursday and alternate Sundays off but was on-call every night of the week. Holidays were only made possible by employing a locum GP to stay at the house while we were away:

Pat, a lovely retired Irish GP, was doing a locum and staying in our house. My Mum had got back from her holiday the day before Pat's stint finished. That night she heard the phone ring and was expecting to hear Pat go down the stairs to do the call, as in those days, night calls were few and far between and were always for something important. But Pat didn't go down the stairs. She knocked on his bedroom door. There was no reply, so she went in. Pat was snoring away with the phone dangling and a worried mother shouting down the phone trying to wake him up! My Mum replaced the receiver and did the call herself. No mention of the incident was ever made, Pat obviously having no recollection. That was Pat's last stint at the practice.

My Dad was well respected and when he drove by, many of the local men touched their forelocks, as they might have done to the local squire in earlier times. As the son of such an important local figure I was frequently asked by patients and family friends if I planned to follow in my Dad's footsteps – my sisters, of course, weren't asked that as female GPs were rare, in contrast to now, when there are more female GPs coming into the profession than men.

Aside from the other professions and businessmen, the most prosperous people in the area tended to be farmers often with many thousands of acres. Shamefully, I remember reproaching my mother for not having a farm to pass on to me so that, whilst other friends could simply take over the family farm, I would be forced to make my own way in the world.

My parents were devout Catholics and brought us all up in the Roman Catholic faith which I have held onto, tenuously at times, all my life. In the absence of a local Catholic school, they sent me, at the age of nine, to a Catholic boarding school run by the clergy, sixty miles away. I only saw my parents at half term because of the onerous on-call duty. Inevitably, at that age, I was a bit homesick. The sense of loneliness, of not being special to anyone in the school, was made worse by the realisation that one of the teachers, then in his mid-sixties, clearly had great favourites, but I wasn't one of them. When the lights went out, he would kneel by their beds for many minutes in the dark and also invite them to his room with the promise of a present. I was never singled out for such special treatment and felt envious and a bit rejected.

Four decades later, after yet another practice meeting about Child Sex Abuse, it suddenly hit me between the eyes, that I had probably been very lucky not to have been one of his favourites. I hadn't wanted to upset my parents by telling them about how jealous I was of the favourites, as this would have revealed my homesickness, so of course never mentioned it to them or anyone else for that matter. Despite being someone who, as part of his work, was on the alert for child abuse, I had not realised what had possibly been happening in my childhood.

I suppose I enjoyed school, though it didn't really cross my mind then to wonder whether I enjoyed it or not. I think living away from home may have made me more resilient in my work and able to keep a stiff upper lip when the going got tough, but my family suspects that it also made me a bit closed-in and undemonstrative. I did enjoy school sport, which there was rather a lot of and which I was fairly good at. It fostered in me a strong competitive streak so that when I played with my own children, my wife called me 'Competitive Dad' after the 'Fast Show' character.

How would my schoolboy-self have been seen by others? Well, if I had to pick one word, I guess it would probably be 'annoying' or maybe even 'arrogant'. I was in the top academic stream in my year, so felt that I was a bit of an intellectual and could therefore challenge the teachers, or indeed anyone, on anything and everything and so frequently did. I think, with hindsight, my sporting prowess probably saved me from some well-deserved beatings.

Eventually the time came to decide about a career. We enjoyed a pretty decent lifestyle at home and of course my Dad had the Jag, so doing medicine seemed very appealing. The only problem with this was that I was far better at the arts than physics and chemistry, which were mandatory 'A' level subjects to get into medical school. I had little choice therefore but to give up the ambition to become a doctor and the suggestion from a career advisory organisation, was that I was well suited to becoming a travel agent. Fate, however, intervened and I did a little better than expected in my physics and chemistry 'O' levels, as GCSE's were called then, raising the possibility that I might just be able to manage them at 'A' level. Around this time, sadly, my Mother had to have surgery for breast cancer. To make matters much worse, a short while later, while she was having a debilitating course of radiotherapy, my Dad had a devastating brain haemorrhage. This was caused by a weakness in an artery in the brain – an aneurysm – rupturing, and as a result, he was in a coma in hospital for three months. He was only fifty-three and had to retire. His speech was badly affected and he became dependent on my mother. Tragically our gardener, who we all loved and was very much a part of the family, was killed in a car accident around this time, so all in all it was a very difficult, very emotional time for everyone. I was greatly saddened to see my Dad physically so diminished and knew it would make him and also my mother, really happy to see me following in his footsteps. That spurred me on to take, what was a huge risk for me, and choose 'A' level sciences. In a less highly charged emotional time I would undoubtedly have played to my strengths and opted for arts at 'A' level …...and my life would have taken a very different course.

My mother, who had qualified at Galway University and had been top of her year academically, suggested I apply for some Irish universities including her old Alma Mater where two of her brothers had also done medicine. By this time, she was running the practice on her own with help from a dispenser. Lots of weak candidates, she assured me, got through the back door to medicine that way. So, I wrote to the Dean of Galway medical school and said that, on the advice of my mother and my two doctor uncles, I felt that Galway would be the best place in the whole world for me to study medicine. With such a pedigree, I was surely guaranteed a place and possibly the keys to the city to boot.

The Dean replied: 'regrettably the medical school is only considering overseas candidates from third world countries and we don't yet regard England as a third world country.'

Then I had some good luck. I randomly applied to St George's medical school in London, and together with another boy from my school, was invited for interview. The standard requirement for medicine in those far off days, was a B and two C's or, if you were lucky, three C's. Now candidates have to have A grades or A star grades of course. Unbelievably, I was offered a place if I just passed my 'A' levels i.e. if I just got three E's. The other boy from my school was not offered a place at all. Even I could manage three E's – just – so, much to the delight and disbelief of my Mum, I got into medical school. Sadly, my Dad didn't live to see that, as he had died from a second brain haemorrhage a few months before.

Years later, I asked the Dean, who had given me the place, why he had turned down the other boy. 'Was he a rugby player?' the Dean asked. He was and a good one at that. 'Well then that would have been why I didn't accept him.' He went on to explain that as St George's was too small a medical school to be competitive at rugby, which was regarded as the most prestigious sport amongst medical schools. The Dean looked for sportsmen (not women – who were only allowed into St George's in token numbers then anyway) who were accomplished in sports other than rugby. This was in the hope of picking up other hospital sports cups. I was too slight for rugby, so played hockey and tennis, and hence was considered perfect, even though St George's didn't have a hockey team. Amazing to think my whole career turned on not being a rugger bugger.

The first year and a half was spent at King's College in the Strand doing sciences and theory, after which we went to St George's Hospital to do clinical studies. I felt a bit stunned to find myself in such a privileged position as, I think, did most of my fellow students, and also wondered whether I had the necessary mental toughness to cope with cutting up cadavers which was required to learn anatomy. On the first day in the dissection room where the cadavers were laid out on tables, we soon found out. Dickie, the doctor in charge, explained that he wanted to show us something and that it was necessary for us to be able to look at it without fainting. He pointed to a white bucket with a lid on in the corner and encouraged us to brace ourselves for the horror that awaited.

'Come up, one by one, look inside the bucket then without speaking to anyone else, leave the room and stay outside'.

One by one people went up, some with an outward show of cockiness, opened the lid and peered into the bucket. To a man or woman, each yelled out with horror and rushed out.

Eventually it was my turn. I'd be the exception and not scream out – hopefully. Or would I? With a show of false bravado, I marched up, opened the lid, screamed and rushed out. As did literally everyone after me. What was in the bucket? Nothing. It was completely empty. Dickie had taught us a lesson.

At the end of the eighteen months, we had to pass an exam to enable us to move on to St George's Hospital and graduate from dead bodies to real patients. My student year group evidently became known as 'Coffey's lot' amongst the lecturers. This, I regret to say, was not because I was a brilliant student or showed outstanding leadership qualities and was far from a flattering description. It was predicated on two events. The first was my notorious performance in the introductory pathology exam taken during the early part of the hospital stage of our training. Older students who I played football with, had assured me, that once you got to the hospital part of training, absolutely no more work was required and that this exam didn't matter at all. Unwisely I had taken them at their word and was subsequently very alarmed to find that others in my year had actually done a lot of work. I went down with all guns blazing. No-one had ever been required to re-sit the introductory pathology exam, but that dubious honour was earned by yours truly and another miscreant in my year, who later abandoned the course and, according to legend, became a South London gangster.

The other 'first' which marked me out, was to be in the first group of students ever to be thrown off a 'firm.' A firm in those days consisted of a consultant, his or her junior staff (registrars and housemen), and the medical students who were allocated to tag along to the consultant's ward rounds and clinics and were taught by the doctors on the firm. Five of us had the misfortune to be allocated to the Professor of Medicine's firm. He was a severe, haughty figure, utterly brilliant but not given to suffering fools gladly, or in our case, at all. He was prone to biting sarcasm and famously said to a hapless student who, for once, had correctly answered a question: 'I see there are gaps in your ignorance'. He finally had enough of us not turning up to listen to the gems of knowledge he sprinkled liberally on his ward rounds, and of the inane answers we gave to his questions and informed the Dean of the medical school that he would not allow us to continue attending his clinics and ward rounds. He only ever spoke kindly to me once when he enquired whether I was really sure I wanted to continue in medicine. I assured him I did – another wrong answer in his view. We were banished to St James Hospital in Balham which had never had medical students, and thereafter we were referred to as 'The Balham Boys.' I had achieved further unwanted notoriety.

St George's was spread across a huge complex in Tooting and the original small hospital at Hyde Park Corner which now, as 'The Lanesborough' is one of the most expensive hotels in London. The college bar overlooked Knightsbridge and Hyde Park and boasted a really wonderful atmosphere and was the most special place to chat over a drink. It was called 'the clubroom' as it looked and felt like a gentleman's club and we loved it. It was also at a disco in the clubroom that I met my wife Jane whom I married in 1976. Henry, the barman, on whom Al Murray's pub landlord could easily have been based, was a jolly good sort even playing in goal for me once when I ran the second eleven football team. So special was the clubroom's ambience that drinking pints of beer felt amazingly natural there and we students were soon proud to realise that we had become quite heavy drinkers, able to down copious pints of beer with impunity and still go to lectures the next day. It was so very, very different from drinking in dreary South London pubs near our flats where, after a few pints, we felt really quite affected. Like all things that are too good to be true, it was. Henry eventually parted company with St George's because he had been diluting the beer to homeopathic levels.

After five, very undistinguished years as a student, the 'final' exams we had to pass to qualify as doctors loomed large. Just before them, exams were held for the various prizes awarded to students who were felt to be outstanding in the year in surgery, medicine or obstetrics. My friends were not high flyers, so I was surprised to find that one of them, Bob, had entered the medicine prize exam. He explained that, of course, he knew perfectly well that he didn't have a prayer of getting the prize, but he felt it would be good practice for finals and encouraged me to enter as well – so I did. Not for the first time with medical exams, I hadn't a clue about most of the questions and so bemused was the Professor of Medicine to find himself examining me for the medicine prize that he took great delight in taking the mickey out of me. The exam didn't seem to have gone well. At all. However, as I have repeatedly told my children, when they have been downcast after a tough exam, you never can tell how it went. My fellow examinees, amongst whom were the supposed highflyers in our year, did not get the medicine prize. Nor did I. It was decided that the standard of entry had been so low that, most unusually, no one was awarded the medicine prize that year. Were Bob and I responsible for dragging the standard down? Undoubtedly, but at least both of us managed to later pass our finals.

I had always wanted to follow in my parents' footsteps and be a GP, so in 1977 I entered a three-year GP vocational training programme in Boston, which was near my Mum's practice, where I gained experience working in a variety of hospital specialities that are important for a GP to be competent in. I was also assigned to be trained in a very isolated rural general practice in Lincolnshire where there was an aptly named restaurant called 'The End of the World'.

I was despatched one morning to visit Harry, a retired farmworker who was very distressed because his wife had disappeared. I introduced myself to an elderly lady who answered the door, who, I assumed, was a neighbour or family friend and then spoke to the old man.

'I'm very sorry to hear your wife is missing' I said.

'I'm his wife' interrupted the elderly woman looking rather upset.

'Oh, it's great news that your wife is back', I said to Harry.

'That old hag - she's not my wife. This is my wife' he said proudly pointing to the attractive young bride in the wedding photo taken many decades before.

Not for the first nor last time in my work I was lost for words. Poor Harry was in a 'confusional state' most probably from a bladder infection.

My heart went out to his poor wife.

Many doctors say they only really learnt about medicine after they qualified. I can vouch for that, and the other old adages that you learn from your patients and from your mistakes. Bit unfortunate for patients that the latter two are so inextricably linked.

I had learnt from my medical student years and the introductory pathology exam debacle that it had been a big mistake not to have been a lot more serious about what I was doing, so had become much more diligent about studying my craft. I have always regarded 'medicine', the specialty that consultant physicians practise in hospitals, as opposed to surgery or gynaecology, to be the bedrock of general practice, so felt it would stand me in good stead if I raised my game in that area. I had also discovered that I was actually quite good at passing exams if I applied myself:

I was within touching distance of passing the MRCP exam – Membership of The Royal College of Physicians – which was the qualification required to pursue a career as a hospital consultant physician. It wasn't required for GPs but would be prestigious to have it and probably help me procure a good GP partnership.

A few years before I had been working at St George's in Hyde Park Corner as a 'house physician'. St George's was due to close and consequently not many patients were being sent there. The very eminent senior cardiologist, called a meeting to discuss the problem and as recompense for not having many patients to gain experience on, said we could tag along on their ward rounds to see patients with rare conditions. These were always oversubscribed to by senior doctors wanting to learn from such giants of the medical world. Was that satisfactory they asked?

'No!' a junior doctor had the temerity to say, 'I want to see real patients, ill patients – I'm not interested in seeing very rare conditions.'

The consultant was flabbergasted. Who was this jumped-up character that could possibly look such a gift horse in the mouth? It was in fact the doctor that was equally flabbergasted to find himself facing the same consultant in the viva for the MRCP. Maybe he wouldn't recognise or remember me?

He introduced himself and then introduced me to his colleague, who would also test my medical knowledge.

'This is Dr Coffey…..' His voice trailed away as, the no doubt unpleasant memory, of who I was flooded back.

'I know Coffey. Yes, I know Coffey, so you'd better start with the questions'

His colleague asked me a few questions that I could make a reasonable stab at. Then he took over and asked me some impossibly difficult questions that I really hadn't a clue about, although of course I did my best to guess the answers. I was undone. He had realised why he remembered me and had exacted his revenge.

Reeling from the ordeal, I composed a letter of complaint to the Royal College of Physicians, about his attitude and his impossible questions.

Never sent it though.

He had passed me after all and I had MRCP after my name. Maybe he felt he had to overcompensate for disliking me, by allowing me a pass. Or, unlikely as it may have seemed, perhaps my answers to him had been correct.

Later I passed the Membership of The Royal College of General Practitioners exam which, all in all, made me reasonably well-equipped to survive as a GP and more importantly, for my patients to survive me.

Chapter 3

Thirty-Six Years of Being a General Practitioner

I joined my practice in rural West Oxfordshire in 1980 and worked for over thirty-six years until my cancer was discovered. In many ways I am a GP cliché. I live in a biggish house, drive decent cars, (though sadly never a Jag), and, of course, I play golf. In short, I'm a stereotypical GP. You might assume I voted Tory and liked to hunt, but like many assumptions, both would be wrong.

There was a lot about my job that I really loved. Treating patients like Peter is a real privilege and rewarding at every level. There is great intellectual satisfaction to be had from applying the science of medicine, doing careful examinations and intricate tests and subsequently treating any revealed illness with the latest evidence-based drugs and hopefully seeing patients respond as a result. The effect sometimes can be almost magical. Equally rewarding is practising the 'art' of medicine, whereby you treat a patient as a person, with his or her particular characteristics, health beliefs, fears, foibles and expectations, rather than as simply a body with a medical condition.

William Osler, an eminent physician and thinker of yesteryear, summed that up with his assertion that:

'it is much more important to know what sort of patient has a disease, than what sort of disease a patient has.'

A few years after becoming a GP, a retired bowel surgeon requested a home visit for his wife, who had had some chest pains. He was an old school patrician in the mould of Harold MacMillan. He was charming and as a colleague, I wanted to give his wife a five-star service. I assessed her and concluded that she had indeed had a heart attack but was stable and in no pain. Nowadays there would be no question that she needed to be in hospital, but in the 1980s it was regarded as a reasonable option to keep older patients at home, if they were stable, to avoid the stress of an admission. The patient preferred to let her husband decide her fate, so, over the only glass of sherry I ever drank at a patient's house, I went through the diagnosis and the option of her staying at home with him.

He looked surprised and startled that the option of her remaining at home had even been raised:

'You do know that we don't have any live-in staff, don't you?' he said solemnly.

I admitted the patient – I'm sure Osler would have concurred!

I didn't really understand the importance of knowing your patients when I first joined my practice in 1980. I felt that my job was simply to diagnose and treat patients, rather I suppose, like Martin Clune's Doc Martin. I shouldn't need to involve myself in a patient's social situation – that was for social workers and the like. However, by the time I finished, I took the polar opposite view and found myself completely in agreement with Osler. What I realised was that the essence of my job, and what gave me the greatest satisfaction, was simply that it was all about helping people. As a prospective medical student, if asked why you wanted to be a doctor that is probably what you would say. Somewhere along the line I'd forgotten that helping people matters more than being able to diagnose rare conditions. Sadly, research shows that doctor empathy declines throughout medical school and during early hospital jobs.

Most people have the instinct to want to help others which is why so many do unpaid voluntary work. To be paid to help people was a bonus. If you pushed me to say which part of the job I valued most, it would to have been present at, and be able to help at, the big moments in people's lives. Few moments are more significant than the end of a life and to be trusted to help then was a real privilege. It helped considerably if the patient was someone I knew well from consultations over many years, so that there was then a deep well of trust on both sides. Then I felt I could make an almost unique difference to them and their families. It didn't always go well, even if I and the end of life team tried very hard, but I always hoped that my patient and his or her family would feel confident that I really cared that the very best was done for them. As the callow youth of 1980 became more aware of what General Practice should really be about, the relationships with patients, often built up over many years and decades, became the source of great satisfaction. That was the reason I did my job for so long.

Brian, was a longstanding patient of mine who was a retired teacher and rather surprisingly perhaps, given his very gentle nature, had been a tank commander in the second world war. He was a considerate, kind and charming man who I felt lucky to have as a patient. When the end of his life approached, I visited him at home on several occasions and on one met the local vicar leaving as I arrived. Oddly enough that was the only occasion in my career when I met a vicar or priest or any religious leader at a patient's house. Maybe they did their visiting in the mornings and we in the afternoons.

It seemed that Brian's spiritual needs as well as his physical ones were being attended to which seemed to be exactly what one would hope for at the end of one's own life.

Unlike my student persona, in my professional life I worked pretty hard because there was a huge amount of work that simply had to be done. You didn't really need self-discipline to do it as there was no way of avoiding the work – it just kept coming – and there was no one else to do it. Oddly perhaps, I didn't really resent this. A full day for me started at 8 am when I checked results and letters that had come in since I last logged onto the computer. Appointments started at 8.30 am and carried on at ten or twelve minute intervals until midday with urgent visits fitted in if necessary. Then there were phone calls to patients or colleagues, interspersed with checking and updating prescriptions and if possible, doing referral letters to hospital consultants. Lunch was often spent in a meeting with the partners either discussing clinical issues or something relevant to the organisation of general practice. Visits were then squeezed in before starting the afternoon surgery at 2.50 pm when the work cycle started again. Another notional break for tea and then into the evening surgery which generally finished around 6.30 pm. Then began, usually a couple of hours, of reading more letters and more results that had come in during the day.

It was pretty full on and it was very rarely possible to get all the work done in a day. Days off and weekends were the times when you could catch up. The aim always was to be right up to date with everything before starting the week on Monday. Not to be on top of your work would add considerable stress to an already demanding job. In later years, the advance of technology meant that we were able to link our home computers to the surgery ones and do this from home, which was a lot better than spending weekends in the surgery.

One Saturday I had cycled the two miles from my house to the surgery and was ensconced in my consulting room beavering away. I came across the blood test of a lovely elderly patient called Rose, who disliked coming to the surgery, so I always phoned her with the results of her tests. I thought I'd ring her there and then to save a few precious minutes later in the week. As usual she was friendly and pleased to hear the result was OK but, after a while, I formed the impression that she wasn't listening and got no response to further questions.

Then I heard loud snoring – or was it just possible that it was noisy, laboured breathing? I tried shouting but still no response. I began to worry that it might be something called Cheyne-Stokes breathing which is an abnormal pattern of breathing that can signify a stroke or some other serious condition.

What to do? I knew the address, but it would have taken me probably twenty-five minutes to cycle to it and in any case, I didn't have my medical bag and equipment with me. To cycle home to pick up my bag and then drive to the patient's house would have taken just as long. I didn't want to call a 999 ambulance as she might just be asleep and the paramedics wouldn't be able to get into the house anyway if it was locked. Her son lived some distance away as well. Thanks to the practice computer I was able to ring her neighbour and asked him to go around and check that she was OK. He was back on the phone a couple of minutes later. 'She's slumped over her sofa with the phone off the hook and is not responding to my ringing the doorbell or banging on the window.'

I called an emergency ambulance and later rang the neighbour to see if Rose was OK.

Sadly, she had died.

I was shocked to think I had actually been talking to her as she died. What were the chances of that happening?

I recounted the story to my then medical student son Duncan, whose black humoured response was:

'Well I knew you were boring Dad, but I didn't think even you could bore someone to death'.

Ouch!

'You must get fed-up with patients interrogating you about a diagnosis they'd got from the internet?' was said to me dozens of times. Actually, it was a false assumption. In most practices older patients tend to see older doctors and certainly in my case many of my patients were well past the first flush of youth and often boasted of how they had literally nothing to do with computers – almost like a badge of honour.

'Bet it was easier when you didn't have those things' was another regular remark as the patient pointed to my computer. Often, I agreed, not wishing to appear contrary, but the truth was the exact opposite. Before computerisation of General Practice, we had to try to read hand-written notes. To be fair to my partners, generally their writing was legible, certainly more so than mine appeared to them, but some entries from previous doctors were impossible to read. More importantly with computers we could work many times faster in many areas and far more safely, particularly when it came to prescribing drugs. If you wanted to prescribe a drug which might interact in a harmful way with another drug the patient was on, the computer would flash up a message:

'Do you really 'dislike' this patient so much you want to kill them off?' or some such message. Suffice to say, it saved millions of harmful interactions that GPs would not have been aware of.

'He's forgotten more about General Practice than you'll ever know' is the sort of thing that used to be said to indicate that 'he', whoever the tiresomely knowledgeable 'he' was, knew a lot about the job I was in. I never really understood that expression as it seems to me that if someone has forgotten that amount, he probably doesn't remember all that much now, but apparently that's not the point. It was always assumed that you would learn a lot when young and gradually forget a lot over time, which was perfectly true. The risk then, for the ageing GP, was that he or she had forgotten a lot and wasn't conversant with the latest advances in medicine. Many years ago, I'd reckoned that atrophy of knowledge would be the catalyst for having to retire. But when I became the oldest GP in the practice, with a computer to hand, I had all the latest medical information at my fingertips. I was like a supercomputer with the wisdom of Solomon, given all my experience that I brought to bear! Well maybe that's a touch of an exaggeration but I could easily look up information very, very quickly. Generally, patients would be reassured to see that you were checking up on the latest knowledge on their condition. Occasionally, particularly when computers first arrived, I was a bit sneaky when faced with a topic I didn't know much about, especially if I saw something other than total confidence in me written on the face of my patient.

'How are you for time?' I'd ask.

'Me? Oh, I've got all the time in the world. Why?'

'Well let me give you a very well written patient information sheet on your condition to read in the waiting room and I'll see a couple of patients while you're doing that, then call you in and we can have a much better, more informed discussion about what to do. Is that OK?'

'Oh yes indeed thank you', the patient would say, invariably slightly stunned by my solicitous approach, before happily going back to read the information I'd given him or her. A few patients wouldn't have brought their reading glasses, but I had a supply of my old ones in a drawer to get around that.

While the patient was reading the information, I printed off and read the same leaflet myself, before calling the now, very well informed and well disposed towards me, patient and agreeing with him or her – as per the information sheet – what to do next.

So far from loathing computers I loved them – when they worked that was.

One of the joys of my work was being consulted by someone you really enjoyed seeing and knew you would miss when you retired:

Harry had had a very difficult childhood and early adulthood, until a former partner had realised his aggressive behaviour was due to a mental illness rather than just Harry being 'a bad un'. I had looked after him for decades and loved the fact that he was one of those people who always saw the positive in everybody. Heart specialists had seen him many years earlier and predicted an imminent demise, so he felt, quite literally, lucky to be alive. He always professed himself to feel better just for seeing me which in medical psychobabble is often referred to as 'The doctor as the therapy' and was very appreciative of my efforts in a friendly humorous manner. For my part I likewise always felt better for seeing him. Although I haven't heard the term referred to before perhaps in Harry's case he was an example of 'The patient as the therapy'

A young doctor in the practice, who saw a lot of my patients after I stopped working, recently asked me rather quizzically whether I socialised a lot with them.

'No,' I replied, 'why do you ask?'

'Well it's just that lots of them seem to regard you as a friend of theirs. Are a lot of them friends?'

'Depends what you mean by a friend,' I replied, 'I guess I did like seeing quite a lot of them and chatting to them, so maybe that does make them friends'.

He seemed quite surprised by my answer. The relationships involved on both sides are becoming much less common now. The intense pressure on GPs now is to deal with problems rapidly and to refer to other services, who do a lot of the work we used to have time to do ourselves. Continuity of care, seeing the same GP all the time, has, as a result, become harder to maintain.

It's not just relationships with patients that are important, it's also those with your colleagues. Almost without exception, the nurses, health care assistants, receptionists, managers, secretaries, health visitors, dispensers and clerks seemed every bit as determined as the GPs were, to provide as good a service for the patients as possible and took the responsibility for what they did very seriously and constantly strove to get even better at their jobs. I worked with some of them for over a quarter of a century and they deserved a medal for putting up with my foibles and idiosyncrasies. We relied on them and they relied on us, and the longer I worked, the more I appreciated their loyalty to the Practice and the NHS. They became much more than just employees. I wish I had made it clear how much I appreciated what they did, but in the hurly burly of the work that was all too often overlooked. I bet most retired GPs feel the same.

Medicine is a notoriously traditional profession – and in the eighties, the senior partner felt it important to keep some distance between the doctors and the staff, but when he left egalitarianism eventually arrived, old fashioned barriers disappeared and relationships became more informal and we relaxed, drank coffee and ate lunch together. When I first started the GPs were, or at least assumed they were, the font of all knowledge and all queries were referred to them. As nurses took over managing asthma, hypertension and diabetes in the practice, we, or certainly I, increasingly found myself asking the nurses about the latest management in their areas of expertise.

We also worked closely with district nurses, midwives and palliative care specialist nurses who were employed by the NHS rather than ourselves. The latter increasingly took over the role that palliative care consultants had previously fulfilled and were a great source of help and support to our patients and ourselves. One of the palliative care nurses, Sam a quietly spoken, humorous Liverpudlian, I later got to know from a very different perspective.

The GPs were more than just colleagues – we were also partners. The way the NHS is organised is that each GP Practice is a mini-business or independent contractor to the NHS, unlike hospital colleagues who are paid NHS employees. In reality we only had one big client – the NHS. The independent contractor idea is a bit anachronistic but essentially it means that in a practice you share financial risks which makes it even more important that you knock along with and trust your partners. With one or two, at times, that was challenging (no doubt for them too) but was always trumped by our mutual reliance on each other. If a partner saw one of my patients and spotted something that I had overlooked and took the appropriate action I was very grateful, not only for my patient's sake but also because my partner had possibly saved my back. That mended fences between partners better than anything else. It was a constant reassurance that we got a second opinion that way. Also knowing that others would see how you had approached a problem to some extent kept you on your toes. If any of us allowed our standards to drop it would have soon been noticed and addressed.

Over the four decades I worked, the doctors' faces changed, but we were lucky that we were always able to recruit excellent partners who you felt you could trust with that most precious of commodities – your patients. The partnership worked essentially because of mutual trust and respect.

Among the GPs we all had areas of medicine which we knew a bit more about than average – which of course meant we also had areas we knew a bit less about than average! It was a large practice with seven partners, so there were diverse interests and lots of expertise. If I wasn't sure how to manage a patient I would ask one of my partners, and they in turn would ask me if they were in a similar situation. One of my partners was very knowledgeable about skin conditions but didn't inject joints, so he helped me and vice versa. As skin conditions are very common, I easily got the better of that arrangement. Working as a team was thus essential to ensure the best outcomes for everyone.

It was encouraging to have very knowledgeable partners of great integrity in the same practice. Knowing that doctors like that wanted to be in the same practice that you were in, was very good for morale.

As younger more 'chilled' partners replaced the older GPs, Jane remembers me reporting lots of laughter over coffee and lunch which were the highlights of the day. We would discuss patient issues, practice business but also spent a lot of time talking about cars. Sadly, as the workload went up, those oases of relaxation became ever more squeezed, until it became rare for anyone to have a coffee break. Lunch became ever briefer and increasingly was taken up with meetings to discuss how to organise the latest changes that were required of GPs. A retired partner observed that when there became less time to socialise at work, people enjoyed the work less and became more stressed.

The work wasn't a bed of roses – far from it. It was pressurised with always more work to do than time to do it in, and, although the vast majority of patients were long suffering and appreciated your efforts, there were a few who were much more challenging in this respect. All GPs have 'Heart sink patients' who are immensely frustrating to interact with, and who, when you see them coming down the corridor to your room, make your heart, or at least your spirits, literally sink because they never seem to be satisfied. There is an ever-increasing workload because, with rapid advances in medicine nowadays, more and more can be done for patients, who are thus living longer and so developing sometimes several complex, chronic conditions. Looking after these patients takes a lot longer than the traditional ten-minute GP consultations allows.

The situation is worsened by politicians, particularly at election times, making all sorts of unrealistic promises about the NHS and constantly re-organising it for political purposes. I feel a sense of relief that I am no longer having to grapple with the latest changes which seem to proliferate week on week. Many of the changes have been beneficial to patients but implemented so badly that GPs and all the Primary Care team for that matter, have become like 'the horse' in 'Animal Farm', just expected to keep working ever harder and harder for longer and longer:

My partner was holding his head in despair. 'What's the matter?' I enquired. He pointed to an email that had been sent to all the GPs and medical departments in Oxfordshire, stating that, because of the desperate pressure on beds in the District General Hospital, 'arrangements had been made' for him to look after quite a number of the hospital patients in a Nursing Home he provided medical cover for. No-one had even discussed this with him, the email being the first he had known of the plan. It was a disaster for him. How would he cope with the flood of complex patients that really needed to be in hospital? I was experienced in local medical politics, so he gratefully accepted my gallant offer to sort it out.

I pressed the 'reply to all' button on his keyboard and simply wrote: 'F... off'

We laughed raucously but he was paralysed with fear lest I hit 'send' or he did accidentally and all the great and the good in the Oxfordshire medical world would receive an email saying 'F... Off'.

Eventually the 'delete' button was hit and thankfully the plan was never executed.

The result of the ever-increasing pressure on GP practices, is that there are now five thousand fewer GPs than there were five years ago. This dearth of eager young doctors wanting to be GPs has caused many practices throughout the UK to close, something that was virtually unheard of just a few years ago. General practice is acknowledged as the most stressful branch of medicine and the concept of 'resilience' is very topical nowadays. It is similar in hospitals as well.

When I think about how many diagnoses and judgements a GP has to make each day, I am full of admiration for my own GP and my former colleagues that they are doing such an awesome job. When I was working, I suppose I was like a hamster on a treadmill just running faster and faster.

Before I retired, I was the longest-serving GP in West Oxfordshire, but despite this, right up till I stopped working, I still occasionally experienced a bit of 'Impostor Syndrome' whereby one sometimes wonders how someone like yourself can possibly get away with doing the sort of responsible job that you are actually doing. It seems to you that eventually you must be found out for the impostor that you are. 'Impostor Syndrome' is common in all jobs, but particularly in medicine – indeed, I've never met a doctor who didn't recognise those sorts of feelings in himself or herself. I guess it's a defence mechanism against overconfidence or complacency. As I write this, I find myself wondering if my poor aptitude for science 'A' levels, failing the introductory pathology exam and the haughty Professor of Medicine banishing me from his firm made me more susceptible to 'Impostor Syndrome' than most and hence spurred me on to work hard. Who knows?

Most GPs retire around the age of sixty or before, but I went on for rather longer. This was influenced by the chance discovery, at the age of fifty-eight, that I had, like my Dad before me, an aneurysm in an artery in the brain which might rupture and cause bleeding. In two out of three patients, such bleeding results in a severe or fatal stroke. My Dad had had his ruptured aneurysm 'clipped'. This entailed opening up his brain and putting a strong metal clip over the artery. Nowadays, aneurysms are usually dealt with by threading a coil up through an artery in the groin under state-of-the-art imaging and placing the coil in the aneurysm which blocks it off. This is a much easier and less risky procedure than clipping.

Coiling was attempted in my case, but unfortunately the shape of my particular aneurysm didn't allow a coil to work. The disappointment of coming around from the general anaesthetic to be told that the attempted coiling hadn't worked was a pretty big blow, mitigated only by the farcical situation of a Registrar, a few minutes later, congratulating me on the success of the coiling! He hadn't checked the notes. I ended up having to have the same operation my Dad had had. There was a risk of having a stroke during the operation and of brain damage, which would have meant the end of my career. Thankfully, it went very well, and although my brain wasn't improved by the operation, it didn't seem to have been made any worse, so I was able to get back to work.

The threat of having to give up work made me realise that, although like everyone else I moaned about the workload, I actually really loved being a GP and didn't want to stop prematurely. I guess I was beginning to understand why someone coined the saying:

The doctor needs his patients more than the patients need the doctor.

When I did return to work, I appreciated far more than before, the privilege of doing what I did.

I stopped work abruptly, however, when I was given the stomach cancer diagnosis.

Chapter 4

The Day the Luck Ran Out

'Definitely doesn't sound sinister,' my GP concluded, after hearing my symptoms and examining me. 'Might be irritable bowel syndrome,' and prescribed some appropriate medication. Just to be on the safe side, he suggested some blood tests. I returned to work reassured that all was well with the world. I'd known there wasn't really a problem, but Jane had insisted I make an appointment.

I'd been having some minor symptoms for maybe six weeks, on and off, which had started with a feeling of being overly full after meals for a few days followed by slightly upset bowels and then a bit of indigestion which settled very easily with Gaviscon.

Oddly enough, when we'd been on a two-week holiday to France, in the middle of the six weeks, where we were wined and dined regally by the friends we stayed with, I didn't get any symptoms at all. We did some fairly strenuous cycling over those three days, which was harder than I'd expected, but I'd needed to carry Jane's and my luggage on my bike and the route was also hillier than expected. However, the symptoms returned back at home, so, under protest, I made the GP appointment. After his reassurances, I put the whole thing out of my mind until four days later, when, because my GP was away, one of his partners rang and explained that my blood tests had revealed an iron deficiency anaemia of 10.8 compared to my previous normal level of 13.5. Anaemia is often the first clue of a hidden cancer in the gut somewhere and would imply that I had lost almost three pints of blood from internal bleeding. It also explained why I had been tired when cycling. The GP said he would organise an urgent assessment where I would have an endoscopy, which is when a telescope-like instrument is pushed up into my bowels to enable a good view of what's going on and one is similarly passed down into my stomach. This was very disconcerting, as I was forced to acknowledge that my symptoms might have a serious cause. I had looked after dozens of patients with iron deficiency anaemia, so knew that bowel cancer was a distinct possibility because it's a common cancer, the first sign of which, is often anaemia and additionally I'd had a change in bowel habit. I also had symptoms which Gaviscon helped, so inflammation of the oesophagus caused from 'reflux', where acid comes up from the stomach, or even a stomach or duodenal ulcer were other possibilities. It didn't cross my mind that I might have stomach cancer, as it was much rarer than the very common acid reflux or even the less common ulcers.

Jane was every bit as worried as I was.

It is a tremendous help to have a network with expert colleagues who know the inside track on a wide range of conditions. I rang a friend who had recently retired from gastroenterology, to ask who I should get to do the endoscopies and he recommended Jeremy. Ten days later I consulted Jeremy and explained what had been going on and how I was maybe just a bit more tired than normal but that it was difficult to gauge as my work as a GP was becoming ever more exacting. After a careful examination, which was normal, he agreed the likelihood of too much amiss was pretty small but estimated the risk of cancer to be about ten percent in view of the fact that I had anaemia and was over sixty.

Over the preceding thirty-six years in general practice I was used to calculating the probability or otherwise of cancer in patients, and of course factored in their age. It was very disconcerting to hear someone increase my risk of cancer because I was now on the wrong side of sixty. But there it was, and anyway I knew that I had a ninety per cent chance of not having a cancer which seemed very good odds.

To enable a clear view of the bowels you have to take a massive quantity of laxatives the day before and on the morning of the procedure. That was a pretty grim business itself. I had to drink large quantities of diluted laxative which tasted revolting and was quite a struggle to swallow. At one point I felt so nauseous I started retching which was exhausting and alarming in case I couldn't get enough laxative down. The overriding fear I had was that the laxatives would still be working when the examination was due, necessitating the procedure to be abandoned so that the laxative misery would have to be repeated. In the event I was okay and after a sedative injection the endoscopies were performed without a hitch.

When I had come round from the sedative, Jeremy came over to discuss the results with Jane and myself.

'Bowels were unremarkable,' he started, in a reassuring matter-of-fact sort of way which made me feel that everything was going to be fine. However, he went on in the same matter-of-fact tone, 'but in the stomach there is a lesion that is protruding and has clearly been bleeding and so explains the anaemia.' At this point he showed us colour photographs he had taken of the inside of my stomach, which revealed what looked like a cow's udder. It looked horrible and seemed to have 'CANCER' written all over it.

'It isn't typical of stomach cancer', he continued', which is usually an ulcer, whereas this has the appearance possibly of a maltoma, which is a lymphoma of the stomach wall'.

Lymphomas are cancers of certain cells in the blood and can occur in many parts of the body, but I had never heard of ones in the stomach.

'Is that worse or better than stomach cancer?' we asked.

'Oh, definitely a better thing to have as it can often just be managed by H. pylori eradication and observation'. [H. pylori is a bacteria and eradication is a two-week course of three pills; two antibiotics and an acid suppressant.]

He had taken a small sample or 'biopsy' from the stomach and would arrange for it to be examined microscopically which would tell for certain what the problem was. The report on the biopsy is called 'histology'.

'So, what happens now is that we should await the histology and have a CT scan which I will arrange as soon as possible, and we should meet up to discuss the results in six days' time.'

He then very kindly gave me a card with his mobile number on, just in case I needed to ring him.

How do you describe your feelings when someone has told you that you may very well have stomach cancer?

I was aware of trying to keep up appearances in front of a colleague and also for Jane's sake. I knew that stomach cancers were usually ulcers so tried to convince myself that it wouldn't be that, but I also knew the old medical adage that 'common things occur commonly' so an unusual-looking stomach cancer would be more likely than a very rare condition like a maltoma.

'Okay,' I thought, 'so have the scan. Should be okay judging from how well I am. In the event of the worst-case scenario, if it is stomach cancer, I guess I can have an operation to remove it and go on from there.' I reflected wryly on the fact that I had been fervently hoping that, if it had to be a cancer, it would be bowel cancer as, if caught early, the outlook is usually far better than with stomach cancer. No such luck obviously. So hopefully, hopefully it would prove to be a maltoma which, although a form of cancer, from what Jeremy said is a condition I could live with - unlike a stomach cancer which usually has a very poor prognosis.

We went home. And started googling and learning all there was to know about maltomas. Like most patients, doctors google medical conditions especially when they know very little about them. Pictures online looked just like the cow's udder protruding into my stomach which was encouraging, as anything would be better than stomach cancer. Definitely a maltoma was what we wanted, it was most definitely a lot better than a stomach cancer. So, assuming the CT scan was okay, which I felt confident it would be, then although very unwelcome in the greater scheme of things, a maltoma would be something I could cope with.

The CT scan was done the next day and only took ten minutes or so. The scanner was like a giant polo mint so wasn't claustrophobic. The radiographer who performed the scan was friendly and seemed to know exactly what he was doing. During the scan, he asked me to take several deep breaths which worried me in case it indicated that there might be something in my chest. He didn't discuss the result and I didn't ask him to, but he didn't appear at all concerned so my confidence that everything would be okay started to return. The consultation to discuss the scan results and get the definite diagnosis from the histology was scheduled for five days after the scan.

I had to get through work before the appointment and was aware that I was a bit tetchier than normal with one or two patients whom I had known for decades. Hopefully they would just assume I had got out of the wrong side of bed that morning, but I was disappointed with myself for allowing personal issues to intrude on my thoughts whilst I was consulting.

I was the duty doctor in the morning before my afternoon hospital appointment, which meant I had to deal with any emergencies that cropped up, and so was a hostage to fortune as far as time was concerned. Usually, the duty doctor's work overran well into the afternoon which would make getting to the appointment on time very difficult, and so ratcheted up the already high tension. For once, however, the work seemed to be manageable with no unexpected emergencies hijacking my schedule.

Then the proverbial... Harry, the 'patient as the therapy' patient, had fallen in the road and been carried into the waiting room and looked as if he had broken his hip. Quickly making him comfortable and arranging a 999 ambulance, I managed to leave in the nick of time.

Months later, Jane told me that as we left for the appointment, she was convinced that life would never be the same again.

At the hospital clinic, as I always do when hoping for a particular outcome to a worrying situation, I whispered a prayer that the news would be good.

It wasn't.

It was anything but good.

It wasn't a maltoma.

It was Stomach Cancer.

Worse still, the scan showed that it had spread far and wide - into my pancreas and spleen and extensively into my liver. Crucially, it had also spread into the portal vein, which carries three quarters of the blood from the stomach to the liver. Jeremy explained that this meant that no operation to reduce the cancer's size and make it less likely to bleed, could be contemplated because the blood vessel was too important to remove.

It was beyond bad – it was as bad as it could possibly be.

I had prepared myself for the possibility of a stomach cancer diagnosis but, given how well I felt generally, I had never imagined that it could have spread so extensively. Essentially, the cancer mass or lump was so large that the radiologist who assessed the scan couldn't be absolutely certain that the itcancer mass was definitely coming from the stomach, as it was affecting the pancreas adjacent to the stomach and also the spleen. In other words, the whole area was like a war zone.

The consultant who examined the tumour under a microscope, was of the opinion that the biopsy showed a poorly-differentiated - where well-differentiated is better – adenocarcinoma or cancer. In summary, her opinion was that it was stage four stomach cancer meaning it was at a late stage – the worst it could possibly be.

So even in the City of Dreaming Spires, where many of the top specialists in the UK choose to work, my abdomen was so messed-up that it necessitated debate about even whether the cancer was in the pancreas or stomach. But the consensus came down clearly on the stomach.

Diagnoses are often not clear cut, though obviously it's better if they are, so that you can be confident of delivering the correct treatment, but the way my luck was running... As surgery was not an option, the only possible treatment I could have would be chemotherapy, which would have to be decided upon by an oncologist, a cancer treatment specialist.

Jeremy had already discussed my situation with an oncologist called Maria, who before seeing me, wanted to know if further tests on the biopsy would show whether the cancer could be treated with a 'monoclonal antibody' drug as this treatment would be more effective than the standard chemotherapy.

Jane, sitting beside me, was crying.

I summarised my reaction to the news by explaining that, prior to coming in, we had felt that a maltoma would be at the best end of the spectrum of diagnoses possible, but this seemed to be right at the opposite end. I sympathised with Jeremy for having to tell me such bad news. What, I asked, was my likely prognosis?

Being 'in the medical game', I knew the standard answer about the likely course of an illness and the probable time to death was usually skilfully avoided in any initial discussion, as it is pretty hard for a patient and his family to take much in after being given a cancer diagnosis. I also knew that hazarding a prognosis for a given individual, as opposed to a population of people, is problematic, as some people do relatively well, and live longer than average, and some, conversely, do very badly. Many patients decide not to ask about prognosis in too much detail, preferring to take events as they come along. However, I wanted to know, as precisely as possible, what to expect. I preferred that to the alternative of going away and worrying that my impression of the prognosis might be unrealistic. So, I asked him how I should explain, in lay terms, the situation to my children and GP partners. I said that my children would be bound to ask how long I might have and other very pertinent direct questions, to which I would like to be able to give as accurate and truthful an answer to as possible.

Put like that, it was a question Jeremy couldn't avoid answering. 'Not years' he started.

I supposed that meant anything up to two years but possibly just a few months. It was a bit too vague for my purposes, so I pressed on. 'Am I likely to be still alive in a year's time?'

'Probably less than fifty per cent likely, though Maria would be better able to gauge things and if the tests show that the cancer could respond to a monoclonal antibody that would be a good thing. However, to get two or three years of life would be an extraordinary result.'

So that was pretty clear. 'Not years' meant 'months' unless I was extraordinarily lucky.

And luck had deserted me of late.

Anticipating the question someone would soon ask me, I continued: 'And when the disease progresses, what will happen?'

'Probably you will lose your appetite and your weight will drop and you will become progressively more tired and, in this situation, often you get pain from the liver swelling which steroids could help. Later you might become jaundiced. You might get stomach compression and the stomach might become stiff, so that you would feel full after smaller meals than usual. You might get further stomach bleeding which radiotherapy might be able to control. If there was spread to other parts of the body later, you would get symptoms depending on which other parts were affected.'

It felt a bit like listening to a teaching seminar to which I was paying really apt attention.

I asked about work and he felt it depended on how I felt, but if one was going to press on with chemotherapy work might delay it. I commented that I had had an ambition to work at least a further three months, till I was sixty-five, but in the course of the last few minutes that had completely disappeared.

Jeremy explained that my case would now be discussed at the Multi-Disciplinary Upper Gastroenterology team meeting. A Multi-Disciplinary Team Meeting – MDT – is routinely arranged to carefully review all the medical facts in a case. Doctors from different specialities meet up and proffer opinions to ensure the best possible chance of a correct diagnosis being made and the best recommendation for treatment is agreed on. So, in my case, stomach surgeons, gastroenterologists, oncologists, radiologists and histologists would all pore over the symptoms and tests and ensure, as far as was humanly possible, that mistakes were not made. An MDT meeting is an excellent process.

I thanked Jeremy for what he had done on my behalf then we shook hands somewhat awkwardly and Jane and I left.

Chapter 5

The Family Conference

How could I possibly have widespread stomach cancer? I had been planning to run the London Marathon if I had got a place in the ballot. If anything, I had put on a bit of weight in the last year or so. I was well, and people with advanced stomach cancer that I had seen never were and always lost weight.

Jeremy thought the reason I hadn't experienced many symptoms was because the cancer was growing into the space behind the stomach.

I didn't have any problem or difficulty believing the diagnosis as Jeremy had been sombre and frank in his explanation and took great care to find precisely the correct words. The seriousness of the moment was all too obvious.

I was visiting Fred. His partner thought he had gone mad. He sitting on a chair with a gun by his side. His friendly demeanour changed when I explained why I had been summoned. He went ballistic, grabbed the gun screamed and rushed towards his partner and me. I ran out expecting to be hit on the head – or maybe even shot – at any second.

That was the only time I had more or less actually looked down the barrel of a gun. This felt far more frightening.

Nonetheless outwardly I remained calm. My main emotion was one of overwhelming sadness. Sadness that I wouldn't have the long life I had expected and had almost felt entitled to. I had always believed myself to be a 'tough cookie' as I kept pretty fit and had run my one and only London marathon just four years earlier at the age of sixty, and so, whilst not exactly invulnerable, I saw myself as odds-on to live to a good age. I'd always felt that if I was not necessarily going to be the 'last man standing', I would at least be one of the last men of my vintage or peer group to be around and certainly not one of the very first to fall. I knew all too well that my time was now very limited and a part of me felt guilty that I had let the people close to me down by being such 'damaged goods' that I would now not even live to an average age. I felt guilty that I wouldn't be around to look after Jane as we grew old together – as I had always seen my role would be – and instead would be abandoning those who counted on me. Jane would become a young widow and the children fatherless, and my grandchild would not remember me and might never even have met me.

Why guilt? I guess probably because when something really bad happens, it's human nature to want to blame someone for it. You could blame God, or the equivalent of God if you had a different faith, but God is not someone you can satisfactorily rail against, so your mind looks around for someone else to blame. Doctors may be blamed if they have been slow to diagnose, or even if they haven't, because they are convenient scapegoats, but in my case, there hadn't been any delay and I knew it. In the absence of anyone else to blame, like many patients before me, I blamed myself.

What had just happened? My head was beginning to swim now that I didn't need to keep it together to interrogate Jeremy and try to squeeze out all the relevant information I might possibly need.

'Come on, let's go down and tell the children – now,' Jane said. 'There's no point in going back home first and there won't be another opportunity for ages to get all three of them together'

It was a very sensible plan and typical of Jane to be so practical and clear-thinking in a crisis. It did feel as if we needed to run to the bosom of our family for succour and support. A reversal of the roles we used to have when the children were young and rushed home if they cut their knee for Mum, or occasionally Dad, to kiss it better. We needed to be among people we loved. We had to ring them to alert them to the need for an urgent family get-together. Fortunately, Jeremy came out of his room and saw us debating what to do and kindly offered us the privacy of his room to make our calls from.

Our three children, Laura, Patrick and Duncan, all live and work in London and conveniently Duncan was temporarily living with Patrick and his wife Lucia in south west London, so Jane rang Laura and told her there was really urgent family business to discuss and asked her to meet us at Patrick's house. Similarly, I rang Duncan and asked him to get home early from work.

'Why? What's going on?' he demanded to know, the anxiety in his voice all too evident.

'Well one of us is unwell and so we want to talk to all of you about it' I replied.

'You or Mum?'

'Me'

'What is it?' – he persisted – not an unreasonable question for a young doctor to ask.

'Don't want to discuss it on the phone – will see you later'

Jane spoke to Patrick and told him that we would be calling in about an hour, which was fine as his wife Lucia was home. Jane explained the news would be upsetting and wondered if he wanted Lucia to hear it initially in view of her pregnancy. He felt on balance it would be better for her to hear it when we came.

On the way down, Jane rang my surgery and explained that I was unwell and wouldn't be in to work for a few days. In fact, I never returned to work and that Wednesday morning surgery had been the last I would ever do.

So Harry, the 'therapeutic patient' who I really liked and who, if you'd asked me who I'd have liked to have seen in my last surgery, would definitely have been there, turned out to be the last patient I ever did consult with.

A few months later, I was walking in a village in another part of Oxfordshire when I came across a man cutting the grass in a churchyard. He seemed to know me and introduced himself as Harry's nephew and let me know that Harry had died a short while before. I was saddened to hear that my old friend had passed on, not least because I would have wanted to attend his funeral but was pleased to hear that he had had a good send off. The coincidence of my last patient being the one that I would have chosen, if given the choice, didn't strike me till over a year later.

In the car, Jane and I debated how we should discuss the situation with the family. Candour and honesty were clearly the only way, but I thought it would be kinder, at least initially, not to emphasise just how grim the prognosis was and in particular that I was unlikely to be alive in a few months' time. Jane's phone went. It was Duncan. A brief conversation ensued.

'What did he want?' I enquired.

'He was upset and very worried by what you had told him. He was crying.'

A huge lump rose to my throat. It made me well up for the first time since I had learnt about my condition. I hadn't expected my strong, resilient son to be so upset at hearing that his Dad was somehow in trouble and it caught me off-guard. In an instant, it brought home to me how important I must be to him. I knew obviously how important he and Laura and Patrick were to me, but I hadn't been prepared for the raw love that this revealed. I knew Jane was devastated, as I would have been if the roles had been reversed, she was my wife and had been through so much that any marriage of forty years entails. But for a son to be so upset without even knowing what was wrong.

I have a great relationship with Duncan and love his company, but we'd never discussed the concept of love and yet here was a literal outpouring of his for me. It was humbling, upsetting and wonderful. Maybe I was a decent human being after all. In fact, this seemed to confirm that I must be. I guess we reproach ourselves for our manifest shortcomings and have a blind spot to qualities others see in us. It makes one sadder to realise that your passing will be bound to have a major effect on someone else though.

We got to the London house as Patrick was getting home on his bike. Laura, Duncan and Lucia were already waiting. Warm greetings and lingering hugs, then we sat around the dining room table with me at one end addressing my 'audience'. I had a hundred per cent attention. Not something that's often happened when I've given a talk – maybe the only other time that came close was when I gave a talk to the North Oxford Rotary club about the health benefits of alcohol.

I quickly went into doctor mode, almost dissociating myself from what I was saying – as if I was explaining the medical problem to a patient and his relatives – very familiar ground for me – and calmly explained that I had been diagnosed with stomach cancer which unfortunately had spread to my liver, spleen and pancreas. I explained that I couldn't be operated on and so the cancer could not be cured. Treatment would be chemotherapy, which I would be starting in a week or two, and hopefully that would extend things for some time. I explained that I'd only had minor symptoms for a few weeks but that sometimes cancers behave like this and that it was simply extremely bad luck that I had got stuck with this. It could have happened to anyone, including someone like me that didn't have any risk factors for the condition. I explained what had happened to get to the point we were at.

Only the sound of loud sobbing interrupted my flow. When I finished, the questions started.

'How long?'

'No-one can say precisely, and it depends what the response to chemotherapy is like, but it is not years sadly.'

'You're not going to do any of that 'I don't want any treatment bollocks', are you?' Duncan asked, knowing much more keenly than the others just how bad the prognosis must be.

'No' I assured him, 'I definitely want to have treatment, so I can be around for Mum and you guys for as long as possible.'

'How long have you known?'

'Really only been certain of the diagnosis for a few hours.'

No-one had pressed me on my prognosis or asked me if Jeremy had ventured a time-line, which was a relief as I wanted to be completely truthful.

A few questions about my symptoms which, as on many occasions from many different people since, seemed to be attempting to make sense of a situation that otherwise made no sense.

What symptoms did you have and for how long? Nothing else? Really?

What seems to happen is that people hope you've ignored some pretty serious symptoms for a long time, so that they can reassure themselves that this sort of thing couldn't happen to them, if they were sensible.

Some people even become quite challenging saying 'Surely there were other clues…?' No, the simple unadulterated truth of the matter was that I had had minimal symptoms for a short while and actually had never felt particularly unwell.

The uncomfortable implication being that it could happen to anyone of the right, or perhaps more correctly the wrong, age.

Then the googly. Three months into her pregnancy, Lucia hesitatingly said, 'I know this may seem a silly question, but you will be here for the birth, won't you?'

It wasn't a silly question at all. It was, as a politician would say when confronted by a question he really didn't want to answer, a very good question. It was October, and the baby was due in April. Some patients at my stage would be dead before Christmas. I knew that and so did Duncan. With as breezy an air as I could muster, I strongly reassured Lucia that, of course, I would be around for the birth. Sounded just a bit hollow to my ear, but in truth I felt generally so well that I should be able to last out at least till April which was only six months away.

My super-smart Laura then took centre stage and exhorted me to be positive and leave space for healing and other positive thoughts. She came up to me and hugged me, as she felt I had looked rather lonely up at the head of the table. It hadn't felt like that, more that everyone else was too stunned and paralysed by the appalling things they were hearing to do anything other than sit tight. Patrick and Duncan had looked devastated throughout the whole thing. Laura then explained that she had heard of this and that alternative approach that could bear fruit in a tight corner. Duncan protested that that would not be appropriate. Expressions of regret and sorrow ensued, and warm promises of total support came thick and fast. Someone would come down every weekend to be with us and support us both. They would be with us every step of the way.

It had obviously been really hard for everyone to hear what was happening. Patrick later recounted that a week or so later, whilst sitting in an airport he suddenly found himself in floods of tears. It was tough on everyone.

There was a wonderful warm feeling of love and support and the explanation of what had happened had flowed effortlessly. They all expressed awe at the way I had explained things so calmly – I was a bit surprised myself but relieved that I had been composed. I had really not wanted to break down during the explanation of what would be difficult enough for the children to listen to, without seeing 'the Big Man', as they have called me since their childhood, in tears.

Looking back now, maybe the experience of being sent away to boarding school at the age of nine and losing my Dad at a young age, had enabled me to develop a sufficiently strong shell to be able to deal with pretty much any situation without revealing too much emotional turmoil.

We stayed for dinner and talked about everything. Duncan was cheerfully ironing several shirts which I had never seen him do before, nor it seemed had anyone else. I commented to Patrick that Duncan had become much more domesticated. No, explained Patrick, it was just Duncan's way of coping with bad news.

The fact that, like my patient Peter, I have a great wife and great children who care deeply and will miss me when I'm gone, means I have the comfort of knowing that for all my faults, mine has been a life worth living. I've subsequently heard other cancer patients, like the BBC's Steve Hewlett and Tessa Jowell MP, eloquently express the exact same feeling and describe the great comfort they got, when staring down the barrel of a grim diagnosis, from the realisation that they really mattered to their family.

I too had a great family. They would kiss my knee and make it better. They would embrace and look after Jane when I was gone.

Chapter 6

Getting Advice

Most people, when presented with grim news, react in the way they do to mundane everyday situations. At least they do when they get over the initial shock. I was no different. When the shockwaves from the final consultation with Jeremy, started to settle somewhat, I began trying to think practically about how best to approach the illness. After all, managing patients' illnesses and trying to get the best possible treatments for them was what I had spent a very long time doing, so surely, I should be able to ensure I got the same for myself?

GPs are focused on spotting cancer early amongst the many less serious conditions we see in our patients each day. A couple of years earlier, our GP registrar had done an audit or survey of how quickly cancer had been diagnosed over the preceding year in our patients and seemingly I had been particularly good at spotting it. In others, at least.

The actual management of cancer is done by specialists and increasingly there are more and more cancer specialists who focus on different areas of the body. GPs take over again when the cancer specialists can't help any more. Then we enlist the help of palliative specialist nurses and consultants. This specialisation process helps ensure patients get the most up-to-date medical advice and management possible. One unintended, but inevitable, consequence of this is that GPs become deskilled as they get less hands-on experience of managing patients in the early stages of their cancer.

The old adage about the difference between a GP and a specialist goes like this:

A GP knows a little about a very wide area of medicine. A specialist knows a lot about a narrow area of medicine. Over time, as more and more medical knowledge is discovered, a GP comes to know less and less, about more and more, till eventually he or she knows nothing about everything. Over time, as more is discovered in his or her specialist area, the specialist knows more and more about a smaller and smaller area of medicine until ultimately, he or she knows everything about nothing. At which point GP and specialist are about as useful as each other.

I knew I personally didn't, and in reality, couldn't possibly, know enough about the management of my stage four stomach cancer. What I really knew about were conditions I saw and treated frequently in my surgery. Stomach cancer was not one of them. Additionally, medical knowledge is expanding so rapidly, particularly in the field of cancer, that a lot, if not almost all, of my knowledge would be out-of-date. First knowledge is perhaps a bit like first love – something that sticks with you – but in that respect what I had learnt as a student in the seventies was woefully out of date. The updating I undertook regularly during my career was not targeted on conditions a hospital specialist would manage but on conditions GPs managed.

I had obviously learnt a lot from seeing the management of commoner cancers by consultant colleagues. One oncologist, Rory, amongst them stood out. He had seemed dogged in his determination to treat new symptoms in his patients when, it seemed to me, others might have called a halt to treatment. The result was that some of his patients did really well and survived, in relatively good health, for a lot longer than I would have expected – granted with my out-of-date expectations. Equally impressively, he seemed to know his patients well and be really involved with them as people. I had spoken to him on the phone a few times about our shared patients and been impressed by his commitment to them. He was exactly the sort of oncologist I wanted to have in my corner, but he dealt with kidney and prostate cancers not stomach cancer. Maybe I could try to tap his brain as to the best way to proceed. Jeremy had referred me to an oncologist but was she the very best person to see? Was there anyone better in Oxford or the UK for that matter? There was no point being diffident and going along with a referral just to avoid any awkwardness as this was my only chance at life or at least prolonging it for as long as possible. Although I felt I knew quite a bit about Rory I had never actually met him but resolved to see if he would allow me to pick his brains on the best way to proceed.

I emailed him: 'I wonder if you'd mind giving me a quick call for a word of advice re oncology asap please?'

He rang the same evening. I explained my situation. He was very sorry and eager to help. He would check on a few things and be back in touch. That was heartening. My sang-froid was definitely returning now. An hour or two later, he rang again and confirmed that Maria, the oncologist I was due to see, would indeed give a very good opinion. He talked animatedly about how research into the genetic make-up of cancers and metastases was in some instances helping to select treatments more effectively than before. To find out if there might be any new treatments being researched, he advised me to also see Arthur, a consultant who coordinates lots of medical cancer research trials in the UK and abroad. He would know about anything else that might prolong my survival. Rory said he would ask his secretary to arrange an appointment for me.

He also gently commented that doctors are often afraid to ask for help and advised that I contact the Oxford branch of Maggie's Centre, a voluntary group set up to help patients and relatives cope with cancer.

However, I had reached out and asked him for help and had been very pleased that I had. And very grateful that he had responded in such a helpful supportive way.

Chapter 7

The Importance of Hope

A few days after seeing Jeremy I was waiting to see Maria, the oncologist, who would advise on the best combination of anti-cancer drugs, or chemotherapy, for my condition.

At least I don't have Pancreatic cancer, I thought, as that was one of the few cancers that would have been even worse than Stomach Cancer. Cold comfort but I was trying to be as positive as I could.

I had managed a number of patients with pancreatic cancer but the one I remembered most vividly was Mary. She was already on the surgical ward when I started my first hospital job and was terminally ill. Hospices for end of life care were still in their infancy then and very thin on the ground, so she was going to be nursed on the ward until the end of her life. I saw her most days and met her devoted husband, who visited every day. She was slipping away painfully slowly.

One day, the A&E consultant invited me to see a male patient he had assessed earlier, who was awaiting treatment. The patient explained that he had been vacuuming the stairs and slipped whereupon the vacuum pipe extension had got caught on his penis, as he hadn't been wearing any clothes at the time. Terrible lacerations had been caused that would require surgery under a general anaesthetic. The learning point was that patients may embellish the truth when it could seem embarrassing. The consultant pointed out that the patient had obviously been using the vacuum tube inappropriately.

I suppose I might have seen some black humour in the situation normally but all I could feel was immense sadness for the patient to be reduced to resorting to such a desperate act.

He was Mary's husband.

At previous consultations when we were being told results of tests and there had been the possibility of good, or at least less bad news, the outcome had always turned out to be the worst one imaginable.

The endoscopy could have been normal. It wasn't.

The biopsies could have shown a maltoma. They didn't.

It was stomach cancer.

The scan could have been normal. It showed extensive spread of the cancer which made it a stage four tumour. The worst possible situation and removing any possibility of surgery.

On each occasion, a wave of disbelief had washed over me, I found myself feeling almost dizzy, distant and reeling with incredulity that I could be in a situation where someone was telling me such terrible things about my health when basically before I'd felt fine. At least this time I knew the situation couldn't get any blacker. Unless that is, the oncologist said that chemotherapy would not be worth trying.

Maria called us in and introduced herself mentioning that she understood I knew her husband. She discussed the Stomach Cancer Multidisciplinary Team meeting and said that there had been an opinion proffered that the cancer might be coming from the pancreas.

It was happening again.

That feeling of disbelief and devastation again.

She went on to say that, on balance, taking lots of things into consideration, she felt the cancer was indeed much more likely to be from the stomach so agreed with the diagnosis Jeremy had come to. However, to be as sure as possible further 'immunohistochemical' tests would be done on the biopsies of the stomach which might clarify the situation a bit, though sometimes it just wasn't possible to tell the origin of a cancer with absolute certainty. Treatment could still be helpful as some drugs were used for both stomach and pancreatic cancer.

Jeremy had mentioned that if the tumour had 'herceptin receptors' it was likely to respond better to chemotherapy.

'Does it have herceptin receptors?' I ventured, knowing in my heart that it wouldn't.

'No.'

She went on to say that the outcome would have been only slightly better if it had been herceptin positive, adding perhaps an additional three to four months in most patients. Given the little time I had left, I would have been so grateful for those three to four months but clearly it was not to be.

So, the nightmare scenario was most definitely happening again. There was some doubt about the actual diagnosis which might never be resolved and so just might mean that I did, after all, have pancreatic cancer. The chemotherapy would still have a chance of working but it would be more of a blunderbuss approach than a carefully targeted one. I wouldn't even have a shot at the extra three to four months that herceptin receptors could have given me.

Maria asked me if I wanted to know the likely prognosis. I did. She was very frank and spelt it out clearly. If no treatment, she estimated six to nine months. If responsive to chemotherapy realistically twelve to fifteen months at best, though a tiny proportion of patients in my situation survived a bit longer. But only forty to fifty percent of stomach cancer patients responded to chemotherapy, and if it didn't respond the prognosis would be the same six to nine months as if I had had no treatment.

So, for the majority of people in my situation, the treatment was actually worse than useless because they ran the gauntlet of bad side effects from the treatment but didn't live any longer. The quality of their lives in their last few months would almost certainly be worsened by treatment side effects – not an encouraging thought. I knew the outlook for me was poor, but I hadn't realised it was that bad. Over the years quite a few of my patients with cancer, eschewing the risk of bad treatment side effects, had very reasonably opted for no active treatment. I know I'd promised Duncan that I wouldn't go in for any of 'that no treatment bollocks' as he had so eloquently put it, but I was faced with very unappealing odds of success with very unappealing treatment, so maybe I was in that situation.

She outlined the chemotherapy she would recommend if I decided to opt for treatment. This consisted of three drugs, two given intravenously in the hospital at the start of a twenty-one-day cycle followed by tablets. Side effects could include fatigue, nausea and vomiting, anaemia, hair loss in most people and a susceptibility to infections. After three lots of treatment a scan would be done and if it showed a response to the drugs a further three treatments would be given followed by a further scan after a while. Two further cycles might be recommended at a later stage depending on how well my body had coped with the side effects and whether I felt able to go through more treatment but after that there would be no more benefit from chemotherapy.

If I didn't respond to the chemotherapy a different set of drugs could be tried, but overall the response rate was even lower than with the initial treatment with only twenty to thirty percent of patients responding to the second set of drugs.

Alternatively, there might be research trials that I could take part in that could help, though she pointed out that, on average, the chances of responding to a research trial are only ten to fifteen per cent. So, I was even less likely to respond to any research trial treatment and the price I might pay for the privilege of trying the treatments was very unpleasant side-effects.

At my request, she outlined the range of symptoms I could develop when the cancer worsened and how radiotherapy might help stop any stomach bleeding. When asked about non-pharmacological things that might help, she stated very clearly that no special diet or supplements had been shown to be helpful and it seemed a shame when patients tried unpleasant food which just impacted on their quality of life with no gain. Physical fitness enabled people to tolerate the chemotherapy better and be more likely to be able to complete the course of treatment but didn't make patients more likely to respond.

Naturally, I was interested in this and discussed running and cycling. Also, we touched on my GP work, which just might be possible intermittently if chemotherapy side effects were well tolerated.

She also estimated that because of the cancer, I had a thirty percent risk of getting a Deep Vein Thrombosis, a clot in a leg vein, or a Pulmonary Embolism a clot in the lungs, the latter which I knew could be fatal, and indeed had caused the death of my mother's father.

Did I want treatment she asked, or did I want to mull it over for a while?

What would she recommend to her husband, who I'd played golf with a number of times, if he was in my situation? I asked. A good way of getting doctors who are trying to be non-directive to open up is to ask them something like that. It doesn't always work though, particularly if you are dealing with someone who is determined that you should make up your own mind rather than be overly influenced by their opinion. In reality it can be bewilderingly difficult for a patient to try to make such an important decision. Most of us, have at best a fairly rudimentary grasp of what statistics really mean. Often it seems best to ask the doctor for his or her recommendation on whether or not to have a treatment.

Maria said she wouldn't exactly recommend anything – that would be up to her husband – but she would hope he might opt to try the chemotherapy as some patients who decline treatment later regret that decision and if the treatment was tolerable it might prolong survival. If the side-effects were unbearable, at least one would know that one had tried and hadn't passed up on the chance of prolonging life.

So, it seemed I was in a situation where patients did opt for that 'no treatment bollocks' but I was getting a guarded steer from Maria to at least give the chemotherapy a try.

I opted to have the treatment. What else could I realistically do? I had to at least try to prolong my life for Jane and the family's sake, even if for quite a proportion of what was left of it, I would be on pretty noxious drugs. I had after all promised Duncan that I would give treatment a go. Maria gave me written information about the chemotherapy she recommended and said that the nurses would contact me with a date to start the treatment the following week.

Jane who had been silent for most of the consultation at the end asked in a faltering way if she could just check what she thought she had heard, namely that the absolute most we could realistically hope for was eighteen months.

'That's correct'.

'That's very hard to take' Jane said with emotion.

Maria agreed that it was very hard and offered to get in touch with the community Macmillan nurse team for support for the whole family through what she said was bound to be a difficult time. As we left, I mentioned that I had worked with a particular one, Sam, over many years and would prefer to be under his wing if possible and she kindly agreed to ask him.

It had been a long and very tough meeting – an hour and a quarter of unremittingly bad news about precisely what lay ahead. It had felt surreal to hear someone speak in detail about just how awful my situation was. Maria had gone into great detail about the uncertainties regarding the diagnosis, adopting a very detached, unemotional demeanour and had been very candid and detailed with her statistics.

Maybe her candour could be seen as a mark of respect to a fellow medic, who she perhaps perceived as being able to tolerate the very bottom line about his condition.

As I listen to the recording of the consultation again it occurs to me that perhaps what she was really doing was outlining the situation from her perspective rather than ours, almost thinking out loud as it were. It felt almost as if she had been explaining to a colleague the challenges my situation brought. Maybe that was how she could distance herself from the very difficult task of having to tell someone, who happened to be a colleague and who knew her husband, just how awful his future would be. She was quite properly determined not to give us false hope and, in that respect, she had succeeded almost too well.

Jane was upset by the consultation. She felt that Maria had not shown much empathy. She hadn't put a metaphorical arm around us and said that she would do everything possible to treat the disease as effectively as she could and make the experience as bearable as possible.

Was that perhaps just a case of blaming the messenger, especially one who had the unenviable position of having to bear such bad news? Doubtless it had been difficult for her too.

Maria had a good reputation for her expertise in my condition and also for being very nice. I really hoped, and expected, that in time a good doctor/patient relationship would develop between us even if the first meeting hadn't been too promising in that respect.

She had however been generous with her time and very thorough and had organised someone to support us emotionally and to put his arm around us.

Although she didn't mention it at the time, we later learnt that she had come to the hospital specially to see me during her holiday which had been really kind of her.

A few days after seeing Maria, together with Jane and my son Duncan, we went, on Rory's advice, to see a second oncologist, Arthur, to see if there was any research that might be of help to me. He explained that none of the experimental treatments were as good as the standard treatment that I had been offered by Maria, so that would be the best first line of attack. The experimental drugs that might be available, manipulated the immune system – the body's defence against infectious organisms and other invaders like some cancer cells – so-called 'immunotherapy.' One trial targeted a cell receptor called 'PD1', which stood for Premature Death 1, and if you could stop the immune cells dying prematurely then you had more of them available to kill the cancer cells. It sounded a bit like a cross between Star Wars and a military based thriller. Some of the terms he used I had never heard of before, but Duncan seemed to have and contributed searching questions which I was grateful for. Arthur talked about the average response time to the standard treatment but said that there is group of patients who do considerably better than that. He had had two stomach cancer patients who he had discharged eight and ten years after starting treatment in similar circumstances to myself. He also had a larger number of patients still alive after two or more years. He explained that there are patients who, for reasons not understood, have tumours which respond far better than average to chemotherapy. He drew a graph shaped like a bell, and the line to the right of the middle of the bell represented those who survived longer – the tail of the graph. One hoped to be in a long tail situation.

Arthur had been very constructive in his approach. He had said much the same sort of things about the outcome with chemotherapy that Maria had, but in a way that left us feeling much more hopeful – almost buoyed up – about the possibility of being part of a long tail. Maria had more or less told us to disregard that possibility, as it was so rare.

She hadn't really offered us any hope.

Robert Twycross, an expert on palliative care, wrote:

'Hope is crucial to maintaining a psychological equilibrium and is particularly important when coping with life-limiting illness.' Another respected Oxford palliative care consultant had similarly maintained that it was important, no matter how bleak a situation was, that a doctor tried to create something positive to give some hope, to make it a bit easier for a patient to carry on.

When I've had a consultation with a patient in similar straits, I hope I've tried to show empathy and explain what the statistics meant. If the statistics were particularly bad, I would urge them to focus on the fact that they could be one of the small percentage of patients who did well with that treatment. I hoped to make them feel they had, at least, a chance of doing well. Hopefully they could be in 'the long tail' and have reasons for optimism.

Maybe Maria thought that it was important to give me, as a medic, the absolute bottom line. Perhaps she had assumed that I wouldn't need any handholding and maybe that had been reinforced by my boarding-school honed outer shell. But doctors are in that respect just the same as everyone else and sometimes, perhaps, because they may have treated patients in a similar situation to themselves and so know just what lies ahead, need even more emotional support. In facing up to the cancer Jane and I had needed some encouraging word or comment that could give us some hope to hang on to and it was unfortunate that inadvertently Jane had been made to feel so upset.

Then again, I never had to tell a colleague that he or she had such a grim prognosis as mine. As I've already admitted, doctors are not the easiest of patients, especially perhaps one like me who asks lots of questions and records his consultations. It never occurred to me – but it has to others – that recording consultations might possibly be seen to indicate a lack of trust in the doctor and so make him or her more defensive when consulting. How would I have felt if a colleague I was treating in similar circumstances wanted to record a consultation? I record all my consultations. I know, from my own experience, that of my patients and from research evidence, that only a small proportion of information at a consultation is recalled accurately by patients and I am anxious not to miss anything important. For many years I have encouraged my patients, friends and relatives to record important consultations. Most are too diffident to do so, and some have asked if they may and disappointingly have been declined permission.

It's not easy being a patient when you are a doctor and it's certainly not easy treating one, especially if that one is me.

Chapter 8

Role Reversal

'From the Cradle to the Grave' is often said to be what General Practice is all about. For perhaps the first fifteen years of my career, we had looked after women during labour, but the pressure of work built up to such a point that taking two or three hours out to attend a delivery became impossible and we now refer women who are at low risk of obstetric complications to our midwife colleagues. Naturally we continued the end of life care and it had always been for me, as for many GPs, a hugely important part of our work. To help a patient have a good death is a very rewarding exercise and can make all the difference to his or her family. It is far from easy and we rely for help from the specialist palliative care nurses also often referred to as MacMillan nurses who are part of the 'end of life team' for their input and advice.

Over the preceding twenty-five years or so, our practice had always had good specialist palliative care nurses delegated to help our patients. One was Sam, a very down to earth, humorous Liverpudlian. He was very calm and measured and always proffered advice in such a way as to make you feel he was deferring to you whereas in reality it was the other way around. I trusted his judgement and always took his advice on management. He was also good fun to be around. He wasn't unfortunately looking after the patients at the practice I was registered at so he would have to make me an exception if he was going to take me on as a patient. He might not be at all comfortable taking me on as a patient, as our long professional relationship might get in the way of objectivity, especially when he didn't have to.

The day after the consultation with Maria, Jane was startled to receive a phone call from someone who introduced herself as being from the local hospice. She went on to explain that although she was actually the palliative care nurse attached to the practice I'm registered at, Maria had spoken to Sam and he had agreed to our request that he look after me when he was needed. He would be in touch and visit in a few days. Jane was thrown by the mention of the hospice as she was far from ready to have a discussion about end of life care. I understood her feelings and didn't particularly want to be visited as early as this but was relieved and grateful that Sam had agreed to take me on as a patient. Nonetheless Jane braced herself and made Sam welcome when he visited a few days later.

Quite sensibly, he went through all the information as if I was completely new to the business of end of life care. He mentioned the names of the consultants who supported and advised him and what his role was and how it involved helping with emotional and physical symptoms. He enquired about our children and how they were coping with the situation and invited them to contact him if need be. He asked about the consultation with Maria and what she had said. He informed me about an allowance which I was now entitled to, which would pay £80 a week and offered me a claim form. Money, however, was not what I needed, so I thanked him but declined.

He mentioned that a third of cancer patients have a low mood and that in a third of them it is severe enough to be diagnosed as clinical depression. How was I doing in that respect? I said I didn't feel depressed, but that sleep was not always easy. He said he would refer me to a psychologist in 'Maggie's Centre' – the local Cancer support clinic for patients and their relatives. Group work at Maggie's might be tricky, he felt, in case I came across former patients. Before leaving he gave me contact numbers and said he would phone on a certain date to see how things were.

It had all felt just a tiny bit awkward, but he had at least broken the ice and was, as always, kind in his manner. It felt weird to be spoken to as a patient by him when there had been so many times when he and I had visited a patient together in our professional roles. That was how I had seen myself for thirty-six years, it was taking some getting used to, acknowledging that I was now the patient. His presence at my home, talking to me about end of life care reinforced that unpalatable reality.

I really was the patient now; there was no getting away from it.

Jane found his visit very upsetting. It hadn't been many days since the consultation with Maria when we had found out just how bleak the situation was and how short a time I had left. Jane was struggling to accept this, feeling that I was just too well to have a stage four stomach cancer. Neither of us had really come to terms with all its implications, nor had we talked through things in enough detail or said enough of the things to each other that needed to be said. I hadn't told Jane that I was sleeping badly, as I suppose I was trying to put a brave face on things, so it upset her to learn that from a conversation I was having with a third party. No-one from our family or very close circle of friends was aware of just how grim things were and yet there I was discussing everything with an outsider.

In short it felt as if the visit from Sam had come far too soon. It was far too close to the mark. It might on the face of it seem churlish to be upset by the NHS organising a visit too soon. I knew that it was good practice for someone like Sam to establish contact well before the clinical situation became very difficult and overall, I was really pleased to have him in my corner. Neither Jane nor I was really ready to accept the situation I found myself in though, and it was particularly hard for Jane seeing me appear, to all intents and purposes, perfectly normal.

She just couldn't believe I could have so little time left.

Chapter 9

Coming to Terms With Everything

So, we'd got our diagnosis with its bleak prognosis and had told the most important people in our lives about it. How could we possibly come to terms with the devastating news that despite me feeling normal, I would, in all likelihood, be dead within a year and very possibly a great deal sooner than that?

My greatest concern was that I would be leaving Jane. We had both hoped and in truth, assumed, that we would have many more years together. She wouldn't in the near future have her husband, who had been with her for so long, to, in my own way, protect, love and look out for her and share decisions about all the happy and sad moments that lay ahead. I should have been around to grow old with her but that was now impossible because somehow, I had conspired to get one of the worst possible types of cancer and been so oblivious to it, that it had spread far and wide and was way beyond any curative treatment.

Jane is amazingly competent and has supported me far more over the years than I her, but nonetheless she couldn't envisage a future without me, any more than I could have contemplated one without her, had the roles been reversed. It struck Jane as particularly unfair that I had always led a healthy lifestyle and had none of the common risk factors for cancer, whilst others who smoked and drank heavily and were inactive and obese, often seemed to 'get away with it'. We knew that sooner or later everyone gets something, but Jane felt that my 'something' had been my aneurysm, so to get this as well, struck her as particularly cruel. Only a small part of me felt the same way as, deep down, I guess I knew that I didn't have a divine right not to be unlucky. In my professional life and in my personal life I had seen many people who were much younger than me with some form of cancer or some other very serious disease, so, at one level, I could accept that it wasn't, in the greater scheme of things, tragic that I'd got cancer at the age of sixty-four. At a personal level, of course, it was devastating.

It was even more overwhelming and distressing for Jane as she was the one facing a lonely old age and, in all likelihood, more than twenty years as a widow. She was heartbroken, inconsolable and struggling not to break down constantly. All our hopes and plans for a long retirement together, all the travelling and holidays we had had in mind were gone. In truth I hadn't been a great one for making long-term plans, perhaps I think, because I have seen so many patients' plans derailed by illness over the years.

Jane and I had faced pretty tough decisions over the aneurysm seven years earlier. The really hard one then was to decide whether to risk having surgery that might itself cause a stroke, or, given that the great majority of brain aneurysms never bleed, leave it alone, and risk the aneurysm bleeding with potentially devastating consequences. Wrestling with this made us realise how much we meant to each other when our future together was threatened and drew us very close to one another. The situation we now faced similarly brought us very close again, except that now there was no chance of a full recovery – the best one could hope for was to live for longer than the average patient did in my situation – which anyway was desperately short.

I feared, given the way my luck had been running, that I would be unlikely to survive for even the average time. I worried that I would succumb to the disease quickly which made me feel even worse about Jane's situation.

I was similarly concerned for our children. I knew they would be able to cope without me, but they would be losing their father at a relatively young age which, as I knew from personal experience, was hard. I had been touched and heartened by their reactions to date, but it would be very difficult for them seeing their Dad succumb to the ravages of cancer, knowing they would never be able to laugh and joke with me again. They would be worried about Jane who would be worried about them. Would I even live long enough to see my grandchild born? Even if I did it was very unlikely that I'd live long enough for him or her to have a meaningful relationship with me, and, if I did, would it be fair to then disappear? Mightn't it be just better to keep a lowish profile so that he or she would hardly miss me? Grandparents are supposed to be around for their grandchildren to provide a special kind of relationship. My grandchild and any subsequent ones would have missed out on that. They would only know what they were told about me.

The term, 'dead man walking' suddenly made sense. Everything seemed to have a temporary feel, a sense of impermanence. Everything seemed futile and transient.

I mourned the loss of some of the small, unimportant things. I'd always loved cars and often found myself thinking about the pleasure owning such-and-such a car would bring when I saw one go past. Now there was not a flicker of interest. No point if you wouldn't have it for long. I needed to get a new mobile phone, but when I rang up about it, I was offered a twelve-month or twenty-four-month contract. Neither seemed sensible given my prognosis so I just left it. Mundane perhaps, even trivial, but I never thought I would have to wrestle with a decision about whether my life expectancy justified a particular phone contract. I was long overdue replacing a particular type of golf club called a 'driver' and before the illness had promised myself a new one. I found myself going to a golf outlet trying a number out with Patrick and Duncan one day. One was promising but what was the point if I'd only get a few months use at best out of it? It wasn't a wish to be thrifty but simply common sense. It was sad, but the joy of trying the golf club with my sons was the thing – the time with them was what had mattered.

I was also forced to contemplate the 'big things' of life. What sort of a life had I led? What sort of a person had I been? Who would care that I was gone? What impression of me would the world be left with when I'd gone? What had I achieved in life? What awaited me after I died? Big, big questions. I was aware of many of my shortcomings but maybe there were others I wasn't aware of. Bit too late to try to change now anyway.

Had I done more good than harm? Probably, simply because my job afforded me lots of opportunities to help people.

I knew some people would really miss me, so therefore my life had, by my patient Peter's test, been, successful. Whether the wider world would miss me or care about my passing mattered far less to me than knowing that my family would.

I imagined probably quite a few former patients would be saddened and that quite a few relatives and friends would write to Jane which would help her and the family and was a comforting thought.

At one level, my life might have seemed dull and predictable. Born to two GPs I became one myself, raised a family then died a bit earlier than the average. There was nothing remarkable about that.

What had I left? What was my legacy?

'Just' a family that were remarkable in my eyes. That was enough. That was more than enough.

The reality of knowing how little time I had left, had shaken me to the core. I have helped dozens of patients face the end of their lives and in the vast majority their end of life care went well, and they had a 'good death'. But in spite of all that, I was worried that I would be in the small number of patients that don't have a good death. I felt that given the way luck had deserted me, I would be bound to have a particularly difficult and harrowing time.

There was no particular logic to those thoughts which emanated from a gloomy pessimism that seemed to have enveloped me. I kept them under rein during the day and didn't discuss them in conversations with Jane, knowing that they would only add to her distress, but each night they emerged and made sleep elusive.

In my case, familiarity with the condition served to make things worse. I had all-too-clear an idea of what was to come. I expected, from observing some patients, that when the final symptoms came, they would do so in a rush. I was scared that the palliative care wouldn't be effective at controlling them, and that I wouldn't be able to cope.

Being a doctor, at least one with my personality and foibles, in this situation, I suspect was probably worse than being a lay person. I had seen the pain in others, the loss of dignity and helplessness that awaited me. On the other hand, I had seen good deaths whereas many lay people had no experience of seeing the end of others' lives and might assume it to be terrible.

Normally when I've had something on my mind, I can work out or worry my way through to some sort of resolution, but for this there simply wasn't one. When helping patients with anxiety, doctors and others sometimes apply an approach called 'Problem Solving' whereby you explicitly discuss all the problems and logically and unemotionally work through possible solutions to them, thereby hopefully, reducing the impact of the problem.

The problem with my condition was that there just was no solution, palatable or unpalatable. There was no way of avoiding dying. I would just have to try to cope as best I could. It wouldn't last forever anyway, it wouldn't last for very long in all likelihood, but it would be a bad way of leaving. I dreaded getting to a point where I just wanted the end to rescue me. I felt that Jane and my children deserved someone with more courage and determination than that.

One of the first friends I had told, a retired GP, like I had suddenly become, had exhorted me to 'make every minute count'. He wasn't the only one to say something like that. But what did that mean? What would count? Obviously spending time with Jane and telling her how much she meant to me, reassuring her that I would do all I could to be around for as long as possible, that would count. Similarly, with the children and others close to me. But you couldn't do that literally every minute of every day. So, what else counted? Do what you enjoy? OK, so I played golf with friends whose company I enjoyed. I don't enjoy golf so much that I want to play it more than once or twice a week. Do normal things? What is normal? Nothing felt quite normal now. Fair enough, surely, to avoid doing things you dislike, such as looking at wallpaper patterns and going to some furniture sale or other. But those were normal things you did because you were part of a couple and one half wanted to go. So, I did go to a furniture sale and it was a waste of time, but it sort of counted because it was supporting Jane and spending time with her.

The sense of dread that what time was left was not being properly used was ever-present. 'FOMO' is a term young people use. It's an acronym for 'Fear of Missing Out' There was an element of this, without knowing quite what I was missing out on. What about TV say? Surely not, as it is a rather mindless thing to do. But it took one's mind off the impossibly difficult present. What about all the classics I hadn't read? Should I start to read as many as possible now? But what would be the point now? I had always enjoyed writing and had envisaged having a go at a book in retirement. But could I finish one if I started? Would anyone read it anyway if I did? Would it be sensible to spend long hours at my desk on it instead of going out with Jane? It would be the only book I'd ever write – a good name for a title perhaps – if no-one else had grabbed it before.

And then there was the issue of work. I regarded myself as lucky to have the job I had. A GP is appreciated by most of his or her patients and like all GPs, I have had many plaudits and letters and presents simply for doing my job. But doing any more of this great job, which I had been full of renewed enthusiasm for since recovering from the aneurysm, was now out of the question. Whatever time I had left had to be given to Jane and the children, and getting my affairs sorted out. In any case it wouldn't be possible to concentrate properly at work now. And I would soon be experiencing symptoms from the illness or the chemotherapy, so it wasn't a practical proposition anyway. But to stop work abruptly without saying goodbye to anyone? That was a sad end to a long career and a part of me felt guilty for doing just that and almost abandoning patients, some of whom, I knew would be upset not to be able to see me again or say goodbye.

My partners needed to know what was going on, so I emailed, stating that I had a gastric tumour and was seeing a specialist shortly and would be able to tell them more soon. I apologised for the bad timing and asked that they kept it confidential for the time being.

They emailed back their condolences and concern. Looking back, it only now occurs to me that it must have been quite a shock for them, but I don't think that my mind had room to realise that at the time. My mind was crossed – criss-crossed – with too many other thoughts.

Soon it would be important to tell the surgery staff what was going on, not only to let them know what had happened but also so that they could tell patients why, after nearly thirty-seven years, I had suddenly stopped working.

My three sisters. They would be shocked and upset. I couldn't simply email them. Or just ring. Or go and see them, as they all lived many miles away. So, I contacted their closest family member to break the news gently to them. Sorted. Rather, just dealt with for now. Concerned, upset phone calls were to come.

Relationships with friends were complex. Old friends one rarely saw were different to ones you saw a lot of. Then there were some people one had known for decades, particularly in the village we live in, who were not close friends but who we saw frequently. The most important group were close, local friends of course, and they would have to be told soon and in person. That would be difficult as some people would be terribly upset and shaken. It would have to be done.

But we didn't really want to tell anyone about our very private, very personal problem. It was altogether too intimate an issue to talk to others outside our immediate family and closest friends. Telling other people about it would make it ever more real and unavoidable, but it went deeper than just that. I felt diminished as a person and as a man. I was embarrassed to have now become a really unhealthy patient even if I felt generally well. We really didn't want to have to go over the whole issue time and again, having to put on a brave, matter-of-fact demeanour. The world and its mother knowing about the crisis in our lives would change everything. We would be regarded differently by everyone. People would be kind and sympathetic and feel sorry for us and shudder at the thought that it could have been them. But who wants that? People would discuss the news and comment about how unlucky we had been. The irony of a medical person getting such a condition on the point of retirement would be chewed over. What rotten luck. I would suddenly become very conspicuous when I walked around the village. Better to stay indoors then, I suppose. And what about the Chinese whispers? Someone would tell the next person and as the story got relayed the whole thing would become far worse than it was. I was desperately unwell... I had become skeletal... I was in a hospice and waiting for the end. I had died... Jane was a widow.

One morning, out of the blue, I received a phone call from Shelley the wife of a friend I'd tried to contact a few months earlier and left a phone message for. She told me she had shocking news. Her husband, George, had died quite a few months ago. Of cancer. What else? It had been uncomfortably close to my situation. An operation had been tried but had been unsuccessful. I was greatly saddened, as many years earlier we had played a lot of squash together and he had been great company. Why hadn't I got around to contacting him much earlier as a few years before, he had spotted me in the street and come over and greeted me warmly? She recounted how upset and angry she was that many of their friends, on hearing the news of his illness, had stopped calling or visiting. Even people who they had regarded as close friends. She called it 'The English disease'. I said the usual thing about how often people are like this because they don't know how to react and what to say. 'But George deserved better' she protested, 'he would never have dealt with his friends like that.' It was true. He was gregarious, friendly and warm. Silently, I regretted that I hadn't known he was ill, as I would certainly have visited him. One thing my job had taught me was that if you asked yourself the question in that sort of situation 'Should I?' the answer was always 'yes'. I tried to be solicitous, but it was rather late in the day. I didn't mention my own situation.

I was upset that I would never see George again. It was quite a blow to be presented with his story, realising that I was in much the same situation as he had been, except that in my case it had been clear from the start that it was far too late for any operation to be tried. Maybe I was luckier than he'd been. George had a much warmer friendlier disposition than me and yet had been shunned by his friends.

Would our phone stop ringing when our news was out?

Would Jane be left like George's wife?

It wouldn't help if we hadn't told people who later found out from someone else, as they wouldn't know if they were supposed to know or not, so probably wouldn't know how to react. One thing seemed clear, we ought to take responsibility for telling people so that they got the correct information. We had to be inclusive, and if in doubt as to whether to tell a couple, bite the bullet and tell them. But not yet, we'd do it when the time seemed right. For now, we just needed to tell very close friends and relatives. Everyone else could wait.

Jane and I had spent a couple of years planning and designing a house to be built in our garden and our architect had been on the verge of going out to tender when the diagnosis came. We had put a huge amount of time and energy, and no small amount of money, into the project by this stage and had been excited that at long last it was soon to start. Knowing I was going to have to undergo gruelling chemotherapy and become more and more ill and quite possibly die before the house was even finished, was it sensible to continue? Could Jane or I bear to have the disruption of living yards from a building site and have to participate in making thousands of decisions? No-one we have ever met who has built a house has said it was great fun or easy. No. It was an easy decision to call a halt, though a very sad one for us. I rang our architect, with whom we had developed a close relationship and told him the news. He was great and responded in the most supportive way. After saying how sorry he was, he said that he would mothball the project and defer the tenders and that we could pick it up again at any point in the future if it proved possible. A big if.

'Lucky,' a GP friend, who is one of the busiest people I know, on hearing our news, rushed round. Before the aneurysm operation, he had been a great source of advice and support and was again now. He reassured me that all the possible problems I foresaw regarding work would be OK and he was right again. 'Lucky' is a good guy to have in your corner, but even he seemed to realise I was in a fight I was bound to lose. He was a little emotional which was something I'd not seen before – perhaps he'd been to a boarding school too – which was disconcerting in a good sort of way. Disconcerting I suppose because it underlined that I had my back firmly pinned against the wall, and good because of the honesty of his response which showed that he cared.

The Will. We needed to check to see if anything needed altering, now that it would soon be needed, so we left a message asking our solicitor to ring us. One beautiful sunny day, we went for a long walk through the fields around the Cotswold villages of Swinbrook and Widford. The golden grey stone of the cottages, the undulating hills and valleys and the flowing Windrush River made you feel glad to be alive. That day it was even more precious, as we both wondered how many more walks on days like this, we would have together. An Australian tourist took photographs of us to capture the moment. It was lovely, and the added poignancy of the situation heightened the feeling. We should have spent many more days like this, but we hadn't. We'd assumed there would be lots of time for walks in retirement. As we walked along the side of an elevated remote field the mobile went off. It was our solicitor calling back about the Will. Everything was in order. No need to worry about that.

Surreal to be discussing a Will in a field, but everything about our lives now seemed surreal.

Financially, we were luckier than most and I knew that Jane would be able to manage OK. Nonetheless she would only receive half my NHS pension when I died. We needed to discuss the situation with our accountant, a friend of many years, to find out what needed to be done. He was helpful and practical, even pointing out that some tax would be avoided if I died whilst still a partner in my practice so advised me not to rush to resign.

Good to have a competent and caring accountant.

Good to know that dying quickly could have some benefits.

Chapter 10

Preparing for my Chemotherapy Nemesis

Jane was concerned that someone reading this might be put off having chemotherapy when it was recommended for them. If that person is you, then please remember that what I have written is personal to me and is not an objective guide to chemotherapy. When I was working, I only became involved with patients on chemotherapy when there was a problem. Chemotherapy patients who didn't have a problem, naturally, didn't need to see me, so my experience skewed me away from a balanced perspective on what undertaking chemotherapy is really like.

Also, remember the adage 'A little knowledge is a dangerous thing'... And probably I'm a hypochondriac like most medics. And that I'm a coward.

'Good morning Paul

Thank you for contacting me yesterday. As promised, I am writing to confirm the time and date for starting your treatment with us. Please present yourself at main reception at 10:30 on 10/11/2016. The receptionist will direct you to level 2 Oncology Suite. We will meet you and take you to one of our rooms where you will spend approx. 5 hours with us.'

The above email from the Sister in Charge of Oncology, went on to describe how some of the drugs would be given into a vein and others taken by mouth, what drugs I should take home and the arrangements for medical assistance if it was required and finished by saying how she was looking forward to meeting me – a sentiment not wholeheartedly reciprocated by me.

It was really happening then. I was going to have chemotherapy.

Chemotherapy is something no-one looks forward to receiving. Patients may be keen to get it over and done with, but that's all. Chemotherapy has serious connotations. You're not offered it for trivial conditions. It means you've got cancer. It's hard to know what a word conjures up in other people's minds but chemotherapy for me conjures up people being made unwell, sometimes very unwell, in the hope that their cancer might be knocked on the head permanently or at least for a while. Having chemotherapy does not necessarily mean that a patient is in dire straits like I was, because it can, of course, be literally lifesaving. For some cancers, the treatment is really very effective. But from where I'm coming from, it's very scary and in my case it's only palliative in that it won't cure me but may prolong my life – if I'm lucky.

I would most commonly see patients on chemotherapy when they had an infection that was caused by the medication suppressing the body's defence mechanisms and so leaving them vulnerable particularly to chest infections, which, if left untreated or underestimated by me, could literally be fatal. Other patients had really grim side effects from their chemotherapy, like extreme fatigue, nausea and vomiting, and weight loss. In truth, I've no real idea what proportion of chemotherapy patients struggled with side effects, but as it was pretty well a hundred per cent of the ones I saw, I assumed I would struggle badly.

I felt pretty low about the fact that I would be embarking on chemotherapy. The very thought of submitting yourself to treatment that could make you feel terrible is daunting. Maria had made it clear that not everyone opted for it, and that not everyone who started the course could cope with the side effects. I wasn't so deluded about myself that I thought I could put up with anything that came my way. Far from it. I was frightened that I wouldn't be able to cope at all well and would give up too easily. I had at least learnt that not everyone has terrible side effects but with the way my luck had been running of late I just knew I would.

On the other hand, three friends had recently coped with chemotherapy. Two had taken a real battering for months from nausea, vomiting and profound fatigue but come through it. One complained very little about it, despite being someone who was not normally stoical – but his skin was messed up, most strikingly on his face, his hands and feet felt cold and numb, he couldn't drink anything cold and he had days when he was pretty well wiped out by fatigue. But he didn't get any nausea or vomiting. Maybe I'd be lucky like that. Maybe I'd be OK.

The acronym for my three drugs was 'EOX'. I had been given an information leaflet by my oncologist. 'Some people might have side effects while they are having the chemotherapy' - meaning literally while the drugs were being given into a vein, either from the actual drug causing, for example, an allergic reaction, or the drug leaking outside of the vein. Afterwards, possible side effects were listed but other than with tiredness, which was listed as a common side effect, there was no indication of how likely it was to get them. Anti-sickness drugs would always be given to 'help prevent or control sickness', so one deduced that vomiting was very likely. There was a long list of side-effects, but the bumph stated that the list was not exhaustive despite filling three-and-a-half pages of A4. Nausea and vomiting were the ones that I feared most, as I had really struggled with the laxatives for the colonoscopy and I figured if something as relatively innocuous as laxatives could almost overwhelm me...

Most people seemingly lost their hair or a large part of it with the EOX. No big deal surely, you might feel in the greater scheme of things, considering what was at stake? But it felt like a big deal for me and did concern me – a lot. Partly for the symbolism – when you see someone you know who suddenly has no hair at all, not even the rim of hair that is seen with normal male baldness – and in my case I'd always had a thick head of hair – then you know they have 'The Big C' – poor bastard. Partly from sheer silly vanity – I didn't want to become a 'slap-head'. I didn't think it would suit me at all and I'd always been rather proud – if one can be proud about something that has nothing to do with you personally and everything to do with your genes – about my hair which had survived the ravages of time far better than the rest of me. And assuming weight loss to boot, a skinny slap head who probably looks exhausted and shuffles around like a very old man. I would stand out like a character from Solzhenitsyn's 'Cancer Ward'. It would be embarrassing and feel a bit humiliating. After all, I was someone who treated patients not the other way around.

I imagined quite a few people wouldn't even recognise me without hair which would be better. But they'd know Jane who would be beside me, wouldn't they, even if they didn't clock me? You'd see the shock on their faces and their embarrassment for not recognising me, then the awkwardness about the encounter and what, if anything, to say. Then Jane would try to make light of things but probably break down. And so on and so on and so on. No doubt people in the street would do as I do when I see someone like that – look away and try not to stare or look interested or, worst of all, sympathetic.

I passed the shop in the main entrance of The Churchill Hospital one day where the wigs were sold and walked past very slowly to enable me to study carefully what was on offer. I didn't go in of course, because I didn't want to appear vain, especially as it seemed that all the wigs were for women. I've read biographies of women with breast cancer describing their reaction to hair loss and also spoken to a few women about how it felt, and the distress of losing their hair was so much, that some said, it was worse than losing their breast, as they saw their hair as a huge part of their identity. A friend who used to provide wigs for cancer patients said that whilst a few men are very concerned, most are not. I'm afraid I was one of the few. I knew you could try applying a 'cold cap' during chemotherapy which makes the scalp very cold and may prevent or lessen hair loss, but I'd heard that was very hard to put up with. I decided that I would appear altogether far too vain if I asked to try one and suspected that I wouldn't be able to tolerate one anyway so just resigned myself to losing my hair.

Still if chemotherapy meant I had a chance of longer survival, there was no real choice. Maria had made it clear that it was at least worth seeing if you could tolerate the EOX, as not everyone struggled badly, and some regretted not taking it when it was too late.

She also said the fitter you were, the better you would be able to tolerate the drugs. So, I started training like I'd done before my aneurysm operation albeit a bit half-heartedly. It helped to feel you were doing something constructive that might help your cause and training was, after all, something I did before some sporting challenge when I was well, so I could delude myself for brief moments that I must be well. Initially I ran on my treadmill and later outside, the first time with Duncan for much-appreciated support. I was pleased a village friend saw me out as it would prolong the impression that I was fit and well. I panted a bit more than usual because of my anaemia.

Essentially, I was the opposite of the professional cyclists and other sportspeople who illicitly take drugs to increase their haemoglobin, which enables them to be less breathless when they compete – in my case the cancer had lowered my haemoglobin.

The family suggested I buy some hats to mitigate the hair loss appearance. So, we all went to Burford and bought a couple of natty flat-caps, a very soft beanie that would be fine for golf and a stylish purple trilby. Additionally, Patrick gave me his fur hat which he'd bought for going to Russia which was super warm. Being well prepared for the hair loss, and the concern and love the family had shown about the whole issue made me feel a lot happier. I was as ready as I'd ever be to face my nemesis.

As instructed, I rang the Oncology Sister a few days before my chemotherapy was scheduled. She said she was surprised to hear from me as she had received a copy of an email sent by Maria to me, saying that in the light of recent test results the proposed date for the chemotherapy may have to be deferred. I hadn't seen it, so I hastily said goodbye and looked Maria's email up:

I would like to update you with the result from the immunohistochemistry, that I have just received. The pathologist has reported that in fact the immunohistochemistry is more in keeping with a neuroendocrine carcinoma rather than an adenocarcinoma as originally thought.

The email went on to explain that the Multidisciplinary Team that dealt with neuroendocrine carcinomas – NECs – would look at all the results the next day and that I ought to see an oncologist who specializes in that type of cancer. She would ring me after the MDT meeting but if I wanted to discuss it before then she would call me later. The email finished:

'I understand that this ongoing uncertainty will be frustrating for you, but it is important to ensure that the treatment, when ultimately given, is going to be optimal'.

That didn't seem to imply that I should be overly pleased about this. My recollection had been that she didn't think the immunohistochemistry would change things, but obviously somehow it had. What was a neuroendocrine carcinoma?

Despite my rather arrogant assumption that I'd seen pretty well everything in my long career, I wasn't at all sure. Patrick and Jane were at home and immediately started googling furiously. I emailed the consultant saying that I'd appreciate a call to get some sort of feel for what this might mean and in particular for whether it might just have a better prognosis. While I was emailing, I was getting the 'thumbs-up' sign from Patrick and Jane – if this new possibility was confirmed it seemed to them to be better than stomach cancer.

Maria rang shortly afterwards and elaborated. As with the face-to-face consultation, she was initially careful not to get my hopes up too much and said that the histologist – the specialist who looked at the specimens under a microscope – felt it was very likely that this was a neuroendocrine carcinoma. What should now happen, she explained, was for it to be discussed in the Neuroendocrine MDT with endocrine surgeons, radiologists and a second histologist to review the findings. By the end of the conversation, however, she did say that this was definitely a better situation and offered more hope as the spectrum of survival for these neuroendocrine cancers (NEC) was much more variable than with stomach cancer. By this, she implied that some NEC patients live rather longer than stomach cancer patients. I was to see the oncologist who specialises in these sorts of tumours the following afternoon.

Chapter 11

Caught in the Cancer NET

Wow! What did all this mean? Was it possible that my luck just might be turning? Did I dare start to hope for a better outcome than had hitherto been promised? Jane and Patrick were clearly excited. My heart began to race. I was a bit confused. Don't get too excited – it's still cancer. The liver is still stuffed with secondaries and an operation won't be feasible. But Maria, who was so wary of getting hopes up, had said it 'definitely offered more hope'. And hope had been in very short supply up to that point.

I started googling. I wasn't sure I knew much at all, if anything, from my clinical practice. It was frustratingly difficult to get a clear handle on NECs. They were rare cancers – which was why I hadn't come across them in my work – that much was clear. Steve Jobs had evidently died from one. As NECs are rare cancers there are only a few hospitals in Europe that are regarded as Centres of Excellence in the treatment of neuroendocrine cancers and happily Oxford was one of them. I wouldn't have to go far then for expert treatment.

We told the news to Duncan and Laura. Weirdly, as NECs are rare, Laura immediately recounted that two of her friends had each had a parent who had died from a neuroendocrine tumour, but both had survived for a few years before doing so. A few years! That was obviously a great deal better than I could expect from a stomach cancer. But they might have been very different to me. Indeed, the one thing that was clear was that these malignancies were very varied in type and outcome. Maybe the outcome would be little better then. I would have to wait till the following day when I would see one of the two neuroendocrine oncologists in Oxford to get some clarity. I couldn't allow myself to be too hopeful lest the old pattern of getting knocked further back with every development occurred again. But surely to some extent this must be good news as very few cancers are worse than stomach cancer.

Keep calm, I told myself, and see what the news is tomorrow. Please let it be good.

Back to the hospital waiting area the next day, to see Michael, a different oncologist, to be told what cocktail of chemotherapy would be best for a NEC. Whenever I had sat in that waiting room before, the news I'd received had always been the worst possible, so I was braced for the inevitable disappointment. I'd made it a point to dress fairly sharply for my appointments, as I thought the better I looked, the healthier I would seem to whoever saw me. There was also an element of wanting to look smart and perhaps even professional, and it made me feel a bit better about myself and more like my previous existence when I was working. At the hospital I observed different doctors with varying degrees of sartorial elegance from dapper to rapper (almost) and mused that at least on the way out I might pass muster for one of them rather than obviously being in the undesirable category of 'patient'. Clearly, I hadn't come to terms with crossing the divide between being a giver of care to now being a receiver.

Michael called us through. A friendly man with a hint of a Wirral accent, he explained that the main tumour mass was involving the stomach, pancreas and spleen, but that it was impossible to say where the primary tumour was arising from. It was academic anyway as there was disease in the liver. [Meaning that wherever the tumour was, as it had spread to the liver, it wouldn't be possible to remove all the cancer from my body]. My case had been discussed at the Neuroendocrine MDT and the pathologist there was quite certain that it was a pure Neuroendocrine Tumour. In fact, about four different pathologists had looked at the histology. He went on to explain that there are three grades of NET tumours with grade one being the best and grade three the worst. At this point I knew that mine would inevitably be a three.

But it wasn't. It was a grade two. The middle grade. This was a break from the tradition of anything to do with me always being the worst possible – grade one would have been a lot nicer though.

The worst type of grade three tumours is also called 'neuroendocrine carcinoma' so it transpired that I had a NET not a NEC. Thankfully. (Please see Appendix 2 for a more detailed explanation about classification of these cancers).

Michael explained that at the MDT meeting, the lead surgeon, Alistair, had been concerned that left alone, the tumour could cause the portal vein to bleed which would necessitate a very difficult emergency operation to try to stop the bleeding, so he felt that surgery to remove the main bulk of the tumour would be worth considering. The MDT recommended that I see Alistair to discuss the possible benefits and risks of surgery. Surgery would be a big undertaking involving removing the spleen in its entirety and part of the pancreas and part of the stomach. The MDT didn't know whether I was fit enough to be able to cope with a major operation, but after speaking to Maria and meeting me, Michael felt I'd be fit enough to undergo surgery. Maybe scrubbing up for the appointment had paid dividends on this occasion.

The MDT also recommended an 'octreotide scan' to see if my tumour had 'octreotide receptors'. These are small areas, present in most NET tumours and NET metastases, which open the possibility of 'targeted liver radioisotope therapy' also known as PRRT – Peptide Receptor Radionuclide Therapy. This entails having an injection of a radioactive substance attached to Octreotide which then attaches to the Octreotide receptors and gives a localised or 'targeted' dose of radiotherapy to the liver metastases. This is much less harmful to a liver than just shining radiotherapy from outside the body to the liver, as that way, inevitably, unaffected parts of the liver get some radiotherapy as well as the metastases.

PRRT sounded impressively hi-tech. I'd never heard of it before, but I definitely liked the sound of it. Targeted therapy, Michael explained, is usually done for grade one tumours but not for grade three tumours for which chemotherapy is recommended. For grade two tumours both treatments can be considered, but he felt in my case chemotherapy would be best to try first to treat the disease in the liver and any residual disease that the surgeon couldn't remove in the abdomen.

Although I would have preferred the PRRT treatment to the chemotherapy after the surgery, the treatment being discussed sounded a million miles away from the gloom and despondency of the consultation with Maria, where the treatment had felt like it was worth a go but not much more than that. This approach sounded much more hopeful. It was active, aggressive treatment which I warmed to the sound of. Maybe the nightmare scenario was beginning to disappear?

Getting a bit carried away, I ventured 'Dare I ask is all of this potentially curative?'

In hindsight and with a calmer mind it was clearly a silly question, as I still had lots of metastases in the liver. Michael gently replied:

'I think it's unlikely, even if you have a good operation, because you have multiple metastases in the liver not just in one or two areas. If you have a really good response in the liver to the chemotherapy and some of the metastases disappeared and some shrank down, then, yes, if we can do liver PRRT then we would, but I can't promise we would ever get to that stage'.

Back to earth.

The idea of the surgery was not to cure things but to remove as much of the bulk of the tumour as possible, so called 'de-bulking', and would mean that the subsequent chemotherapy treatment would have less tumour to deal with, which could lead to a better overall outcome. The operation would also make my situation safer, as left alone the tumour could grow into the portal vein or a blood vessel elsewhere and cause heavy bleeding which could be immediately fatal.

I returned to the question uppermost in our minds. How much time could I realistically hope for? It was impossible to say, he replied, as it depended on how quickly the tumour was growing and its response to treatment, and he would only be able to assess that over a period of time. He did have patients with grade 2 tumours like mine. The tumours progressed very slowly and were controlled with monthly injections. Some of the patients lived for five or ten years. On the other hand, he explained, he had patients where the tumours were growing much more quickly which made it a lot harder to get control of the disease and who by implication lived nothing like as long.

So, the old banker – what should I tell my children?

'That it is significantly better than stomach cancer with liver metastases, where the prognosis is surviving for less than a year even with treatment, so I'm sure it will be better than that. How much better at this one point in time I cannot tell and would be literally plucking figures out of the air. Over time, you get a feeling for what is happening with the disease. On the whole, they tend to grow more slowly than stomach cancer. Your tumour could have been present for a long time, even years.'

He asked how long and what symptoms I'd had and, listening to the tape now, I realise that I waffled on a bit in the annoying way that some patients do, doubtless because I was completely unprepared and caught off guard by what I was being told. I wasn't expecting to be offered any surgery as a result of Jeremy, the gastroenterologist, telling me that surgery was out of the question when the diagnosis was stomach cancer.

I mentioned to Michael that in the past, when patients had liver secondaries, they were sometimes just metaphorically patted on the head and told to make the most of the time left.

'But that was the past, now we are much more aggressive in our treatments.' He replied, 'It all depends on whether we can get all the disease out from the primary tumour which is where you need Alistair's advice'

'Was this sort of surgery often undertaken?' I enquired

'Yes' was the straightforward answer. 'Whenever the NET MDT meet, they make these sort of recommendations'

'If you were in my shoes would you have surgery?'

'Unquestionably, if I could have that primary out I would.'

'Does Alistair do a lot of this kind of surgery?'

'Yes, it's his bread and butter – he's doing it all the time'

'If it was you, you'd be happy to go to him?'

'More than happy.'

So, no sitting on the fence from Michael – a straightforward unequivocal recommendation to have surgery which was brilliant. I explained that I was very pleased to hear about the surgical options and would be very happy to see Alistair, who, Michael explained, I would be able to see in about a week. I mentioned that I had been really pleased to see that Oxford was a specialist centre for NETs and asked how many cases they saw. As a European Centre of Excellence for NETs, Michael said they saw about 150 cases a year. That seemed an impressively large number for a rare condition and that was very encouraging.

He finished by saying that we would meet up again, after the surgery and the MDT meeting had been held, to discuss the outcome of the operation and the octreotide scan which would probably be done after the operation.

Compared with the absolute bleakness of the initial diagnosis, being told that it was a NET almost felt like a miracle and for the first time with any of the appointments we left happier, a lot happier, than when we had gone in.

What had just happened? What was going on?

Surgery and aggressive surgery at that, was now on the cards. I would certainly go for that option even though I hadn't given a moment's thought to what would be involved in surviving it and then recovering from it. After all, I had coped with a surgeon removing part of my skull and then delving deep inside my brain clipping arteries. It couldn't be any tougher than that surely? I was fit and having done the marathon I felt showed I had pretty good endurance for pain and discomfort, so I didn't have any doubts in my mind that I would get through the surgery OK. I'd have to in any case. The great thing was that I was going to have the sort of energetic, active, aggressive treatment that had not been possible with a stomach cancer and there was a definite chance it could make a real difference and give me a chance of more time with Jane than had seemed possible before.

'We can then deal with the liver metastases after the surgery' Michael had said. That sounded very encouraging, as if he felt that he could sort the liver out. That was very good to hear. I'd always had the impression that when your liver has a lot of metastases in it you are not long for this world. Michael had dismissed this generalisation as being out-of-date and didn't seem to think that was necessarily the case at all. Fair enough, he hadn't promised to be able to sort it, but he definitely sounded reasonably confident and the PRRT, the targeted liver approach, was clearly cutting-edge treatment and might be possible for me. I had to have chemotherapy first, of course, which was not that great, but it sounded like there were real options which could make a really significant difference to how long I might live. His seemed very different to the stomach cancer treatment, which might make a few months difference at best, provided it worked at all, which, of course, in the majority of people it didn't.

This was really good news. Really, really good news. It felt like a reprieve.

It wasn't of course. We knew it was more like a stay of execution. Still on Death Row but some of those guys there had been waiting a long time. Maybe, just maybe, I could be one of them. Two or three years would be wonderful compared with the year or so which had been the best I could really have expected before with stomach cancer. In two or three years you could live a little instead of just dreading each day passing bringing you inexorably nearer towards the end of life care. I could also get things properly in place for Jane. We were stunned. We hugged and laughed and tried to take it all in.

We must tell our children. We had guarded hope. We mustn't get too far ahead of ourselves.

Jane was concerned about having to wait for a week to see the surgeon, not just because she wanted to get on with the treatment, but also because she was mindful of the risk of a heavy bleed which surgery would eliminate, but Alistair was away at a conference so wasn't holding his usual weekly clinic.

Who was he? I'd vaguely heard of him and seen his name on letters about patients but that was about all. I couldn't form any sort of mental picture of him. The internet would fill in some of the gaps no doubt. I had done my best to get Michael to say how good he was. He'd said he'd be very happy to have Alistair operate on him and he definitely would go for surgery in my shoes so that really said it all. Alistair's surgery could make a very real difference.

Jane had never been able to fully believe or accept that I'd got stomach cancer as she had felt I was just far too well. This diagnosis seemed far more credible in her mind. Lots of thoughts and ideas raced around our heads, about living longer, being able to go on more holidays and really to live a more normal life for longer than we'd dared hope possible. My luck, our luck, had turned. We had a real sense of wonderment and gratitude, it felt like a miracle. We felt our prayers and those of so many other people who had told us they were 'whispering' had been answered. Jane suggested that on the way home we call into the Roman Catholic church we sometimes went to in Oxford – but it was locked.

Peter, the patient who was so impressively steadfast and eloquent in the way he dealt with being told that his X Ray showed he had stomach cancer, later had an endoscopy of his stomach. In contrast to his X Ray the endoscopy report came back as being entirely normal. I requested a formal review of both tests, which concluded that the X Ray report had been incorrect. Peter did not have stomach cancer. I explained to him what had happened and that he did not, after all, have stomach cancer or any cancer for that matter. He received and reacted to this fantastic news in the same calm and measured way that he had when the shoe was on the other foot.

'If you can meet with triumph and disaster and treat those two impostors just the same...'

Peter could and did.

I wasn't quite as fortunate as Peter, and there hadn't really been a mistake per se, just a working or provisional diagnosis which was revised when all the tests came back. Admittedly I could have started chemotherapy for stomach cancer before the correct diagnosis had emerged, but I hadn't. The important thing was that I didn't have stomach cancer.

When your diagnosis of stomach cancer is changed, almost any other cancer seems like a blessing.

Chapter 12

Meeting the Surgeon

I wasn't going to look this gift horse in the mouth. When offered the option of a debulking operation, I wanted to grab it straight away even before meeting Alistair or knowing exactly what he proposed to do. So keen was I to get on with the operation that I rang his secretary to ask her to let him know that I was definitely keen to go ahead and was hoping he could start to make arrangements as soon as possible. His secretary was friendly but explained that getting operating theatre slots for this sort of operation was very difficult. She said she assumed I wanted it before Christmas – which was seven weeks away. I was struck by sudden despair, panic and bewilderment as I had been expecting the surgery to be either the next week or the week after. How could I possibly be expected to wait up to seven weeks, for what seemed a manifestly urgent operation? Michael had explained that there was a risk of major bleeding from the tumour growing into the portal vein, which could even be fatal. Even allowing for my personal stake in the matter, that seemed to make a seven-week delay unacceptably dangerous.

Patients often came to me requesting help to get an operation done sooner than was being offered, and in an instance like this, I would have been a strong advocate for them. It seemed bizarre. It felt almost nightmarish. I had just been told I had a chance at some life, but this felt like the lifeline that had been thrown to me was being pulled away again. I wasn't expecting any priority over others in the NHS queue just because I was a doctor – my condition just seemed to merit an urgent operation. I had even told the secretary that I could fund the operation myself and have the operation done on a private surgical list.

For most of my career, on the rare occasions I needed any hospital treatment, I would see my GP and be referred. I didn't ask for any form of priority, but it happened as a matter of course. The prevailing mindset used to be to give people who worked in the NHS some priority with appointments and operations on the basis that they kept the NHS going, and without them the already hard-pressed NHS service would struggle even more. It was also regarded as a professional courtesy from one colleague to another and to be 'the one perk of the job'. We all hoped for and generally got, this extra consideration, which meant usually being seen fairly promptly, usually by a consultant, rather than by a less experienced member of his team and, if one was available, a room to oneself if admitted to a ward. This was often referred to as 'privoid care' essentially private-like care without payment. However, providing that sort of privileged access gradually became harder as tighter management of hospital clinics and operations occurred and quite properly a more egalitarian approach to health provision replaced it.

About ten years before my 'Medical Waterloo', at a practice meeting one of my thriftier partners surprised us by mentioning that he had taken out Private Health Insurance. A consultant friend had pointed out to him that, for the reasons I've mentioned, it had become virtually impossible to give colleagues and other NHS workers special consideration. This caused disappointment if the doctor who needed treatment had been counting on the old-fashioned traditional arrangements, and embarrassment to the consultant he had been referred to that couldn't provide any special treatment to a colleague.

My partner felt that it was just more straightforward to pay for health insurance and then actually be able to go to a colleague and for him or her to be properly paid by the insurance company. He argued that it would be good for the practice if he was able to access quick care as it would mean he would not be off work for so long and the remaining partners wouldn't have to cover his work for so long either. I think my partner hoped that the rest of us might follow suit. I was the oldest in the practice, hence the most likely to need medical care at some point. I had very mixed feelings about it, wondering if it would be hypocritical of me to have private treatment when I worked in the NHS and was both a strong supporter of and campaigner for it? Would it be saying that I deserved to be seen more quickly than my patients? Would it seem almost like a betrayal? I supposed I could have the security of private cover but not use it unless the wait for NHS treatment was dire or I was in a lot of pain. If I did buy private cover, as I enjoyed very good health and assumed that would continue for many years, wouldn't it just be a very expensive waste of money? I couldn't deny that it would be good for my partners and patients if any absence for illness was as short as possible, and also it would save the awkwardness of hoping that any colleague I saw could give me priority and sort me out quickly.

It did seem fair that any consultants that treated me got paid rather than me being able to take advantage of their good nature. I also reasoned, although this might appear to be post-rationalisation, that if BUPA paid for an operation it would be sparing the NHS the expense and would mean another patient was treated earlier. I was surprised to find that the cost of basic private health insurance for Jane and myself was affordable and much lower than I'd expected, so, with some misgivings, took it out.

I was very pleased that I had when my neurosurgeon was not able to find an NHS slot for my aneurysm operation anything like as quickly as he wanted to. He was very relieved to be able to do it privately much sooner, which was good for my morale and meant I got back to my NHS work a lot sooner. The treatment I received then was exactly the same as if I'd been an NHS patient – my neurosurgeon treated all his patients in the same – extraordinary – way. My treatment was just 'self-funded'. I don't think any treatment I received was any different because I was funding it. I was in a bed on an NHS hospital ward and there was certainly no red carpet or luxury food.

The NHS can't fund everything that patients want or need, so for example, some people have to pay for fertility treatment themselves. They attend a normal NHS clinic and get the same treatment as everyone else. There is no difference. Some expect special consideration but soon learn that there is one standard for everyone – which is just as it should be.

I had been surprised by how relatively calm and accepting of the fact that I had extensive cancer I had been. I had noticed, however, that I wasn't able to cope with stress and uncertainty anything like as well as normal. The realisation that I might have to wait seven weeks for my operation was very unexpected and almost surreal. Stress and the uncertainty floored me. It felt intolerable. It was almost as if I'd been keeping the lid on my fears, and this setback had blown the lid off. I explained my concern to Alistair's secretary who did her best to assure me that, of course, he would arrange things as quickly as he could. But the damage was done. I felt shattered that I could be expected to wait so long. Surely the secretary must have got the wrong end of the stick?

A few days later, we met Alistair. A smallish, slim man with a quiet manner – the absolute antithesis of Sir Lancelot Spratt – that booming, loud, caricature of a God-like surgeon in the 'Doctor in The House' films. He asked what family I had and what my children did, showing particular interest in Duncan who was doing orthopaedics in London as a junior hospital doctor.

'Was I still working as GP? Where was my surgery? Who was at home with me? Was Jane medical? He wanted to know how this all came to light and what had made me have a scan and so on? Was I generally healthy?'

He outlined what he planned to do. He drew a picture of the tumour to illustrate the options.

'You've got a NET in the pancreas which has attached itself to the stomach and spleen. There is a metastasis in the splenic vein (the splenic vein is a smaller vein than the portal vein and feeds into the portal vein like a tributary into the Thames).

Liver metastases don't necessarily make things inoperable.

The likelihood is that the disease is not curable, but because it is a NET the likelihood is that you could be managed for a long time with different modalities of treatment, provided we can address this bit here' – pointing to the tumour mass on the picture he had drawn.

'If we don't, this is likely to invade the stomach and cause bleeding requiring an emergency operation when the disease overall may be inoperable. I've seen you walk in and you don't have any other comorbidities, so you are fit enough for an operation now.'

I had of course done my usual trick of buffing up as much as possible so that I looked reasonably fit – it seemed to have paid off again. Rather like a successful job interviewee perhaps, but maybe this was just a form of 'magical thinking' or perhaps 'desperate-in-a-corner thinking'. Whatever it was, I continued to try to look my best at appointments.

Alistair described the treatment options.

'We could give you chemotherapy first which might shrink the tumour and make an operation easier. However, the MDT felt that might be risky as the tumour might progress despite the chemotherapy and make later surgery impossible.

The second option is to do surgery now – it is not going to be curative but will reduce the bulk of the tumour and take away a lot of the risks from the tumour.

Surgery would entail trying to get to the top end of the metastasis in the splenic vein, removing it and also taking a cuff of stomach away, all of the spleen and two-thirds of the pancreas.

The third option is to do nothing but that is not sensible.

Doing surgery initially is the recommendation of the MDT.

Surgery will entail a General Anaesthetic and an epidural for pain relief.

Bleeding is a risk. The pancreas is notoriously bad for leaking which happens in about a third of patients. We put a drain in for this, but any leaks can become infected and could become septic. You can get stomach leaks also. Removing the spleen reduces your immunity. Try to get your flu vaccinations tomorrow. You can also get the same risks that can occur with any op, for instance, chest infections and wound infections and deep vein thromboses.

Mortality risk – the risk of dying from the surgery – is two to three per cent risk with this operation.

Morbidity – something going wrong – is about forty per cent, usually something like a wound infection.

If you have the operation you are in hospital for seven to fourteen days, depending on complications and pain control.

It takes about three months after the operation to get back to feeling the way you are now. Initially you will feel tired and worn out. Depression after the operation is also common There is a one in three risk of developing diabetes over the next two years.'

He asked some more routine questions about any previous medical problems and asked about general fitness, and whether I did any sports.

I told him I did a bit of cycling and running and golf.

'Golf is not a sport' he interjected lightening the mood momentarily.

'Do you want to have surgery?' he asked.

'Yes, as you and the MDT people recommend it'

'But what do you personally think?'

I explained that we were relieved to find out that it was a NET and that debulking was an option, and Michael had left me in no doubt that in my situation he would have the operation done by him. If this gave me a better shot at longer survival, then it didn't seem I really had a choice. Obviously, I was a bit daunted at the thought of the surgery.

Alistair said very quietly that he'd personally be terrified at the thought of undergoing the surgery required.

'If you were my father – although you are too young to be him – I'd have no problem with you having the operation'

'You'd have the operation in my shoes?'

'Yes.'

'We've got a bed next Thursday. Is that Ok?'

Phew - no need to wait for many weeks then.

'Yes, sooner over and done with the better'

'Do you do many operations like this?'

'Yes'

The latter in a very matter-of-fact but confidence inspiring way.

He asked if I had something called an 'Advanced Directive.' This is essentially where you write down what you would like to happen to you in the event of grave, life-threatening illness. Often people will say they don't wish to be resuscitated.

No, I didn't have one. Had never even occurred to me, even though dozens of my patients had them. Was I in a situation where I ought to have one maybe? No, it didn't bear thinking about or even speculating along those sorts of lines.

'We'll do some blood tests today and will call you to the ward a few days before the operation for checks and swabs. Afterwards you will need an Intensive Care Unit bed.'

We then went to his secretary's office where he discussed arrangements with her and gave me a form to get some bloods done at the clinic.

So, there it was. My fate was sealed. In just nine days I would be under the knife. A very big operation that was being proposed. It was too big to be done in the small Oxford private hospital where there was no Intensive Care Unit so it would be done in the NHS Churchill Hospital where there were many more facilities. It all hinged on whether he could get the metastasis out of the splenic vein and whether it had spread further along into the portal vein. If it had and if he couldn't get it all out, he wouldn't be able to prevent a build-up of pressure in the circulation which would cause varices, which are like knotty varicose veins, only in the stomach and oesophagus. They are very dangerous because they often bleed heavily. If he couldn't do all he wanted, he would do whatever seemed best at the time.

He seemed pretty confident he could sort things, though in a quiet understated sort of way which inspired trust. But could he really do all that? He definitely seemed to feel it was eminently doable. He didn't seem concerned or have any doubts in his mind about his ability to do the surgery. After all he did lots of this type of operation.

In the best Osler tradition, he had spent a long time initially trying to find out a bit about me as a person and what sort of support I'd have from my family. In hindsight, he was checking my suitability for a very big operation. I couldn't really have been in a better situation with regard to home circumstances and family support. He had checked my fitness out and my mindset. He was keen to know what I felt about the surgery not just whether I felt I ought to have it. He repeatedly checked to see if I had any questions. Without me realising it at the time, he had conducted a very thorough consultation.

But was this all a bit too good to be true? After all, we'd been told an operation was not feasible before because of the portal vein metastasis. Was what he was proposing a bit cavalier, a bit over the top for someone with liver metastases?

He most definitely didn't seem the cavalier type. Was the fact that I was going privately perhaps influencing him to recommend an operation that was not sensible? Would he still have recommended it if I'd been an 'ordinary NHS patient'? Was that an unworthy thought? Yes, most definitely. I felt a bit shocked and ashamed of myself for entertaining such thoughts.

Negativity and pessimism had forced their way into my mind in the light of the setbacks I'd experienced earlier. I reminded myself that Michael and the MDT team had recommended surgery not just Alistair, and Michael had said that Alistair did lots of these sorts of operations. I had no way of checking out the negative thoughts about the operation anyway. I guess I could have sought a second opinion but what if that second opinion was against surgery? I had to 'gamble' on Alistair and his colleagues being right.

In short, I had to do what hundreds of my former patients had had to do – I had to trust my surgeon.

He said that if I had been a relative of his, he would have no problem with me having the operation. He told me he would personally have the operation in my situation. Michael had said the same and confirmed that he would be happy for Alistair to perform the operation. It was in a good unit for NET management. What he proposed to do would give me a far better chance of more time than the other options. What more could I ask for? Jane had also been very impressed by him. I was surprised by just how impressed I had been. He just exuded a very quiet air of confidence that he could do what was clearly technically very difficult surgery. I was happy to entrust my care to him. I felt very strongly that I could trust him.

I was now nervous at the thought of what lay ahead as I realised the magnitude of the proposed surgery. However, I thought that whatever was entailed I could and would cope with. The doubts I had about coping with chemotherapy didn't surface at all. Cocky? No. Confident? Yes – some of Alistair's confidence had rubbed off on me. Overly confident? With hindsight, most definitely yes.

Chapter 13

Preparing for Surgery

In the event the operation was to be done within two weeks, on 24th November 2016. We'd worried that surgery would be delayed for too long, but all of a sudden it seemed almost too soon. It was imminent. In nine days to be precise. Things needed to be organised.

The first priority was to let our children know what was happening and why. They were all due down the weekend before the operation anyway.

The exercise I had begun doing in preparation for the chemotherapy I started to do with a great deal more purpose just as I had done before the aneurysm operation. Before the aneurysm had been discovered I had been training for the London marathon, so I re-started the same training in what time was left but more intensively than before. It had seemed to pay dividends then, so I had to do the same again. It also helped take my mind off things. I was exerting a measure of control in that I was doing something that ought to help me. Although I hadn't even heard the term then and just did this instinctively, getting as fit as possible before an operation is now called 'Prehabilitation' and is recognised as being important in aiding recovery from an operation. I was also trying to eat a bit more than usual in anticipation of losing a lot of weight after the operation and was taking iron tablets for my anaemia which were proving to be a penance as they made me nauseous and played havoc with my bowels.

I knew my life would literally be in the hands of an anaesthetist and had been reassured to hear from Alistair that he always worked very closely with one in particular. It turned out that he wasn't able to do my operation on the allotted day, so Alistair's secretary emailed me saying that another experienced anaesthetist would take his place. Then it turned out that he couldn't do it either, so she told me that Donald, who was an anaesthetist and an 'intensivist' i.e. he looked after very sick patients on Intensive Care, would be the choice. This was beginning to be a bit worrying. I was down to the third choice who was someone who split his time between intensive care work and anaesthetising rather than someone who exclusively did anaesthetising. The only intensivist I knew had dropped most of his anaesthetising to do intensive care work and I had wanted ideally to have someone at the very peak of his powers, who was doing lots of anaesthetising.

I knew that for large operations it was good practice for anaesthetists to do a pre-operative assessment of patients and enquired when that would be done. The secretary explained that anaesthetists don't always do an assessment until the day of surgery. This concerned me a bit, so I explained that I hoped and rather expected to meet the anaesthetist before the day of the operation. She would pass the message on. Was I being too demanding, too pushy? I didn't think so, but I felt uneasy about the whole thing. Before my aneurysm, I'd met and been assessed by my anaesthetist and had taken a lot of encouragement from meeting her.

A day or two later I was contacted to go to the Upper GI – Gastro-intestinal ward at The Churchill Hospital to meet Donald and would then be checked over by one of the surgical team. This was to be the first of my trips to The Churchill Hospital and more specifically to the Cancer and Haematology Centre within the Churchill. It was to become, if not a second home, somewhere I have been to many times, but whenever I do, I still feel apprehensive.

It's huge and like every hospital in the country, the thing that everyone who works, or is treated there, agrees on, is that there is woefully inadequate parking. Many years earlier I'd had a patient with severe depression tearfully tell me, that despite arriving half an hour before his appointment, he had been unable to find a parking spot and so had come home and was desperately upset about it. I knew parking was a problem, but it turned out to be much more of a problem than I'd imagined. On most days it's awful but on the two days of the week when the majority of the outpatient clinics are held, the parking is truly horrendous. The stress begins well in advance of the car park. To reach The Churchill you first have to run the gauntlet of the Oxford traffic which takes forever, as sneaky road works with temporary traffic lights pop up everywhere and take an eternity to get through unless you leave hours more time that you should, in which case inevitably you sail through the traffic arriving hours early. The ultimate frustration is when you find yourself stationary in a queue hundreds of yards before the hospital car park. Often there are spaces in the car park but they're not visible to the drivers by the entrance who thus have to wait till a space they can see becomes available, as if they take a chance on finding one further away, they may be forced out of the car park by the one-way system and have to start queuing again. Disabled drivers are no better off because they can't get past the queue blocking their way into the car park even if there are lots of empty disabled slots visible. Jane comes to all the appointments so, if we are motionless, I abandon her and walk from wherever we have come to a halt, but this isn't an option for very frail patients.

Once parked, you have to walk the hundred or two hundred yards to the main entrance, most of the way exposed to the elements and, for some reason, the wind has it in for you. It whips along ferociously making your shivers of apprehension even worse. That walk feels bleak and buffeted against the backdrop of the Churchill massif makes you feel small and insignificant and even less in control of your destiny than you felt when you arrived.

I'd read about the opening of The Cancer and Haematology Centre a few years earlier. The 'Cancer Centre' name had been chosen deliberately because that was what was mostly treated there. The name had been a bit controversial at the time because the 'C' word is one many people prefer to avoid – a bit like the way actors prefer to refer to 'Macbeth' as 'The Scottish play.' 'The Cancer Centre' seemed somewhat – no completely – in your face. That was the point though, to try to remove the stigma associated with the 'C' word.

That first visit is etched in my memory. I was going into the hospital department of the Cancer Centre which broadcast to the world the fact that I had cancer. Me. Someone who didn't do the patient stuff. I did the treatment stuff. The old thoughts about how I saw myself refused to go away. This was an alien place; I didn't want any part of it. What if one of my patients spotted me? What would I say? Should I nod a greeting or say Hello? What would I say if I did? How would I answer the inevitable question about why I was there? Just as bad – perhaps worse – would be if I saw a colleague, or rather he or she saw me? Should I speak or just nod? I felt incredibly self-conscious. Surely the whole place was looking at me and wondering... In reality I've never spotted a patient of mine there and only once a colleague and he was Alistair who I was always pleased to meet.

At the appointed hour I reported to the ward desk and explained to a young male nurse that I was a bit early for an appointment with Donald.

'Oh, hi yes I'm Donald. Nice to meet you.' So not a young male nurse, but a very youthful consultant anaesthetist/intensivist

Twenty-five minutes later I had experienced a perfect consultation. Disarmingly and a bit unexpectedly, he started by saying that he was sorry that I had got stuck with my condition. He was the first of the six consultants I had seen to empathise at the start of a consultation and had done it better than anyone else and his words were surprisingly comforting. I guess it made me think that he had considered what it must be like for me to find myself in a tight corner. The cliché about anaesthetists is that they choose their specialty so that they don't have to talk to patients much, so I was most definitely not expecting one who could consult in such a kind manner. He then very thoroughly and methodically went through everything from coming in on the day of the operation to the process of being anaesthetised. He described the pros and cons and risks of the epidural I would have for pain relief, the main risk being that it might not work. He described under what circumstances I might require a blood transfusion. He went through all the tubes I would wake up with in the Intensive Care unit, which I would be in for a day or two after surgery. He would personally be looking after the Intensive Care Unit on the Friday, Saturday and Sunday after the operation, which would provide good continuity of care as he would know a lot about my physiology by then. He described the precautions that would be taken to lessen the risks of chest infections, clots in the veins of my legs and in the lungs.

'You sound as if you have done lots of these?' I ventured hopefully.

'Yes – intensivists often do big ops because our skills translate readily to the surgery and post-operative recovery.'

So, I had been completely wrong in being apprehensive about him, he was in fact perfect for me. He may have been the third anaesthetist to be asked, but he was clearly first rate and I felt lucky to have him on my side. It was very comforting.

Shortly afterwards Alistair himself came into the room to go through the final arrangements. He went through all the information I needed to be aware of to enable me to formally consent to be operated on. Most of that had been discussed before but he sombrely explained that, if at the operation he discovered something that might make the operation unacceptably dangerous, he would get the opinion of another consultant surgeon and between them they would decide on the best course of action. The chances of this happening were slim. What did he mean by 'slim?' 'Probably less than ten percent.' That old 'ten percent' that had been the estimated risk of cancer right at the start.

Lightening the mood a little, he said that he would remove my gallbladder 'for no extra charge' as it was likely I might at some stage be put on a drug that could cause gallstones. Would I mind talking to medical students after the surgery?

'No problem'

'Will your [doctor] son be coming in?'

'Good I will get a chance to meet him. I will ring Jane after the operation to tell her how it went. The first three to five days after the operation won't be very nice but we will try to reduce the discomfort as much as possible.'

He explained that there was a small risk that there would not be an Intensive Care bed available on the day, which would necessitate cancelling the operation.

Cancelled operations are very tough on patients and the Oxford Hospitals have more than their fair share of cancellations. I had a patient in whom a weakness in the wall of his bowel – a diverticulum – had burst with the result that the contents of the bowel had been discharged into his abdomen causing a lot of mischief internally. He had required an emergency operation to form a colostomy to give the abdomen a chance to settle down. The plan was to re-join the ends of his bowel thereby removing the colostomy after a few months. He was duly invited to come in for the re-joining operation only to have it cancelled six times despite ever increasingly strident letters to the hospital from me. My first aneurysm coiling operation was cancelled on the day, so I knew all about cancelled operations and the havoc they wreak on patients' peace of mind. I would just have to pray that there would be an Intensive Care bed available on the day.

Jane and I felt further encouraged by this second consultation with Alistair. He had discussed the worst-case scenario and told us that he wouldn't just decide what was best for me but would, as a matter of course get a second consultant, to help with the decision. That seemed to be a very enlightened, considered approach. He warned me that the first few days would be tough, but they would do what they could to make it easier. He had remembered my son and was pleased that he would meet him. It all felt good. It really felt that he would do his level best for me and my family. He had been friendly and interested in the family and his understated confident manner was again very reassuring.

I had a very good anaesthetist and a very good surgeon in my corner, and a great wife and family. If there were no unexpected complications found at the time of the surgery I would, I supposed, be fine. Hopefully.

Chapter 14

A Pre-Op Party

All the children and their partners would be down for the weekend before the operation. I knew it would be the last time they would see me in apparently rude good health for some time. It would be the last time anybody would see me in good form for that matter. That thought and because all the family were there, made me feel that it would be good to have an impromptu drinks party on the Sunday lunchtime. We loved it when Laura, Patrick, Duncan, and their partners, came to a party at our house and saw village friends who always were pleased to see how they had grown up. Like everyone else, we were ridiculously proud of our children, but the way they had responded to my situation had been very special and made us want them around as much as possible.

It would be the last opportunity for quite a while for us to have a party. We'd been intending to have one for many months but as so frequently seems to be the case in life, never quite managed to get ourselves organised to work a date out well enough in advance. Now there was only one possible date. It would be at less than a week's notice for people but that couldn't be helped. We'd say it was because all the family were down rather than because we thought it would be a long time before I'd be fit enough to have another one. It would take our minds off other matters at least for a while and the children could help with the drinks and nibbles. I emailed or phoned a good number of village friends, almost all of whom could make it – probably more in fact than if we'd given them months of notice. We were all agreed not to mention anything about my diagnosis and imminent operation. Laura – a bit unusually – took lots of photographs and everyone enjoyed themselves, more so seemingly, because it had been such a last-minute arrangement. It was a bit of a strain for Jane I think, but she was happy because she knew I wanted it to happen. Months later, one of Jane's close friends said that Jane had looked a bit strained and she had wondered if something was going on but no-one else seemed to have been suspicious. We had ticked the box of being sociable and repaying many past invites which I felt important to do for Jane, in case it turned out to be our last joint party.

At the back of my mind was what Shelley, my late friend George's widow, had said about people not calling or being in touch when they heard about his cancer and how angry and upset she had been over this. It was partly why I wanted to throw one last party.

Bit desperate I admit.

I surmised that if we didn't tell people in advance about the surgery, they would hear the Chinese whispers and get inaccurate, exaggerated information about what was happening. I also guessed that some closer friends might be a bit surprised, dismayed or even hurt that we hadn't felt it right to tell them our news so that they could offer help. Maybe they would take that as a sign that we didn't really value their friendship. Maybe they wouldn't know how to react. Maybe that was what had happened to George and Shelley.

In a few days' time, it would be apparent that I was in hospital recovering from major surgery. It would inevitably have emerged on the grapevine.

After my aneurysm was diagnosed, I naturally told my three sisters. All of them decided to get themselves checked and my youngest sister Helen, was found to have a small aneurysm. Because it was small, it was decided that it didn't merit anything to be done other than to have a repeat scan, to see if it was enlarging. If it did, and got to a critical size, it would need coiling. Sadly, a short while before the repeat scan was due, Helen's aneurysm bled and she had to be rushed into Leeds General Infirmary and have it coiled. Her husband Simon sent an email out each day with an account of how she was progressing to a large number of friends and relatives which meant he could ensure everyone knew what was happening without him having to take numerous phone calls. Happily, Helen made a full recovery.

I decided to borrow Simon's approach and personally email local friends, many of whom had been at the impromptu party, and relatives, so that the correct story emerged and to suggest that they email Jane rather than ring her. I included pretty well everyone I could think of and after carefully preparing it beforehand sent it out on the morning of the operation just before I left the house. I called it and subsequent follow-up emails 'From The Horse's Mouth' explaining that I wanted to try to ensure they got the correct information. I tried to keep the tone light referring to my NET as an 'exclusive' type of cancer for which I'd be having major surgery. I finished the email:

If any of you remember the Mamas and Papas' song 'Dedicated to the One I Love' the line after 'Each night before you go to bed my baby, Whisper a little...'

Be good if you whispered as they did!

The song goes: 'Each night before you go to bed My Baby, Whisper a little prayer for me My Baby'. I'd felt too awkward or embarrassed to ask people directly to pray for me, but actually I hoped they would.

At the same time, I emailed staff at the surgery to let them also know what was happening, again trying to say difficult things with a light touch. I wrote that I guess some people might have been wondering, because I'd stopped working so abruptly, if I'd been struck off or suspended from practising medicine or whether I had finally lost the plot. I pointed out that I'd be away from work for several months, possibly permanently, and suggested what they might tell my patients. I finished with:

Despite my default grumpy demeanour, I have enjoyed working with you all immensely and loved the buzz of working with such a great team in a great practice for a great bunch of patients. Keep up the good work and don't let the bug...rs [running the NHS] get you down.

Sending out the emails had the desired effect. We got lots of replies and good wishes and promises of 'whispers' as a result which was heartening. Everyone seemed to appreciate being informed personally and often said thanks for being told. Jane had lots of emails with offers of help. Later Jane and Laura sent out 'bulletin emails' updating people on progress

Emailing like this had definitely been a good idea.

After the party and the children returning to London, we had just three days before the admission. Three days before I would be a proper patient and properly poorly from the operation as Alistair had forewarned us. Three months it would take to recuperate, he reckoned. I assumed I would be quicker than that because I was arrogant enough to think I was a pretty tough customer. Nonetheless the shadow of the operation loomed large. As it got ever nearer, I became a lot less confident and had moments of wondering whether it was sensible to have it at all. Maybe I should call the whole thing off. Maybe I would emerge from some sort of nightmare back to good health. Maybe the operation would be cancelled, and I would get a temporary reprieve. I knew I would be clobbered by the operation and would be physically diminished afterwards. I felt sorrowful because I knew I was heading for something that would hurt and weaken me and knowing that I was doing this voluntarily, made me sad – it was almost as if I was mourning the passing of myself from a well person to an ill one. Many times, I've seen on the TV news, the faces of prisoners on the way to some form of incarceration or physical punishment, with a look that seemed to mirror the way I felt myself – a deep regret about what awaited them. There was a sense of injustice that you were going to be hurt and maybe very badly, possibly even fatally, if things didn't go well. And you were allowing it to happen.

It was akin to the feeling you had as a schoolboy awaiting the physical punishment by the teacher, as we used to have back in the day, with a wooden bat, knowing it would hurt but, in this instance perhaps, heightened by knowing you had done nothing wrong yourself. I hasten to say that whenever I was beaten by a teacher, I had always done something wrong. On just one occasion I was marginally less culpable than the other boy, who was throwing tomato ketchup over me when we were caught literally red handed. It had started as I shook the tomato ketchup bottle without realising that the top was loose and had inadvertently sprayed him. His instinct was to retaliate and spray me with sauce. Naturally, with such a mature approach to life, he also became a GP.

I guess most patients feel a sense of unfairness about being ill and having to undergo unpleasant treatments and investigations. It's always seemed remarkable to me that patients in this situation so rarely howl at the moon at the unfairness of it all.

Maybe they do, but just privately at night.

The air was heavy with despondency and gloom, but I tried not to show fear because others, and particularly Jane, were going through a pretty grim time as well. Was I crazy to subject myself to this extensive surgery? We'd been told right at the onset that the portal vein was involved, which therefore made surgery impossible. Admittedly that was when the diagnosis was stomach cancer. Alistair said the splenic vein rather than the portal vein was involved. How could he be so certain? Why hadn't I pressed him about that? Had I just accepted the message that I wanted to hear from him? He had said that if the tumour had worsened there was a possibility that the portal vein might now be involved and that if it was, it might be too dangerous to fix it, in which case he would do whatever seemed the best thing to a colleague and himself. So, if I was unlucky – and goodness knows I had been pretty unlucky of late – I might end up having a massive painful scar and very little actual surgery and then my quality of life, for whatever time was left, would be considerably diminished for several months.

That had happened to an uncle of mine who had been thought to have operable lung cancer but when he was opened up – which entails breaking lots of ribs – his disease was found to be too advanced for surgery to be done. In effect he'd had all the drawbacks of painful surgery with none of the benefits. It had also happened to my late squash friend George. Could this happen to me? Obviously, it could. I was putting an enormous amount of faith and trust in Alistair. Maybe I should have got a second opinion before agreeing to his proposed surgery?

On the other hand, I knew from long experience with other patients, that a second opinion is a dangerous beast. What do you do if one advocates surgery and one doesn't? Get a third one? Or a fourth? In any event I knew I would go for the opinion that seemed to offer the best prospect for the future which would be surgery – if it was successful. And Alistair had given me the impression of being very confident in his ability in a quiet impressive way. Michael spoke very well of him too.

I was tough.

I could cope.

I would cope.

But what about the fact that there were lots of metastases in the liver? I'd been brought up with the idea that once a cancer had spread to the liver that was basically that. I had known of patients with one or two liver metastases being operated on, but my liver disease was far worse than that. Were the surgeons effectively going to be fiddling while Rome burned? On the other hand, Michael had pointed out that things are different now and he was in no doubt that, in my shoes, he would go for surgery. Also, the MDT meeting had recommended surgery. But were they being misled by Alistair's confident manner?

But, but, but...

I knew I couldn't answer all the questions and that with time racing on I'd get to the day of admission, when I'd be overtaken by events and end up going into hospital and having the operation.

And it really was happening. Thursday morning came around. I sent off the 'Horses Mouth' emails, had a light breakfast and went to face the music. 'Butterflies' hardly describes how I was feeling. Very apprehensive and frightened, but on the outside composed – on the outside only.

Duncan drove us into the 'Upper GI' ward at The Churchill Hospital in Oxford. I was shown into a side room and asked to put the theatre gown on. Problem was, we couldn't figure out how to get it to stay on. It turned out to be a gown for patients who have Bariatric – weight reducing – surgery who are inevitably two or three times larger than normal. A normal size gown eventually materialised. The room was clinical and uninviting but did at least have a TV and best of all an ensuite bathroom. It was exactly what I expected and was fine as far as I was concerned.

The operation was due at 2 pm which came and went with no sign of anyone coming to take me down to the operating theatre. A further hour went by. It was beginning to look as if I wasn't going to be called down for surgery that afternoon after all. I started to entertain ideas of escaping to fight another day. That prospect seemed pretty good from where I was sitting. But there was to be no escape and eventually I found myself walking the short distance from the ward to the anaesthetic room accompanied by Jane and Duncan and one of the nurses. Donald was waiting and went through the plan for the epidural and anaesthetic and got me to sit on a trolley and lean forwards while he inserted the epidural. He warned me that I would probably experience a 'tickling sensation' in my legs and moments later I got a searing, agonising pain in my right leg more severe than any pain I'd ever had. It knocked the breath out of me. He promptly withdrew the needle and the pain went after half a minute or so. Tickling was never like that. Sweating and panting from the shock of the pain I braced myself for the next attempt. After a few minutes, Donald tried slightly higher up in the spine. This time it was OK. Then there was a needle in my arm and a gas mask over my face and I was unconscious to the world.

Chapter 15

Recovering From the Operation

Nothing had remotely prepared me for how I was to feel when I came around from the anaesthetic and found myself on the Intensive Care unit. Jane and Duncan greeted me as I opened my eyes and joyously told me that the operation had been a complete success and everything Alistair had hoped to be able to achieve, he had. It was brilliant.

I couldn't have cared less.

All I knew was that I felt utterly terrible – unable to move and in too much discomfort to be able to rejoice at the news. I was groggy, desperately thirsty, my abdomen hurt and, as a result of a tube being inserted into my airway for the anaesthetic, the right side of my throat was terribly sore, especially when I swallowed. Of course, in trying to avoid doing just that, I ended up swallowing far more frequently than normal. Those symptoms were, however, nothing compared to the nausea. Nausea, the like of which I have never before nor since experienced. Nausea hardly seems an adequate enough word to describe the deep, grim, all-pervasive queasiness that completely enveloped me and consumed my every thought. Bad as the other symptoms were, compared to the nausea, they were also-rans. I hadn't signed up for this. No-one had mentioned nausea as a possibility so I reasoned that it must mean something had gone badly wrong. I explained how I felt to a nurse, who didn't however seem concerned by the nausea and duly gave me an injection into one of my tubes, I don't recall it making much difference.

I had, in total, seven tubes in various parts of my body; one through my nose into my stomach, one into a neck vein, one into an arm vein, two drains on either side of my abdomen to enable any fluid that was leaking internally to flow out into two bags, a catheter into my bladder and an epidural tube into my spine. The nasal tube was the worst and felt like a giant clothes peg on my nose; the bladder catheter was the best as it meant I didn't have to even think about making the effort to pee but did require me to beg everyone to move the bedclothes gingerly as a sudden yank on the tube...

I had a 'PCA' or Patient Controlled Analgesia machine connected to the neck vein and if I pressed it, a shot of morphine was released into my bloodstream. The idea was that it would enable me to control any pain I had. It could only be used once every five minutes, to prevent overdosage, and I was encouraged to use it liberally. However, this brilliant-sounding device didn't seem to help at all, and I suspected that the morphine released just made the nausea worse and as nausea easily trumped any pain I had, I didn't use it much. Jane later explained that probably the reason it didn't seem to help was because I would doze intermittently so never gave myself enough zaps to make much difference.

Donald, and later Alistair, both looked in on me, and enthused about how well everything had gone, and how pleased they were with how I was doing. I took no great encouragement from this, as all I knew was that I'd never felt worse in my life. I was like a helpless new-born baby, unable to move or do anything for myself, but with the agitated mind of a sixty-four-year-old who knew too much for his own good, yet not enough to appreciate the bigger picture, namely that I had survived the operation and all I had to do now was concentrate on getting better. No, I didn't see that at all. I had definitely not bargained on feeling so terrible and for the first of many occasions, wondered why on earth I had allowed this to happen to me. Had I been mad to submit myself to this operation? Could I endure feeling like this another moment? Would it last a few minutes or hours or days or, God forbid, weeks?

I'd had three discussions about the operation and how I'd feel afterwards but I'd never imagined feeling like this. Much later, I thought it was probably just as well I hadn't known how I'd feel otherwise I would have been even more frightened in the days before going into hospital. Maybe I would have chickened out. No, I wouldn't have chickened out because my imagination could never have stretched to realising what it would be like to feel as bad as this. On reflection now, I remember that Alistair had very quietly said that he'd have been terrified at the thought of having my surgery. At the time I thought he was just saying that to be kind – sort of implying that I was very courageous to have the surgery. In hindsight, maybe he said that because he really knew how awful I'd feel after the operation. Yes, I think that was it, but in my eagerness to have aggressive treatment and with my gung-ho – but sadly misplaced – sense of my own resilience – I hadn't appreciated that he really meant what he said.

I'd coped OK with the mother of all headaches that my aneurysm operation caused, so had arrogantly and naively assumed I would be able to cope with a 'belly operation' especially as I was to be given an epidural to numb my abdomen. But this was in a completely different league, an altogether different level of grimness. What a fool I'd been to think that I could have so much surgery done and just breeze through the post-operative period. This was unbearable. No-one could bear this. I certainly couldn't. But I would have to. There was no going back. The Rubicon had been well and truly crossed. Would I have the operation again, knowing now how I'd feel afterwards? Yes – or at least yes, I'd like to assume I would, but in that first day or two after the operation, I would probably have said 'no'.

What made it seem particularly difficult was that I was entirely dependent on 'the kindness of strangers' – the nurses and doctors on the ICU. Of course, they were all highly-qualified, paid professionals rather than random strangers, but the main thing was I was entirely in their hands. Without those hands, there wouldn't be any me.

Sleep was the best way of coping, when it was possible between the frequent checks of blood pressure, temperature, oxygen level and the rate of breathing. I was drowsy from the anaesthetic the first night and could frequently take refuge in sleep, so it wasn't as bad as the second night. The first fleeting moment of happiness I experienced after coming around was when a dampened sponge was put into my mouth to suck which moistened the desiccated landscape of my mouth and fractionally reduced the soreness in my throat. It was absolute bliss. Happily, I was offered a second one straightaway.

Thereafter, while awake, I lived for one thing and one thing only – the sponge. I didn't dare to be too demanding fearing that I might risk losing the goodwill of the nurses but gradually became emboldened enough to hang out for three at a time when the sponge was offered. I would have liked even more, but in my agitated mind felt asking for more than three sponges might push the nurses' patience to the limit. I'm sure now that the nurses would have willingly given me far more than three at a time, had I simply asked, but on the ICU, and on many subsequent occasions, I was very conscious of not wanting to appear to be over-demanding. The irrational fear of the elderly, helpless, new-born meant I felt that pretty much my actual survival depended on me not being disliked by the nurses. Crazy in hindsight, as the extremely high levels of professionalism and compassion shown by everyone I met meant that they would have treated all their patients in an exemplary fashion, even an over-demanding man-baby, but it was most definitely what I felt at the time.

A few hours after coming around from the anaesthetic, it had become pretty clear that I couldn't bend my left knee. At all. I could move my foot perfectly well, but the knee movements had gone AWOL. Absolutely what a stroke must feel like, I mused, but uncharacteristically for me, I felt quite detached from the issue and was almost indifferent to the matter – nausea demanded too much attention to leave any room to worry over a 'minor matter' like a stroke. Donald was summoned to evaluate matters and explained that it was bound to be due to the epidural and was definitely not important but, if it persisted overnight, I would have to have an MRI to ensure a clot hadn't occurred at the epidural site. He assured me he had never had that particular complication, but it would be mandatory to do a scan if it persisted. The apparent illogicality of insisting there was nothing wrong but needing to get it checked, is a logic I know very well from my own work and could therefore readily accept, but I dreaded the thought of having to be moved onto the scanner and lie in an uncomfortable position in a claustrophobic tube, for an unknown amount of time, as it was taking all my determination to cope with just lying on a bed. An MRI scan was bad enough at the best of times, but at the worst of times? Hopefully the knee would have come back to life by the next day.

Of course, the next day the knee stubbornly still refused to move so I had to have an MRI. It was bad being moved on and off a trolley with the inevitable yanking on my catheter and the discomfort and indignity of being moved and unable to help myself at all, but there was no way of ducking it. Just as Donald had predicted, there was no clot. The 'paralysis' was cured by reducing the rate of the epidural and thankfully when the rate was increased again the paralysis didn't return.

I think the second night after the op was probably the longest of my life. I was still in the ICU and as there weren't many patients on the ward that night, a staff nurse was assigned to look after me. The only way of surviving a few hours would be to get some sleep. To achieve this nirvana, this temporary reprieve from the cruel world I inhabited, I would have to be in as comfortable a position as possible and particularly have the pillows correctly aligned so that my head was neither flexed nor extended. It was absolutely vital – the most important thing in the whole world to me at that time – as a few degrees out either way would make sleep difficult and without sleep there was no escape from the nausea. The problem was I couldn't move at all and so needed to ask my nurse to arrange the pillows. Happily, she was very patient and longsuffering and got the pillows just right and later in the wee small hours, at my request, told me her life-story which temporarily distracted me from the misery of thinking just about my own predicament. Also, while I had her full attention, I could easily slip in a request for a pillow repositioning or even a sponge. During the day I knew I could ask Jane or Duncan to adjust the pillows whenever I liked, which took the pressure off, but at night I feared I would only get one chance. I dreaded my visitors leaving as it signalled the start of the seemingly everlasting night and so I counted down the hours and minutes until they were due to reappear, which always seemed much later than I hoped, due to the vagaries of trying to find a parking space at the hospital.

After the second night on ICU I was moved back to the side-room on the Upper GI ward and again everyone who came in and looked at me, my abdomen, my blood tests and observations enthused about how well everything was going. The throat remained sore and another issue had arisen. Hiccups. Frequent, very unwanted and powerful ones, which I dreaded as they threw my abdomen upwards with a resultant sharp pain over the scar. They were caused by air settling under the diaphragm. Sadly, they were inevitable and I dreaded them just a little less than the nausea.

What I was blissfully ignorant of, but was of very great concern to Jane and Duncan, was that I had become very swollen from retained fluid in the tissues under the skin, so-called oedema. Evidently, I looked like the old Michelin man figure with a bloated face and neck and legs. I wouldn't have been encouraged by seeing myself, as when I've seen that sort of appearance in patients, it often seemed to have been just a short while before they died. Alistair explained that it was due to a protein in the blood being at a low level from the operation and from not eating, and reassured Jane and Duncan that it would settle – which it must have done. The oedema was at its worst on the ward when I had been starved of food for some time. All I noticed were fingers like sausages and a swollen wrist, which I thought must be due to the drip leaking into the tissues beneath the skin. Seemingly, I was lucky that my testicles didn't become hugely swollen.

The stand-out caring person I came across during my stay was a Health Care Assistant. On my first ward night he repeatedly came in and seemed really anxious and determined to make me comfortable in any way he could. He seemed to rejoice in being able to help. About five days later, he popped up again and was similarly caring, but by then I really didn't need much help at all. I sensed almost a disappointment that he couldn't do more for me at that point and felt a bit guilty about it. He had studied anthropology, which led to his research. He worked in a bookshop before coming over to the UK with his wife. He planned to do a nursing course in time and will make a tremendous nurse when he qualifies.

Later, I reflected that the transformation from being as helpless as a new-born baby to an almost fully independent man with a fairly calm mind, over the course of just a few days must be very rewarding and also weirdly interesting for nurses and doctors to observe.

I liked to describe myself as a 'coal-face' GP, meaning that I was an ordinary GP doing bread and butter GP work, as opposed to being an academic or research GP. Maybe 'bog-standard' would be a better term. 'Coal-face' makes the job sound harder and more challenging and somehow perhaps more heroic, like the wartime miners. We 'coal-face' GPs have a category of patient who answers negatively to every possible thing you say and comes up with yet another unsolved or not considered problem. We describe this as the 'Ah! But...' syndrome. It goes like this:

The doctor: 'I'm pleased to say the Chest X-ray is normal'

The patient: 'Yes, that's good but I have a pain in my chest'

Doctor: 'We've already ruled out any problem with your heart'

Patient: 'Ah but it hurts when I breathe in'

And so it goes on, and on and on, with the patient producing ever more symptoms to counter any good news he or she receives from the increasingly desperately frustrated doctor, till the penny finally drops that he or she isn't going to convince the determinedly unwell patient that he or she is doing well.

'Ah! But...' patients are a royal pain. In reality, they are just very anxious individuals who feel the need to question lots of issues and perhaps a perfect, more compassionate doctor would not be so dismissive of them. It's pretty hard to be perfect at the best of times and well-nigh impossible in the overburdened NHS. So, when one of the two surgical registrars, or anyone else for that matter, having told me I was doing famously, heard me say: 'Ah, but I feel very nauseous', they would beam and say 'We'll prescribe an anti-emetic to take care of that'

I would counter that I was already on one.

'So, we'll try metoclopramide as well then.'

'But they tried that yesterday.'

And so it went on.

Eventually I would let the poor registrar off the hook and shut up, accepting that the nausea would not be going away any time soon. Realising that I was that 'Ah! But... patient' was a sobering thought to conjure with. Not only had I crossed the great divide and become a patient, but probably in the eyes of others I had become one of the most annoying types of patient. Are 'Ah! But...' patients just a pain or is it because their attendants never address their real fears properly? You start to see things differently when you are one.

Different people or teams of people came in to check on me seemingly randomly and independently of each other – the registrars always the first before they went to the operating theatre and then perhaps the nurses from the ward then maybe the anaesthetists checking on the epidural, then a dietician, then a physiotherapist, then maybe a consultant surgeon and so on. Eventually it became apparent that their agenda is basically to make sure that the surgery is working, that nothing is leaking or infected, rather than to deal with every symptom I might have, as they know that time takes care of everything else.

Which it did.

Eventually.

My agenda was firstly the nausea, secondly the nausea, and, finally, the nausea, which ultimately, of course, was actually far less important than making sure that the surgery was working ok.

Weeks later a retired partner suggested speaking to a mutual friend who had had a very similar – but even more extensive – operation than mine. My symptoms reminded her of what our friend had experienced. She had had nausea for over a month, and had been shocked and totally unprepared psychologically for how terrible she would feel after the operation and had experienced exactly the same determined optimism from her doctors and nurses that she was doing really well, despite her feeling like hell on earth at the time. It was hugely interesting and put my mind at rest. I think because no-one had seemed particularly concerned by, or even all that interested in, my nausea, I had thought they must be thinking it was all in my mind, so hearing that it wasn't all that rare was reassuring. Maybe I wasn't a hypochondriac with low moral fibre after all, and maybe my symptoms – which were less severe than hers – would eventually stop as hers had done.

Life on the Upper GI ward was in some ways interesting and challenging. There were all sorts of things to try to get my head round and try to work out the best way of getting through the days and more importantly the nights. Each morning, the nurse allocated to look after me, would introduce herself or himself whilst checking my observations or 'obs' – blood pressure, pulse, blood sugar level and so on. Sometimes the blood pressure or the sugar level would be a little high which, though minor in the greater scheme of things, caused me a mild degree of panic because they had never been high before. Invariably there would be great relief when the next measurement, as always seemed to be the case, was absolutely fine. I just wasn't used to the vagaries of being a patient, I guess. It always seemed to be very important to make a note of my allocated nurse's name. A written note. The drugs and the anxiety engendered by my situation meant I couldn't trust my memory alone to retain that information. If anything needed doing it would have to be done by my nurse and if I could say who that was, it would enable Jane to get hold of the right person and lessen the wait for whatever needed doing. Also, when my nurse came it felt more respectful and more in control to be able to address him or her by name. I also figured that it might help get my nurse onside. I knew from my own experience as a doctor that it was easier to go the extra mile for a patient you liked and vice versa, though professionalism means trying your best for everyone. I also scribbled down the names of the other key players such as the registrar that had called, or the dietician, as I would often be asked by another team member what had been said and by whom. I made a careful note of when I had been given my painkillers or anti-nausea tablets so that I knew when I could ask for more – otherwise there could be a delay while the nurse checked back to see who my nurse was and if there was any debate about whether I was having them too early; it put me in a stronger bargaining position. All the nurses were good, but some seemed particularly compassionate and determined to lessen the misery of my situation. If one of these were allocated to be my nurse again, I felt a great sense of optimism for the day ahead.

Crunch time again was of course the night. I had to be at just the right angle and have the buzzer very close to hand to be able to summon help. The window had to be open enough to feel a very slight breeze of restorative air but not enough to make me cold, the door to the corridor ideally needed to be shut to lessen the noise and ideally the curtain across the door glass to stop the light coming in and the pillows had to be precisely pumped up to just the right level and so on. I had to be able to reach a glass of water which had to have a lot of ice in it and also to be able to grab the notes I had made of people's names and which drugs I'd had. It was a very precise operation to get it all right. I wouldn't let my weary visitors go till everything was in place. I was nervous that if even the smallest detail was wrong the night would be a lot tougher to negotiate and that I would struggle even more than I had to. I guess when so much of your life is controlled by other people, the small things you can control yourself become much more important than usual.

On the first day on the GI ward, I was helped out of bed and into a chair for an hour or two. On the second day, a physiotherapist came to get me to take a short walk. To be honest, it seemed a bit much to be expected to walk at such an early stage, but I sensed there was little to be gained by pointing this out and resigned myself to having to do as I was told. Various tubes were lifted and carefully held in different positions, particularly the catheter tube and with the physio holding my arm, I ventured out into the corridor and shuffled along for a few yards, bent almost double, as any other position pulled on the wound too much and was painful. It was very hard going, but the physio pronounced himself very satisfied that I was now 'mobile' and should do several walks a day from now on. Jane and Duncan were delighted and determined to build on this.

'Straighten up and take a deep breath and a deep cough' Duncan insisted 'It will lessen the risk of a chest infection, which is vital to avoid.'

So I did as instructed, again and again, at his behest and didn't get a chest infection.

The next day Donald announced that he would remove the epidural. Although I had been deeply disappointed by the epidural which I had thought would prevent all pain and didn't, I knew that it was far too soon to remove it. Nonetheless he removed it and of course it was fine – it didn't worsen anything at all.

Next to go was the bladder catheter. The memory of one being removed after my craniotomy operation was daunting. It had been exquisitely painful as the long tube came out then but this time there was no pain at all. So much for 'experience' informing one. Without a catheter, I had the odd experience of peeing into a bottle – it always felt slightly risky lest it spill, which I was very careful to make sure didn't happen.

The next thing to be removed the following day was the nasogastric tube. It was supposed to lessen the nausea, so again, in my mind, it was obviously going to be disastrous to remove it as the nausea was still very prominent. It was removed, which was bliss and of course the nausea didn't get worse.

I knew I would be at considerable risk of getting a clot in my leg – a deep vein thrombosis – or even one in my lungs – a pulmonary embolus – so was shown how to inject blood-thinning heparin into my thigh. More intrusively, but reassuring, was the flotron device which was attached to both calves and was intermittently pumped up with air to push the blood through the leg's veins. It was worn over white stockings, which made me feel like a pantomime dame and a pretty unappealing one at that.

Chapter 16

Fork Mashable

I wasn't initially allowed to eat after the operation, as the stomach and other parts that had been sliced and diced, needed time to settle down a bit before they would be able to cope with food. Food was the last thing I wanted anyway because of the nausea and the tube from my nose into my stomach being in the way, made food seem even more unappealing. I knew, of course, that I needed to eat to survive. I was in what's called a 'catabolic state' from the operation, which meant that my body was using up a lot of energy and hence calories, as it tried to repair the 'damage' done by the surgery. Several days of total starvation inevitably meant pretty rapid weight loss, which itself could slow the healing rate down. It would be vital to start getting as many calories down as soon as possible. Management of my diet was therefore a key component of the recovery and was in the hands of a very competent dietician.

Three days after surgery it was decided that I could start food again. Initially it was to be ice cream and jelly only. I had fond memories of that particular combination when I'd been given it after having my tonsils removed at the age of four and on other occasions when recovering from some childhood illness or other. It had always hit the spot, so I eagerly anticipated the forthcoming treat. But this ice cream and jelly wasn't the stuff of my memories...to pack the vital calories in, the ice cream and jelly had been made incredibly sweet almost like neat honey. Unfortunately, I don't have a sweet tooth and so after eagerly swallowing some down I pushed it away in disgust. Then, in response to concern from Jane, I tried again and again as we both knew a lot depended on me eating. Like my survival. So, most of it eventually went down. It was to be my staple diet for the next day or two.

Soon I was allowed other 'treats' from a menu called 'Fork Mashable' which was essentially deliberately sloppy, liquidy food like soggy cottage pie or fish pie that would slip down and not be too irritant to an inflamed recently-operated-on stomach. It was, perforce, a very limited menu but was made to look more extensive by cunningly switching the order of the same foods on the lunch and dinner menus. My dietician encouraged me to take some high calorie drinks between meals. Again, they seemed impossibly sweet, but in the greater scheme of things were vitally important. Most mornings she came around and like everyone else checked the fluid draining from my abdomen. Her eagle eye spotted some fat in the fluid which indicated that there was a small pancreatic leak. This wasn't too much to be concerned about but necessitated reducing the fat content of my food for a couple of days. To make up for the drop in calories I had to up my carbohydrates, which meant eating even more of the very sweet food. Breakfast was cereal but because a gallon of milk was always added to the bowl before it got to me, the Weetabix was virtually liquid, which of course made it easier to swallow. The Weetabix was almost as difficult to find as it is to find a sliver of soap in your bath when, as a result of falling asleep, you've been in it far too long.

As part of the operation, I had had a third of my stomach removed where the tumour was pressing into it. This procedure is called a 'Sleeve gastrectomy.' In different circumstances it is performed to enable people to lose weight – so-called 'Bariatric surgery' – the idea being that the stomach feels full up with a much smaller amount of food. It's a pretty drastic procedure for a patient to undertake for weight loss because of the much higher risks with an operation and anaesthetic if the patient is obese, but it's actually very effective and can transform the lives of some patients. The combination of nausea, the small stomach capacity and the process of catabolism resulting from the operation, plus the tiny amount of food I could initially have in my diet, resulted, in further rapid weight loss. I knew I was likely to lose weight but hadn't realised what a struggle it would be to eat any food when I felt permanently sick.

As the days went by, I started to be able to walk further on my own and be less bent over. More tubes were taken out and I could eat a bit more. My survival seemed to be less in the hands of others and more in my own again. A smidgeon of confidence began to return. I could, at times, almost forget what I was in the midst of and just concentrate on getting over the operation. I started to feel better about myself and could see that I had made big strides – literally – in recovering. In medicine there is a concept called 'locus of control'. Patients who need to see a doctor for matters that most people wouldn't, who need a lot of reassurance about relatively minor issues, are described as having an 'external locus of control' i.e. that is outside themselves. Essentially, they rely and depend on others to keep them healthy, and if they are not, will tend to blame other people. At the other end of the scale are patients who have an 'internal locus of control' they are very independent-minded about their health and will assume responsibility for remaining well. They will see a doctor only when they have tried everything else they can think of. They dislike being dependent on others. I suppose I was nearer the 'internal' end of the scale and had disliked being so dependent on others. Now I was getting my locus back nearer to myself again.

I studiously avoided looking in the mirror. I didn't want to be confronted by the beaten-up old man's face that would be reproaching me for submitting myself to such extensive surgery. The world and his mother examined my scar and raved about how impressive it was, but I didn't personally want to see it. To look at the scar would somehow force me to see that I had been diminished by a process inside me. I didn't need or want to be confronted by the indisputable evidence that something big and bad had happened to me. I had showered, initially with the help of one of the nurses and then with Jane's help, but I wouldn't risk a look in the mirror. Then one day by accident I caught a glimpse of a gaunt, stooped, far older man than myself, with a vivid purple red scar right across the whole of his tummy covered over by mauve glue staring back at me from the mirror. As I had expected, the surgery had reduced me physically – quite literally there was less of me than before both on the inside – which was of course good – and on the outside – which felt sad. I looked terribly frail and haggard – a lot worse than I'd imagined I would. I wondered if I could ever get back to the previous version of myself.

I certainly felt better than I looked, but there was a long way to go to get over the surgery.

By the fourth or fifth day, I was becoming more confident and spent increasing amounts of time in the patients' lounge. I had shed the hospital gown and was sporting new pyjamas and the rather natty new dressing gown which Jane had insisted I get. It could almost be passed off as a smoking jacket. The effect of abandoning the pantomime dame look, wearing pyjamas rather than the hospital gown and looking smarter, was good for morale. I felt less like an invalid and more, I hoped, like a sophisticated David Niven-type character from a 60's movie. In reality I expect I looked more like an elderly Hugh Heffner! Jane had been sending regular 'from the horse's mouth' emails out regarding my progress, but Laura volunteered to relieve her of the duty and sent out the following:

Clinical observations - 30 November - 1st December 2016

Tea and Sympathy? Not Bloody Likely

Patient has been seen prowling the corridors of the Churchill Hospital, cat-walking in his smart silk smoking-jacket/dressing gown, showcasing his Autumn/Winter 2016 sartorial style (when confronted, he suggested that he was simply looking for the Churchill Christmas cards to send to his 'fans')

This observation of stylish recovery was compounded by the following exchange, witnessed in the Upper GI ward. Patient, to another very smartly dressed patient:

Patient A - 'you're looking very dapper'

Patient B - 'I'm just trying to keep up with you'

- the Patient was visibly satisfied with this conversation, reassured that he remains Alpha Patient on his ward.

Patient's improvement appears almost directly correlated to Patient's increasing demands. These include a late-night 'SOS' call to Patient's patient and ever-loving daughter to drive late at night through the freezing, frosty roads bringing various strictly unnecessary items that the Patient suddenly decided he wanted immediately. Patient was reprimanded and reminded that 'acting like a boss' is only something people get away with on Instagram.

Patient's wife was commended by medical staff for going above and beyond in service to the Patient. Patient's daughter is now recovering from the Patient's recovery in London.

The Patient has also been increasingly dictatorial and has been re-exerting his control through demanding: (1) which chair Patient's visitors should sit in (and forcing visitors to move if they have chosen the 'wrong' option, even if they are already seated, a game seemingly inspired by musical chairs) (2) that the Patient's son name his unborn child in tribute to the Patient – regardless of gender of said unborn child. The notes read that the name put forward is not 'Paul', but instead the patient's preferred nom de plume on the golf course – namely 'Genghis'.

The doctors and other clinicians have now indicated a very clear interest in getting shot of the Patient and sending him home.

Patient's family have indicated that they would be happy to have him home, provided various behaviour changes are put in place. These include: (A) an agreement that the patient is to relinquish his expectations of room service, an ensuite, and leg massaging devices in bed (B) that the Patient reminds himself that he is not Beyoncé and cannot act like a diva just because he's starting to feel stronger.

The Patient was last seen drinking tea and holding forth in the visitor's room of the ward.

By now the nausea was a little improved, the hiccups had gone as had all the tubes bar the drains in the abdomen. Alistair came in each day always pronouncing himself very satisfied with progress then one day, somewhat to my concern, said I could probably go home the next day if all remained well.

'Hang on! Hang on! Hang on! – isn't that a bit precipitate? Surely a few more days would make sense especially as the days are passing more easily now?' – I wanted to say but didn't, recognising this to be the way of the 'institutionalised patient' that is, the patient who prefers to stay in the safety of the hospital rather than get home. By now, the ward existence had become easily bearable. I could enjoy the telly and my book and socialise a bit with the other patients and receive and enjoy the company of visitors.

Home would not be nearly so secure. But that's where I found myself the next day.

Chapter 17

Home

It was of course, symbolically, very good to get home. It was also a great relief for Jane not to have to wait in line for sometimes up to an hour before she could get to a parking spot at the hospital. I'd made it through the immediate post-op period without a major complication thanks to the skill of my surgeon, my anaesthetist, the care of the ward staff and also the encouragement and badgering I got from Jane and Duncan to keep walking and take deep breaths and cough strongly. We'd been sent out with a removal van's worth of dressings and a variety of anti-nausea pills, painkillers, a stomach acid suppressant and penicillin. The latter antibiotic I was instructed to take twice a day indefinitely because my spleen had been removed as a result of the tumour growing into it. Without a spleen you are more susceptible to infections, particularly bacterial ones, so I felt very threatened by anyone with a cough or cold or even a sniffle. Still do really.

I also felt very threatened by the thought of a blood clot, which was definitely on the cards because of the long operation and the enforced period of immobility afterwards, and also because the mere fact of having cancer increases the risks of one enormously, so I was aware that I had to move a great deal despite the discomfort that caused. Initially I could only manage a lap a day around the garden, then fairly quickly that increased to two, then three laps, each time trying to straighten up a bit more and pretty soon I was able to go for a mile walk. I had been given routine blood-thinning injections, called dalteparin, to jab into my thigh for a total of four weeks after the operation. I'd often thought that to inject yourself would be very difficult, but weirdly they were almost painless, and I was pleasantly surprised by how easy it seemed.

Another 'threat' were my platelets. These are cells in the blood which make the blood 'stickier' and mine were more than double the normal level as a consequence of having my spleen removed and, to a lesser extent, of the operation itself causing inflammation. The danger from excess platelets is that they can cause a stroke. A quarter-strength aspirin was advised to lessen the stickiness, but I was very wary of taking it as I was on the blood thinning injections and the combination of aspirin, which can cause stomach bleeding, with an injection which would make any bleeding a great deal worse, is not an enticing one. Additionally, the aspirin seemed to give me indigestion.

I'd been warned that the most weight I should lose was ten percent of my normal weight, so was concerned to try to shovel in as much food as possible, as I was pretty close to that already when I left the ward. The trouble was that anything more than very small amounts of food caused such an unpleasant, painful, feeling of fullness in my stomach that I had to lie down for an hour or so afterwards till it passed. I also felt very tired and dozed a lot of the time. The main bugbear, however, remained my old nemesis nausea. I took the prescribed pills for it, trying different combinations but although they helped, the mornings were always difficult. Surprisingly, to me at any rate, food seemed to reduce the sensation a bit, but decent amounts of food were purgatory because of the very early and intense feeling of being overly full.

I'd come home on a Friday and my son Patrick and daughter-in-law Lucia came down the next day for the weekend. The Saturday was relaxed with lots of rejoicing and congratulations on getting to this point so quickly and quite a bit of laughter too. Then, on the Sunday morning, I suddenly experienced a very bad lancing pain in my stomach in and around the scar. It seemed to come with increasingly severe waves of pain, then abate a bit, then start building up again. It made me retch. It was shockingly severe. And worrying. Something must have gone disastrously wrong. My guess was that it was bowel obstruction. Why hadn't it happened on the ward when we could have summoned help easily? Would I have to go back to theatre to be opened up again? I assumed I would. Would I have to go through the same grim process that I'd been through after the actual operation? Maybe. But don't panic.

Maybe it might go as quickly as it had come. Give it ten minutes or so. But the pain. The pain made me groan and at times cry out. I remember musing that this was what childbirth labour pains must be like. And I had to frequently rush to the toilet ready to vomit. It was terrible. And terribly worrying. It had all been going so well and everyone had been so confident that it would, as a matter of course, just continue to go well. Then again, I'd had a lot done to me and so there was a lot that could go wrong. And going wrong it most certainly was.

Alistair had very kindly given me his mobile number for just this sort of event, so I rang it and left a message asking for a call. Meanwhile, my medical brain cranked itself up a bit and I felt that maybe the answer would be to take a suppository to see if that might clear the presumed obstruction. It did or at least appeared to do so as the pain receded remarkably within an hour. At which point, with impeccable timing, Alistair rang. One of the great skills of medics is to give symptoms a chance to settle which on the whole there is a very good chance of if left for long enough. There was no need to rush over to see him now because the pain had gone but if it returned, I should ring again. Miraculously it didn't.

I mentioned earlier that a friend had had similar surgery a year or two before. Turns out she had to cope with this exact type of pain every day during the first few weeks after her operation. Once again, I had got off comparatively lightly.

When a surgeon does a big abdominal operation, he or she will often put a 'drain' in. This is a tube to encourage any blood or fluid produced by an organ like a pancreas that has been cut, to come to the skin surface rather than stagnate in the abdomen where it might become infected. The drain is removed when there is no or very little fluid coming to the surface. I'd had two drains put into my abdomen – one on the right and one on the left – and several times a day on the ward, the amount in each drain was measured and the fluid was inspected. Gradually as expected, less and less fluid came out, particularly from the left drain so it was pulled out and a dressing covered the area where it had been. At night, a couple of days later whilst I was on the ward, the dressing became soaked and it was apparent that a lot of fluid from the area where the drain had been was coming up to the skin. 'I'll just change the dressing for now but if it doesn't settle, I'll get a wound manager' decided the overnight staff nurse. I knew there were specialist nurses in all sorts of areas including those who advised about skin infections, but I hadn't come across ones who specialised in the management of post-op wounds. Still hospital practice moves on rapidly, and wound experts seemed a good concept and it seemed eminently sensible to get as senior an opinion as possible, so I looked forward to meeting the wound manager if need be. The dressing got quickly soaked again so the same nurse returned alone with a dressing pack and proceeded to take out the 'wound manager' and stick it over the offending area. The 'wound manager' was not a person at all but in fact just a fancy dressing with a small bag to collect or 'manage' the fluid problem. You live and learn.

By the time I came home both drains had been removed and I had a 'wound manager' over the site of the right drain. The hospital adjudged that, given Jane's background as a nurse, and later as a university senior lecturer on the Oxford Nursing course at Brookes University, that there was no need to involve the district nursing team in checking the wound and changing the dressings. Considering that her patient was the one described all-too-accurately by Laura in her email, Jane had quite a daunting task on her hands and was understandably a bit nervous. She was fastidious in doing everything possible to reduce the risk of causing an infection but felt very rusty and apprehensive, as it had been decades since she'd had an abdominal wound to dress. And now she had a pretty big one at that to contend with. The dressings needed changing every other day but the 'wound-manager' one was tricky because she had to cut a hole in it large enough to allow the fluid to drain through the hole in the skin but not too large in case the dressing leaked. They hadn't been around in her day, so she didn't feel very confident about them.

One morning there was no fluid in the bag of the wound-manager that had been changed the night before. Had Jane inadvertently sealed over the hole with the dressing? What would happen to the fluid that had been draining if it was trapped inside? Would it become infected? Would it build up to such an extent that it might cause damage internally or burst out elsewhere? These complications were after all the reason a drain was put in. I was worried, though Jane felt it probably just meant the fluid had dried up, but of course she couldn't be certain. She needed advice as we didn't want to take any risk that might set my progress back.

Jane telephoned the practice nurse, but she hadn't come across wound-manager dressings before either, so advised asking the district nursing team, who more commonly saw patients in the early days after a big operation, to assess the situation. Jane therefore rang the district nurse office, requesting a district nurse assessment. To her dismay, her request was declined on the grounds that there hadn't been a referral done to them by the ward. Jane was not expecting that, partly because she had been told to contact them by the practice nurse – which was in effect a referral – but mainly because over the years I had frequently recounted to her how amazingly helpful our practice's district nurses were, and she knew I held them in high esteem. But, like most parts of the NHS, their workload had gone up and their workforce hadn't, so they were fighting a losing battle to maintain the previous levels of service. Invariably in these sorts of situations, the managers trumpet a 'reorganisation' to 'streamline the service' and make it more 'efficient', and inevitably whatever service is affected is told it has to stop doing some work that it had been doing up until then. The poor foot soldiers on the ground, the clinicians, in this case the district nurses, get the flak from the patients when they expect some help and are declined. Morale drops, resignations increase and the pressure on those who remain goes up. The same had happened in general practice. There were many things that we used to do that we couldn't anymore, because there were just so many new areas of work we had to take on, that had been passed onto us from the hospitals, as their time became similarly squeezed. We also had frequent new initiatives that were being asked of General Practice by the Department of Health to fit in. So, for example, we used to do obstetric deliveries, look after patients in a local community hospital, perform lots of minor operations and freeze minor skin conditions but had had to stop them all.

The experience of being unable to access help from the district nurses confronted me with the limitations of the NHS in a way that was up close and personal and as someone who had worked for over forty years exclusively in the NHS, I felt a particularly deep sense of disappointment. I guess I was really experiencing more of the frustrations of what it was like to be a patient.

Jane, it turned out, was right. There wasn't a problem – in fact it was good news – as the operation site improved, the drain had simply dried up.

I had just panicked.

Chapter 18

Getting Better

My goal from this point onwards was to get back to a semblance of fitness as quickly as possible so that I could get started on the dreaded chemotherapy, without which, the pernicious liver metastases and any other metastases elsewhere in the body were being given free rein to enlarge and multiply. Before I could start the chemotherapy, I needed to be to be well enough to cope with the nausea and vomiting, weakness and other debilitating side effects the drugs frequently caused. It was daunting to think that I would be voluntarily submitting myself to a treatment that might make me feel terrible and worst of all, invite my old vomiting nemesis to have a field day.

Before the operation I'd been told by Alistair that it would take, on average, three months to get back to pre-op fitness, but at that stage I'd confidently assumed it wouldn't take me that long. After all, I was the person who everyone said had coped so well after my skull had been cracked open and my brain operated on a few years earlier, the same person who then, two years later, at the age of sixty, had run The London Marathon. Years earlier I had coined the adage 'Ageing is for others' as I was very active, still had a full head of hair and was surprised by how really well I felt. I joked ironically about this concept to friends but managed to half convince myself that it was true in my case. Sadly now, the old saying 'pride comes before a fall' was horribly apt. Getting back to pre-op fitness most certainly didn't happen with a rush if it happened at all.

After a week or two at home I was able to walk a reasonable distance but was slow and not even able to stand up fully straight because of the painful pulling on the scar. I was surprised and a bit alarmed that my weight was slipping down ever further. I still couldn't eat much without needing to rest afterwards to cope with the horrible feeling of stomach distension and was further enfeebled by the wretched nausea which didn't seem to want to lessen, let alone go away. I resigned myself to the assumption that my weight would probably never get back to its pre-op level and that I'd just remain wafer-thin, not in itself a problem, but more for the fact that it would reveal to the outside world that I'd had cancer and had that 'cancer-look' about me. I'd been sent home with lots of the repellent high-calorie drinks and been told to take a couple a day or even more depending on what my weight was doing. It always needed a bit of mental preparation to take them, as although they were not long drinks, they usually made me retch. What was, however, surprisingly acceptable, was whole-nut chocolate bars! My former partner brought a huge one whenever she visited, which was thankfully pretty often, and not only was she good for my spirits but so were her chocolate bars. I had very slight misgivings about eating so much chocolate, because I was at risk of getting diabetes as a result of having two thirds of my pancreas removed, but such misgivings were easily overcome as I rationalised that the overall nutritional benefit of the chocolate outweighed any downsides. Friends went walking with me which was a morale-booster, though apart from walking I wasn't up to much other than dozing and watching TV. Being compelled to watch several hours a day was no great hardship, particularly as my daughter, Laura, had downloaded Netflix to improve the variety and quality of my viewing. Guilt-free Netflix fests with chocolate – there had to be some upsides to convalescing from surgery.

Guilt-free telly brought to mind nights many years ago, when I would be on-call for our large practice. My way of getting through the stress of being on-call was to stretch out in front of the TV with a phone more or less clamped to my ear and hope to doze off and wake up hours later with half of the night over. Kind of sad to wish a night away, but that was what on-call did to you. I sort of wished the days away again now, as I knew that with each one that passed, I must be recovering a bit more.

One of the fairly common complications of surgery is depression. I saw this in many patients and explained to them that it was similar to people who have been mugged or assaulted for any reason, who often feel low for a while because I suppose, they have been living their lives happily not thinking about death, when, out of the blue, they are brutally reminded of their mortality and their own frailty. 'Surgical mugging' was an expression I coined to describe what had happened to people who found themselves with painful scars as a result of being 'cut-open' or 'assaulted' by a surgeon, which was made in some respects worse, because they had brought it on themselves by allowing themselves to be 'knifed'. Fortunately, I didn't get depressed about what had been done to me by Alistair. I guess I was lucky not to have a predisposition to depression but mainly because I had such great support at home from Jane and the family and from friends. I knew my devout Irish relatives had been 'whispering' very loudly on my behalf which was also a comfort and I'd done a fair bit of 'whispering' myself. Maybe all that helped too. The combination of social factors and my lack of a tendency to depression are called 'bio-psychosocial factors' and are well known to make a major difference into how patients recover after an operation. Patients who fear that any pain signifies a problem, and so avoid walking for example, are much more likely to develop complications like blood clots in the legs or lungs – deep vein thromboses or pulmonary embolisms. Knowing about all this, by virtue of being a doctor, was a definite advantage though as you will realise from the tale of the dried-up wound manager dressing, it didn't stop me catastrophising at times.

I did feel a bit rueful that my poor old body had a massive livid scar right across it and was quite frail. The recovery was a lot tougher than I had naively and somewhat arrogantly, assumed it would be, and worryingly much slower than I'd expected. This mattered as I needed to start chemotherapy as soon as possible. In one respect, time was dragging – four weeks had seemed like four months – but in another, it was going too fast, as too much time was elapsing with nothing being able to be done for the disease in my liver until I was well enough.

Over the next four weeks or so, slowly, and quite literally painfully, things improved. I began to be able to eat more. My weight steadied out then slowly increased. I started to be able to stand up reasonably straight and walk further and faster. I began to jog a little on the treadmill, which I had bought to train for the marathon years before and was still, somewhat to Jane's despair, located in an area off the kitchen. And, little by little, life started to look up. I could go for longer, more varied and challenging walks. I could get out a bit to friends' houses, be driven, and eventually drive myself, to other villages and even eat a small meal out. I socialised a bit and we had a black tie Christmas dinner party for very close friends. The dinner jacket was rather loose, and I had to lie down after the meal for thirty minutes, but it felt like passing a milestone. No alcohol though. I had lost the taste for it completely. Even the nausea abated a little. I still needed two different types of anti-nausea pills and, first thing in the morning, occasionally found myself with my head hanging over the toilet bowl retching furiously, but, increasingly, food seemed to help. It sometimes felt as if it was a contest between me and the nausea to see who would win in the mornings. If I got down to eat quickly, I would usually be able to head off the nausea with breakfast.

It had eventually dawned on me that I couldn't treat the convalescence like it was some sort of endurance event with the aim of impressing, everybody by 'how well' and 'how quickly' I had recovered. Nausea is a particularly malevolent adversary and refused to give in easily. I basically had to wait for it to tire and give up, which it finally did.

I 'launched myself back into the village' by going to a neighbour's New Year's Eve party. I felt very conspicuous at first and had to bunk off early, but it was another hurdle cleared. Going on longer and longer walks, often with people I wouldn't normally have walked with, or who I hadn't seen for some time, became something increasingly to look forward to, and it was heartening to have such people go out of their way to get in touch. My fear of people avoiding me, or leaving Jane to cope alone, dissipated. I felt immense gratitude and relief that we had apparently managed to involve our friends in a way that meant there was none of that awkwardness that might lead to the kind of isolation that George and Shelley had so sadly experienced.

Chapter 19

The Magician

Eleven days after being discharged from the ward, Jane and I went for an early check-up with my surgeon Alistair. I was looking forward to the appointment and wanted to look smart and as far removed as possible from the person he'd seen a lot of in a hospital gown looking gaunt and unwell. Hopefully, he would think I was doing brilliantly and tell me which would in turn make me feel better because he had said it. In the time-honoured tradition of slightly desperate patients, I made little of the negatives about how I felt and emphasised the positives. Spouses and partners of my own patients had often expressed frustration to me that their partners weren't telling me just how bad they were feeling, preferring to put a gloss on things. I could better appreciate why now. You really want and actually need to hear from your doctor that you are doing well. The converse is not only hard to take, but actually unthinkable, so you embellish your story a bit.

Alistair reassured me on the weight front that I would still be catabolic from the operation so couldn't expect to regain much weight yet. That would follow in time. Similarly, the bloated feeling after small amounts of food would definitely improve. He seemed very happy with my progress, which predictably lifted my spirits.

Then he explained that 'the margins of all the specimens removed were clear' which stopped me in my tracks. It meant that where he had operated, he hadn't left any tumour behind in the abdomen. Alistair had evidently managed to remove everything malignant from what had been the war zone of the area around my stomach, that had been so messed up that the experts hadn't been able to tell from the scans whether the trouble was in my stomach or my pancreas. It didn't mean that there was no tumour left in the abdomen – even he couldn't possibly lay claim to that Nirvana – and he explained that probably glands in the abdomen and even in the chest might well have been affected that he hadn't been able to see or get to, but it was way better than I had expected and as good as it could possibly have been.

Alistair said he wanted me to get back to normal as soon as possible including going back to work. Doing normal things makes you feel normal, so this was a very good topic to raise. It would encourage me that I could get back to normal in case I harboured any doubts. I guess he assumed I would want to get back to work though I wasn't really sure I did. He explained that he would like to see me again in three months then probably six-monthly for a couple of years, then perhaps a yearly follow-up with him that might be dovetailed with a yearly follow-up with Michael so that I was seen twice a year.

He was talking about two years of follow-up then yearly ones as though that was to be expected. That was a minimum of three years. Did he really expect me to be alive in three years? I had doubted him a bit when he had talked so matter-of-factly about removing this and that from my abdomen. So why doubt him now? But three years. Just like that. Could that really be possible? If it was, it would be fantastic, amazing, extraordinary and whatever other words you could think of to mean miraculous.

My sons already regarded Alistair with 'total awe' and felt that 'he walked on water.' There was no question that he was a remarkable surgeon. In addition to being a magician, I was beginning to think Alistair could be psychic as well.

'No other experience duplicates the intimacy, candour, physical access, and vulnerability of seeing a doctor', wrote the medical thinker Daniel Federman.

For someone like me, who had spent over forty years being the doctor, the experience of being on the other side of the consultation with Alistair was extraordinary. He was the person who had given me a glimmer of hope. He had said that he could operate and remove all sorts of tumour and tumour-affected organs – apart from the liver of course – and he had delivered in spades on that promise. Not only did he imbue me with a sense of trust and confidence in his ability to do virtually anything he put his mind to, but his quiet friendly manner made me feel that he really cared about me as a person. I have subsequently heard similar warm sentiments from other patients of his.

It was a good example of 'the doctor as therapy.'

Over the years, like all GPs I'm sure, a number of my own patients had said they always felt better for seeing me and I felt now that, if I had given them even a fraction of what Alistair had given me, then I'd made the right career choice all those years ago and was very grateful that I had.

Chapter 20

Very Unexpected News

I was due to have a consultation with Michael, the NET oncologist, several weeks after seeing Alistair, to arrange the chemotherapy. Before the operation, I'd been given a fairly good idea which drugs I would have to take and of course had looked up the likely side-effects which were pretty daunting. Nausea and vomiting, which whilst not affecting literally every patient, were always mentioned as the most common side-effects of all three of the drugs I would receive. I gloomily assumed, in the light of the severity of the nausea I'd experienced after the operation, that I'd be more susceptible than most to those side-effects. The thought of doing anything likely to induce more nausea let alone vomiting and possibly lots of it, was a far from pleasant one and made me wonder again if I'd be able to cope with the chemotherapy treatment and end up having to abandon it.

The worries about hair loss that I'd had when I was due to start chemotherapy before re-surfaced to a certain extent, but I was a little more sanguine now and had an eclectic mix of beanies and hats. I'd probably lose further weight as well. But other people coped, didn't they? So why not me? My preposterous 'Ageing is for others' adage really seemed ironic now. The confidence, the cockiness, that I had before the operation that I could cope with anything, was long gone. This wasn't an endurance race but more like a fight that I knew I would get beaten up in. I would just have to pray that I could eventually get up off the canvas.

Before the appointment I had to have two scans done in the nuclear medicine department of The Churchill Hospital two months after the surgery. They were to be done on consecutive days to see the extent of the disease left in the body and also to see if the metastases in the liver and any elsewhere had the special octreotide receptors that Michael had mentioned when we met him before the operation. I was to have an injection in the morning then be scanned four hours later and go back again twenty-four hours after that for the second scan. The Churchill Hospital felt like a very different place now. I had spent probably the most significant eight days of my adult life there and whilst no one that I saw knew me and it was just as large and impersonal as before, now we had history together. A part of me, admittedly a malign, most unwanted part of me, had been left there.

It felt surreal to be sitting in The Churchill waiting for a cancer scan. That feeling was boosted by watching a flat screen in the waiting room showing soundless day time TV.

Right on time I went in to be weighed by one of several radiographers. I was then invited to sit in a cubicle and a radiographer inserted a venflon needle into a vein over my wrist. I then had the radioactive octreotide, which was carried in a special container, injected into the venflon. I was invited to return four hours later for the first scan.

The scan itself was very different to the one I'd had before the operation in the private hospital and now I felt very different too. With the first scan I'd been very confident that nothing much would be found and felt like a fit guy just having a belt and braces check. It was also quick and comfortable. Chastened by that experience, and knowing my liver was extensively affected by metastases, my mindset now was completely different. Now I felt like a 'cancer patient', or 'victim' like so many of the people who pass through that department must be. It is in The Cancer Centre after all. This scan was really quite uncomfortable as I had to keep my hands and arms behind my head for the duration of the scan which seemed far longer than the actual forty minutes or so that it took. What thoughts did the radiographers have about their patients I wondered? Did they feel sympathy for their patients, or did they just concentrate on performing their work professionally not allowing their minds to wander too much? Probably the latter, I surmised. After all, in the main, that was how I had performed a lot of my own work.

The scan would be scrutinised by a radiologist who would send a formal report to Michael and he and his colleagues would discuss it at the MDT meeting before he saw me to discuss the next steps on the 1st February 2017.

The 1st February arrived. Usual drill; buff up and get to the Manor Hospital in plenty of time. I was by no means back to pre-op fitness, but I was well on the way by now and anxious to get on with the treatment to the liver and any other metastases. Jane was dreading the consultation. So was I. I had braced myself for an uncomfortable discussion about the chemotherapy and had carefully prepared a series of questions about how the drugs would be administered, what to expect and what to do if there were difficult side-effects. I was apprehensive about having the treatment at the private Manor hospital rather than at the NHS Churchill hospital, because the chemotherapy unit was far smaller there, with fewer doctors on hand. My experience of The Churchill had been so positive that I felt confident that chemotherapy administered there would be done very well. Not for the first, or the last time, I felt some misgivings about being a private patient. It would have been possible to get the treatment done on the NHS at The Churchill if I'd asked, but I was a bit reluctant to dump myself on the already hard-pressed unit there.

A brief enquiry from Michael established how I was doing, then, as he had done at the first consultation, he bowled me a googly. The scan, he explained, had shown that Alistair had managed to remove everything malignant, apart from the liver metastases, and there was now no other sign of any other cancer on the scan at all. The liver was positive for the octreotide receptors, so the recommendation of the MDT was that I have PRRT treatment for the liver metastases, rather than chemotherapy.

I was stunned. Jane was stunned.

Nirvana after all. I was not going to have chemotherapy.

I was not going to have to have chemotherapy and was mighty relieved. I didn't really have a clue what was involved in having PRRT and what price one had to pay in terms of side effects, but I assumed it would be a whole lot better than chemo. I was shocked by the unexpectedness of what I had just heard. If I'd had a hat on, I'd have thrown it up in the air.

If the PRRT failed, then chemotherapy would come on the menu again but not for now. Michael had indicated at our previous meeting that he couldn't guarantee that I would ever be at the stage where he would be able to recommend PRRT. And yet here we were already. How amazing. How wonderful not to have to face chemotherapy. I was completely unprepared for this and nearly all the questions I had so carefully prepared were irrelevant now.

This was the second time – in just two meetings – that Michael had given me great news. Was he my talisman? Would he always be so?

I was starting to have a good feeling about him. The bearer of bad news is traditionally shot, so shouldn't the bearer of good news be revered? Michael had had nothing to do with the amazing surgery Alistair had pulled off, but he was the one telling us about it and what it meant.

Quietly, Jane asked if the treatment could be curative?

'I think it's unlikely' he gently replied, 'because of the amount of disease in the liver.'

The treatment would be in the NHS as the private hospital didn't have access to this sort of treatment, which was in fact a relief. I'd feel safe in the place where I'd come through amazing surgery.

There was, he explained, a waiting list for the treatment which unfortunately was longer than normal because there'd been some trouble with the drains from the room in which the radiotherapy was administered.

Drains? Drains delaying my precious treatment. Bit bizarre. I thought in my career I'd come across pretty well every reason, every excuse possible, for NHS delays, but drains were a new one even for me.

When would it be?

He really couldn't say, he really didn't know. It would be as soon as possible.

What about the metastases on the liver scan?

'The largest had increased by about a centimetre from five to six centimetres but in fact the others looked pretty much the same as before. It's certainly not out of control or rampant. It's behaving like a well differentiated grade 2 tumour.'

So, there was no real urgency to get on with the treatment then?

No, he wasn't concerned from a clinical point of view about the delay. In any case he thought it likely that I had had the metastases for years – maybe as much as three or four years – so in the greater scheme of things the wait was not that long.

I might even have had them when I ran my marathon I found myself musing.

Checking that she had understood things properly, Jane asked:

'Do you feel this is good news?'

'Yes. You've had a fantastic result in terms of surgery. I was really worried that the surgery wouldn't get everything out. Also, being octreotide positive is good, as it gives you other options [to chemotherapy.]'

She asked if, in the light of the scan, he could now better comment on prognosis.

'It was difficult,' he said, 'as we know it's growing slowly but I'll be better able to judge in the light of the response to the PRRT treatment'.

He described what the process of the treatment would entail, including some checks on my kidneys to make sure they would be able to deal with the treatment and so on.

Jane returned to the question of the delay but there was nothing that could be done about it, so we left.

Jubilation.

Shock, but good shock.

'Over the moon' about the results and the revised treatment plans which did not include chemotherapy and all the imagined horror chemotherapy might have entailed.

It took some time to sink in.

The feeling I had, after first being told that I could have really active surgical treatment for my condition returned. Close to euphoria, mixed with disbelief, bewilderment, gratitude and humility. 'Words can't express…' is a phrase I've heard several times from a friend when referring to the gratitude she feels particularly towards her surgeon and also to her NHS life-saving treatment. To find the words to describe emotions you've never come across before, arising from a situation you could never have expected to experience, is, to use British understatement to its best effect, 'challenging'.

I felt incredible esteem and even more respect for Alistair, whose skill had made it possible for me to have a far, far more acceptable treatment now than had been planned. It felt as if he had almost been my saviour. How wonderful it must be to be him and be able to make such a difference to people's lives I reflected. Did he realise what a difference he made I wondered? He didn't seem to have an ego, just quiet self-confidence. I would make sure he did realise just how great the work he did was. I'd planned to write to him anyway, but I'd wanted to make sure I chose my words very carefully.

Paradoxically I'd already written to Donald, the anaesthetist who had been superb, to thank him but I had been waiting for some kind of special inspiration before writing to Alistair and as inspiration rarely passed my way, I had been waiting a while. Perfection may well be the enemy of the good and prevent you from expressing something at all, but I was determined to write more than just a good letter to someone who had done so much for me.

Paul Coffey

Chapter 21

The Impatient Patient

On the rare occasions when you have a good round of golf, you always feel that your score could, and by rights, really should, have been even better. You missed a few short putts you should have sunk or something completely out of your control made you fluff a shot. Perhaps someone had moved a millimetre and made it quite impossible for you to hit your shot properly! In other words, you are not content to live in the moment and savour the wonderment that you didn't hit quite so many awful shots as you normally do, but feel that it should have been better.

Maybe that's how Jane and I started to feel when we came down to earth. It was great that I was going to have PRRT but it would have been much better, if it had been scheduled for a week or two's time. A minimum of four weeks delay seemed a bit long and it might be as much as eight weeks. Michael had indicated that he didn't feel the wait was really much of a problem and anyway all his other patients were having to wait that long, so there wasn't anything he could do about it.

But then he wasn't the one with metastases growing in his liver.

The whole point of private self-funding was to try to avoid NHS delays. The catch was that there wasn't a private nuclear medicine Department in Oxford, so my treatment had to be done in the NHS Hospital. BUPA would be paying for the treatment which, at about ten thousand pounds a go, was a saving for the NHS, albeit less than a drop in the ocean of money needed to run the NHS.

The person who would know how long the wait would be was Catherine, the superintendent radiographer in charge of the nuclear medicine department, who was very friendly and helpful. She elaborated on the drains explaining that because of the need to get rid of radioactive waste – meaning urine and faeces – safely, the drains were actually very important. It wasn't simply a matter of waiting for a plumber. Because of this, the wait was far longer than normal and the earliest she could get me in would be in seven weeks. Unfortunately, she explained, she had to order in the radioactive medication for each patient well in advance of the treatment, as the dose was tailored to the patient's weight and clinical condition, so even if someone cancelled – which they rarely did – it was hardly ever possible to bring someone else in to fill the cancellation slot.

Seven weeks. Jane was even more unhappy than I was about the delay in getting on with the treatment. I completely accepted that I couldn't jump ahead of someone else already on the list for PRRT just because I was self-funding and wouldn't have wanted to even if I could. But surely my clinical situation demanded more urgent treatment than a seven week wait? My disease had progressed since the previous scan, so didn't that make it urgent? Michael had indicated that the progression since the first liver scan was not too much to be worried about – it was just one metastasis that had gone from five to six centimetres. Six centimetres? That's huge. That's a twenty percent increase over three months, so during the wait for the PRRT, at that rate, it could increase up to about 7.5 centimetres. That was ridiculously big. But equally wouldn't everyone on the list be concerned that their wait was too long also?

I've never had a patient who wanted to wait any length of time for any treatment. The more serious the condition, the more necessary it feels to get cracking. Even if the treatment is not urgent or life-saving, all patients prefer to 'get it over and done with' so that they can get on with life. Being on a waiting list at times feels like suspended animation, with real life on hold. But waiting seven weeks for treatment of my worsening cancer?

When Alistair's secretary had implied that I might have to wait up to seven weeks for my surgery, I thought she must be mistaken. Happily, she was. But Michael was not mistaken. I must wait my turn and that was the end of it.

Or was it? Surely, as a medic, I could work something out. If I could get the PRRT treatment or ideally just the first one done quicker elsewhere, that would be the ideal thing. It would also be one less on the Oxford waiting list, which would be a win-win for everyone. That would be a smart solution. Having private insurance gave me that option.

The Churchill Hospital in Oxford is one of only a handful of hospitals in the country where you can be given PRRT treatment. The Royal Free in London is another. I rang The Royal Free and with surprising ease was soon talking to an oncologist who was sympathetic to my quandary. Yes, they would, in all likelihood, be able to get me treated rather more quickly either in the Private Wing of the Royal Free or otherwise in a NET Unit at the private Wellington hospital in North London. She seemed a bit surprised that chemotherapy wasn't being offered first and explained that they had stopped using the particular type of PRRT, that was being proposed by Michael, in favour of one that she said was safer for the kidneys – but she said that wasn't really an important issue. I would be under the care of a particular consultant who was the Royal Free NET specialist, so she very kindly emailed him there and then about my situation and copied me in. He responded the same evening saying they could probably get me in in about three weeks, but they would go through their normal rigorous approach of discussing my case with all the scans, histology and operative notes at their MDT meeting and then make a recommendation for treatment. He listed a whole host of other treatments that might be recommended including, of course, chemotherapy.

What an idiot I'd been! I should have realised that The Royal Free consultant, would not simply agree to give me the treatment the Oxford MDT recommended. No, he would, as a professional and expert himself, want his MDT to carefully review my case and decide what they felt would be the best treatment for me which might or might not be PRRT. In other words, I would be given a second-opinion on the best treatment for me. Good or even brilliant if you want a second opinion but actually I didn't. I was more than happy with the treatment Oxford had provided and with the proposed treatment. I just wanted it sooner.

What if the Royal Free MDT recommended chemotherapy rather than PRRT? That would really put the cat amongst the pigeons. Whose opinion should I go by, theirs or Oxford's? I certainly wouldn't want to have to traipse all the way over to London for the chemotherapy I had been so overjoyed in avoiding in the first place. Furthermore, what if the treatment they recommended didn't work and I needed another type? Where should that then be done? Who would decide, The Royal Free or Oxford? Or would I have burnt my boats with Oxford and be stuck having to go to London?

Many times, patients have asked me if I would recommend that they have a second opinion. Unless I thought the advice they had received in Oxford was wrong, which was very rare, I would point out that it could be difficult if the second opinion differed from the first. What should my patient do then? Seek a third one and go with the majority? But what if the third opinion was also in some way different…? In any case, with the MDT model for major treatments, patients effectively get more than one opinion routinely now anyway. A second opinion may initially seem like a sensible thing that couldn't do any harm, but the reality is not always so simple. So, no, I did not want to have a second opinion and possibly end up having to take chemotherapy.

So, feeling somewhat chastened by my actions, I resigned myself to the seven-week wait.

Sometimes being a medic and having the wherewithal to direct your own treatment can be injurious to your health. Sometimes too much choice enables you to shoot yourself in the foot.

Is it perhaps better not to have private insurance after all?

Chapter 22

There's More to Life Than Cancer

Having Irish parents, but being born and brought up in England, I could, theoretically at least, have played sport for Ireland or England, and so am always a bit conflicted when Ireland play England at rugby as to who to support. When I'm with Irish relatives I staunchly support England and when with my sons, Patrick and Duncan, who unhesitatingly support England, I support Ireland. Don't know what Norman Tebbit would have made of that other than that, generally, I must be a bit contrary, disloyal and probably not to be trusted. I'd been offered three tickets for a Wales Ireland Rugby International in Cardiff by a friend and because of the PRRT delay was able to go with Patrick and Duncan. It felt pretty special to be able to take them after all I'd put them through and even Wales winning the match didn't matter too much.

The treatment delay also afforded Jane and me the chance to go to a hotel near Laugharne in Wales, that had Spa facilities, which we planned to take full advantage of. The first morning we were both booked in for a back massage and both duly filled in the requisite Health and Safety forms beforehand. I naturally wrote that I'd had surgery for a NET. As seems to be the case with many forms you have to fill in, no one had looked at it, because just as the massage was about to start, Jane double checked that it was OK for me to have a back massage. The masseuse looked aghast at the mention of cancer, hurriedly excused herself saying that she needed to check with her senior and was back a minute later explaining that because of my treatment 'obviously' it wouldn't be safe to have a back massage. It was the first time the NET had barred me from something and the fact that the massage would almost certainly have been harmless anyway made it feel worse. I was now a 'cancer patient' to be handled and dealt with differently to the general population. It felt dispiriting and almost like a kind of microaggression but probably had more to do with their public liability insurance. I was now a risk, someone to be wary of.

We cycled and walked, and visited all the Dylan Thomas sites in Laugharne, enjoyed amazing food at the hotel and spent time in the swimming pool where I was confronted with just how weak my 'core' had become as a result of Alistair's slicing and dicing.

The weeks slipped by, then a momentous event occurred that put everything, including the NET, into the shade. Theo Patrick Andrew Coffey was born on the 21st of March in Kingston Hospital. He had required an Emergency Caesarean Section, but he was OK. He was perfect. Our first grandchild. We were ecstatic, relieved and overcome with excitement just as we had been decades earlier when Laura had come into our lives and later Patrick and Duncan. Lucia was tired and sore, but you would never have guessed what she had been through. She is an amazing athlete and I guess her fitness and the excitement had enabled her to come through the section far better than most. Patrick was equally ecstatic in a way I'd never seen him before.

At any time, the birth of a first grandchild would be a cause for great rejoicing but in view of what the family had recently been through this meant so much more. Theo symbolised the future and for a while all the worries, pain and stresses of the preceding few months were put aside. We rushed down to Kingston to see him later that day. In the Special Care Baby Unit with a drip in one arm, bruising on his face bearing testimony to the attempt to deliver him with forceps, he looked fragile and helpless. He was helpless. I thought of how I had likened myself immediately after the operation to a helpless new-born and there he was, just like I had been, but not tormented by an agitated mind, nausea and pain. I thought back to the moment that Lucia had asked at the family conference in October whether I would live to see her baby being born. I had and it was great. Just great. We were so thankful for the events of the 21st of March.

The next visit to a hospital would be quite a contrast.

Chapter 23

NETs Haven't Read the Cancer Rule Book

The PRRT treatment was scheduled for the day after Theo's birth. The instructions were to have a blood test in 'Oncology Outpatients' before having anything to eat that morning and then to present myself on the Oncology ward by 9.30 am. That meant getting to The Churchill by about 8 am. 'Oncology Outpatients' eluded us for a while because it's actually called 'Chemotherapy Outpatients'. A smartly-dressed woman, already waiting – what cancer did she have I found myself wondering – explained that I should take a ticket from a machine, exactly like at the supermarket cheese counter, and when my number was displayed, I should go through for the blood test. The blood test form had been incorrectly filled in which delayed matters for over an hour and made me late arriving on the ward. The sense of being out of control the delay had caused, cranked up the tension I was already feeling almost to panic levels. I feared that if I missed the time I was supposed to get to the ward by, my treatment would be cancelled. The old me would have realised that was ridiculous but he had long gone. The new me didn't cope anything like as well with stress.

After half an hour Catherine the superintendent radiographer, arrived and took me through the ward, down one turn then another, until finally, tucked away in a corner, was the lead-lined room that was designed to keep radioactivity away from the rest of the ward. It was really a cell. There was a window but at just below ceiling level, designed only to let light in. The night before Jane recalled that we watched Steve McQueen in the film Papillon pace out his solitary confinement cell. Jane says I automatically did the same when I entered my cell. Catherine explained the 'house rules.' Only I could use the ensuite bathroom and whenever I had the urge to have a pee I had to sit down and afterwards flush the loo twice. Sitting was mandatory to ensure that no urine found its way onto the floor which was lined with paper anyway. There was a bold line on the floor by the bed. I wasn't to stray over that line and Jane was to stay behind it at all times, as was everyone else unless the treatment required otherwise. There was a telly and a fridge. It wasn't the Ritz and if I'd been deluded enough to think my BUPA insurance would entitle me to luxury accommodation, I'd have been very disappointed, but it was better than Papillon's cell. Catherine gave me a sandwich for lunch and a menu for supper to fill in. She noted the book I was struggling to read and enthused about how good it was and asked what Jane was knitting and delighted in the news about our one-day-old grandson, when Jane explained it was a hat for Theo. She was really warm and lovely.

A bit later a young, very pleasant, doctor came to clerk me in. The time-honoured tradition of writing lots of notes about any patient admitted to the ward was one I had done as a young doctor a million years ago.

A drip was set up in my arm and a bag of fluid run through it to prime my kidneys to start working at maximum power so that when the radioactive PRRT was injected, the kidneys would get rid of it as quickly and efficiently as possible. I was also given a couple of injections through the drip to counter the likely side effect of nausea. Michael arrived and checked the dose with Catherine and waited in the room – behind the bold line of course – until it had all been administered. His presence was mandatory seemingly because of the radioactive PRRT being administered. Next, I was given a diuretic drug which further made the kidneys work hard. It was a small dose of a drug I had prescribed hundreds of times to patients, but the effect was immense. I had to rush out to the toilet almost constantly for an hour or so, which was easier said than done tied up to a drip. What it must have been like for all the patients I had prescribed far bigger doses of the diuretic to, I could only imagine and in my mind, I apologised to them for the literal inconvenience I must have caused them.

An hour or two after the radioactive PRRT had been given, a physicist appeared and explained that he would like to measure how radioactive I was. That was easily done by pointing what looked like a speed camera, but was in fact a gamma camera, at me. He got a reading and explained that the idea was to see how quickly my body was getting rid of the radiation. I would have another reading a few hours later to check that things were on course. Were they currently OK, I naturally asked? 'Oh yes'. I asked him what sort of level he would expect the next reading to be and he mentioned a figure. It was beginning to dawn on me – surprisingly late in the day you might perhaps think – that Michael, Catherine and all the others involved, took this radioactivity thing quite seriously. I hadn't really stressed about it at all because, as far as I was concerned, anything was better than chemotherapy.

Finally, another bag or two of fluid was run through. Supper didn't appear. I wasn't entirely surprised as the 'cell' was so hard to find that I could imagine it being easy to miss if you were pushing a large food trolley along. I was therefore given an emergency supper, which was a sandwich. Hospital sandwiches never fail to disappoint, but you don't really come to hospitals for the food, do you?

A different physicist duly arrived and took another reading, but it was much higher than his colleague had predicted.

'Should I be concerned?' I asked.

'Oh no, it's very variable. We'll do another one in the morning before you leave' and he left. Shouldn't have enquired too much about the first one I deduced. I couldn't believe that my kidneys weren't getting rid of the radioactivity in the light of the torrents that I had produced – all sitting down as instructed. The drip stopped a few times and had to be tweaked a bit by the nurses but was finally finished just before midnight.

It had taken a lot longer than I'd expected but then again, I hadn't really known what to expect. I could have asked I suppose but sometimes – not often in my case – you have to give your attendants a break and not ask them about every single detail. I'd only experienced very mild nausea and had been given something for it, which seemed to have settled it. The whole experience had been a lot less grim than I'd anticipated. In fact, it hadn't been grim at all. The main tribulation had been the telly. Only BBC1 and a couple of dreary Freeview channels worked, so I watched the news repeatedly. Which was terrible. That day the Westminster Bridge terrorist incident had occurred, and I saw and heard every shocking detail repeatedly. Jane rang my mobile and told me that Duncan, who was working as a junior orthopaedic surgeon in The Chelsea and Westminster hospital close by to The Houses of Parliament, had stayed on late at work to help deal with some of the casualties. Not for the first time I felt enormous pride that he was doing what he was.

The night passed OK – bit boring being in the cell but I was pretty happy that the treatment had been so easy to cope with and reflected that, had I been having chemotherapy, I would, I assumed, have been in for far worse side effects. This I could easily cope with which was a big relief as I was due to come back for the second dose eight weeks later.

My first morning visitor was the physicist – this time the reading was far lower than before and evidently well on track. Next was breakfast – I'd been remembered which was good. One of the dilemmas you have when in a hospital bed is whether to risk having your shower and missing the breakfast person and hence being unable to choose your cereal, or wait too long and miss your shower because the people who are collecting you come before you're ready. Not the most important dilemma of all time perhaps, but an example of how you lose control of the small things as well as the big ones.

Catherine duly breezed in and removed the cannula from my arm. I was packed up and ready to go. 'How had the night been?' 'Fine other than for the telly,' I joked. 'Oh, we must get that fixed' said Catherine who escorted me from the ward as I was still radioactive and had to keep my distance from other people. Felt a bit like close protection security would feel, I mused.

Steven, a man of about my age, had been my patient for over thirty years and rarely saw any doctor other than myself. In recent years it has become ever harder for patients to see just one GP unless they were really determined to and willing to wait, sometimes for quite a while, but he had always wanted to see me. The devil you know, I suppose. Whilst reading work emails at home, a month or two earlier, before I had irrevocably decided to retire, I was shocked to see that he'd attended hospital after having a fit and been diagnosed with a metastasis as a result of a lung cancer. I knew he had never smoked which meant he had been extraordinarily unlucky to get lung cancer and for it to present with a symptom caused by spread terrible.

Part of my shock at reading about Steven's condition was my immediate sense of guilt. As his pretty well exclusive doctor, I worried that I might have missed something, some symptoms or examination finding that could have led to an earlier diagnosis and a better outlook for him. I hurriedly looked through his notes. There was nothing that looked even faintly suspicious of a mistake which was a huge relief. On the other hand, since there were only my notes, could I have failed to pick up on some clue and simply not recorded it? Anything was possible but I certainly hoped that I hadn't somehow failed him.

However unlucky I had been to get stuck with my cancer, Steven had been even more unlucky.

My medical student friend, Bob, the one who had encouraged me to enter for the Medicine prize at St George's, had been unluckier still as he had died many years earlier of exactly the same thing in his forties, the first person from our time at St George's to die.

'Hello Doctor Coffey' – a friendly, slightly insistent, greeting appeared seemingly from nowhere. I looked around and there was a familiar face. It was a patient I had known for well over thirty years. I'd looked after both of her pregnancies – or rather in truth the midwife had, with token assistance from myself, and I attended the birth of one of her children. She was Marie, Steven's wife.

Naturally I stopped and returned the greeting. She explained that she thought I must be in because she had spotted Jane leaving the ward the previous day – and I suppose had been looking out for me. What was I doing on the ward? I explained in general terms that I'd had some radioactive treatment but didn't go into any detail. She explained that, sadly, Steven was in a side room having radiotherapy and was very unwell.

'Well, if it's OK with you both I'll just put my head round the door and say hello to him' I said to her. She looked very pleased, maybe a bit relieved and maybe even a bit reassured to hear this. But Catherine intervened. Sorry. No. It wasn't possible. I needed to keep walking. I wasn't allowed to say 'hello' because of my radioactivity. They were polite but firm.

'Sorry I'm too radioactive evidently – wouldn't be safe for you' I hurriedly tried to explain as I was whisked away.

For a few seconds I had been back in my familiar and much more preferable role as doctor and as part of that, a comforter for the sick and their relatives, rather than in my new role as the recipient of care. It had really seemed to matter to Marie that she got the chance to speak to me. Her husband had been my patient for so many years and she knew that he would have wanted to say 'Hello' and perhaps more importantly, a 'Goodbye' as well.

I felt bad about the way I had been rushed past Marie on the ward and rang her up when I got home to explain the situation a bit more clearly. She expanded a bit about Steven's illness explaining their shock about it all, as he had indeed been perfectly well until he'd had the fit – he hadn't had anything wrong before at all – which at least made me feel a little easier in my mind. We talked about her children supporting her and what they did now. I wished them both well though it sounded as if Steven would not live very long. Sadly this was the case and a week or two later she sent me a message, through the surgery, to say that he had died. I wrote with my condolences. I always felt a measure of sadness when a long-time patient died, but this time, he and I had had a shared experience of the oncology ward and so it felt a bit more personal and a bit more important to write.

That meeting on the ward with his wife and the subsequent unfolding of events sums up what General Practice is quintessentially about at its best. It's about relationships, trust on both sides, effective communications and caring – the doctor for his or her patient, and, to an extent, the patient caring about his or her doctor. I guess I had been so wrapped up in my own world that I'd temporarily forgotten about what a special job I'd had.

So, with my escort, I arrived at the nuclear medicine department where I was to have an octreotide scan. Michael had explained that the idea of the scan was to check that the PRRT had been taken up into the liver efficiently so that it would have a chance to work. He'd explained before that there was a possibility that the scan might show up small secondaries that had not been visible on the first octreotide scan. I had my fingers crossed that this wouldn't be the case.

Back onto the scanner then – I was becoming quite used to being scanned now, if not exactly comfortable with the procedure – then when it was done, Catherine took me down to out patients where I met up with Jane. We sat slightly apart from other patients as a nod to my radioactivity and Jane sat the requisite number of inches away from me that was considered safe for her.

Soon we were taken through to Michael. He said the scan was really good. The radioactivity had been taken up very well by the liver, which meant it had a good chance of working and then he showed me a smudgy looking scan of my liver – the black smudges being the metastases which were lit up by the uptake of radioactive Yttrium. There did seem rather a lot of black, but Michael explained that the scan wasn't really useful for assessing the extent of the metastases. He did point out however, that there was a small black pin prick sized area in the pelvis which most likely meant there was a metastasis in a lymph gland there. He couldn't be certain that it was in a lymph gland and would rely on the radiologist to decide precisely where and what it was. He'd ring me with the radiologist's report. It wouldn't alter the treatment approach. Immediately after the second PRRT, he'd be able to arrange a CT scan to precisely locate where it was. The fact that the metastasis had been lit up by the PRRT meant it had already been treated.

He seemed quite unfazed by the new metastasis so maybe I shouldn't be either.

But I was. It felt very threatening.

Michael reassured me that it wouldn't alter anything. It was tiny particularly in comparison to the liver which was my main problem and the PRRT was dealing with that, how effectively we'd know by the scans done a few weeks after the second PRRT.

I relaxed a little and mentioned that at a talk given by the Oxford NET professor I'd got the impression that NETs were a chronic condition. Was that correct?

'Absolutely. For the vast majority of patients. If this was an adenocarcinoma of any other organ, you would be talking about a very finite amount of time i.e. months, unless chemotherapy had a big impact. Whereas with NETs I have a patient that's now twelve years out from diagnosis, and that's not unusual if the NET is behaving in an indolent [slow growing] way. Now, not everybody's NET behaves in an indolent way, but we are only just starting to get a handle on your disease and it's over the next few scans that we will get a better idea of how it's behaving. These NETs haven't read the cancer rulebook, so they don't follow exactly a fixed pattern all the time.'

'So five years wouldn't be preposterous?'

'No, but again it depends on how it behaves. If it turns out that yours is relatively slow-growing, then five years is not at all unusual.'

'And your patient with twelve years' Jane asked, 'with liver metastases?'

'Yes – with a liver stuffed full of disease but it just sits there and may get a tiny little bit worse over time'.

The metastasis in the pelvis was undoubtedly a disappointment, but seemingly the more important issue was that the liver had taken up the radioactivity very well. Michael had seemed very pleased so presumably overall that was good then. He'd made it clear that if I was lucky enough to have a slow-growing NET, liver metastases or no liver metastases, I could live for several, perhaps even many, more years to come. He didn't elaborate on what would be the situation if I was unlucky.

Living for years with lots of metastases in a liver seemed counter-intuitive to everything I'd understood about cancers and liver metastases, but NETs didn't conform like normal cancers...

They hadn't read the Rulebook

Chapter 24

Panic Stations

I drove home after the clinic appointment with Jane sitting in the back on the other side of the car to minimise her exposure to my radioactivity. We had been given written instructions, as well as being told, what I should and should not do, when I could see other people, especially Theo, how long I needed to use exclusively one toilet and how many nights – three seemingly – I should sleep alone. I had to wear a wrist band with a radiation sign for a while afterwards, which would guarantee me a seat to myself if I sat on a bus I imagined. I was even told that I might set off a radiation alarm at an airport for several months afterwards.

At home, I lounged around feeling distinctly like a malingerer for a few days, until nausea kicked in and I had to re-start the anti-nausea pills. I also became a bit tired. Tiredness or fatigue is a difficult thing to be certain about. Are you just feeling tired because you know you might get that side-effect and it's become a 'self-fulfilling prophecy' or are you exploiting your situation and taking the opportunity to be lazy and get away with watching Netflix and garner a bit of sympathy? I could certainly manage to 'whip' myself into playing golf when I wanted to. There were quite a few remarks made about 'glowing in the dark' and not needing to turn the lights on as well.

But what was really bothering me was that I couldn't forget I now had a secondary in my pelvis. Was this going to be the first of many until I became, like many of my patients before me had been, riddled with metastases? These negative, catastrophising thoughts, coupled with trying to divine whether Michael's apparent lack of concern was just an act or not, went round and round – my medical background making me hypervigilant to nuance and possible downplaying of setbacks. Eventually I decided that Michael would always play a straight bat so probably I was getting way too het up and calmed down. After all, he had said things were good.

After being back home for a week I had a call from Phil, the Net specialist cancer nurse, who rang to see how I was getting on after the PRRT.

As a specialist cancer nurse, Phil was an expert on NETs so was able to reinforce and explain, very clearly and in a supportive manner, the complex issues that had been discussed in the clinics. I told him that I was a bit nauseous and a bit tired and that I was waiting for Michael to let me know the verdict on the pelvic metastasis. Had he seen the report, I wondered? He had and would read it to me if I wanted him to, which of course I did. He explained that the report referred to a small amount of uptake in the left side of the sacrum which was likely to be 'a small bone metastasis'.

A bone metastasis was a shock. Over the years I had seen lots of cancer patients who developed bone metastases and could not recall any of them surviving for very long afterwards. Bone 'mets' in my experience tended to be the harbinger of very bad things to come. Usually they required radiotherapy to the metastases to alleviate the pain they seemed to invariably cause. Had I been through all the traumas of the operation only to have an indication that I was on the downhill run now?

I've repeatedly been asked whether being a doctor has made my own medical experiences easier or harder. The honest answer is I can't be certain, but in situations like this, having experience of seeing some patients struggle badly with the set of circumstances I now had, does make things worse. You recall the patients who had difficult, painful, bad outcomes and, of course forget about, or never even knew about, those who had good outcomes because the latter didn't need to see you at all. I may have had patients with bone metastases for years – it was just that I couldn't remember any.

Phil hastened to try to put it in perspective. Overall, he said, the impact of the bone metastasis he expected to be negligible. A number of his patients had bone mets. Often neuroendocrine bone mets didn't cause pain. Many didn't require any treatment as they were very slow growing. In fact, it was pretty rare to have to treat them specifically. They didn't usually spread. There was no need to do further scans as they wouldn't influence my treatment, whatever they showed.

Phil had been reassuring. I felt slightly uplifted by talking to him. He'd said at the end that, if I remained worried about the bone met, I should talk to Michael, so I did.

Michael repeated what he'd said before when the metastasis had been thought to be in a lymph gland, namely that it had no real implications for me, would have no effect on how well I did, or how long I'd live. Those things depended on the situation in my liver. If I got any symptoms – which he doubted – it would be local pain. He would arrange a CT scan of the area the morning after the next PRRT as well as an octreotide scan and anticipated that these scans would either be the same or possibly not show any metastasis if the PRRT had worked well. He didn't expect me to get lots of other bone secondaries as he would have expected more by this stage if I was going to get any. It hadn't really mattered whether it was a bone or lymph gland secondary.

He outlined the plan, which would be that six to eight weeks after the second PRRT I would have a whole-body CT scan and an MRI of the liver to see what, if any, effect the PRRT had had. In some people the first scan after treatment is unchanged or stable but the subsequent scan three months later shows some improvement but even that scan may be unchanged, which is fine, because it shows the disease is stable.

Reassuringly, he said that fewer than five per cent of patients after being treated with PRRT would have worse scans.

Jane asked where else you could get metastases. Anywhere in theory, he replied, but the liver, the lungs and the bones are by far the commonest sites with NETs.

'The lungs are fine then as nothing is showing?'

'Yes, but the scans will only show metastases that are big enough, they won't show cells.' meaning that are tiny.

'I get the impression that you think that things will go well?' Jane ventured just before we left.

'I've no reason to think they won't go well' he said.

'And most do go well?'

Quietly he replied 'Yeah.'

Panic over. No reason in my case for things not to go well – mostly they do.

Get over the preconceptions about a bone metastasis and get on with things. So, I did.

Funny how adaptable humans are. Even one like me. Many times, I've marvelled at how quickly patients adapted to something that I felt would be quite difficult to come to terms, like a colostomy bag or a catheter into the bladder. Similarly, when patients became diabetic and had to have daily or twice daily or more frequent insulin injections, most soon seemed to be able to do it without batting an eyelid. I'd always thought that must be really hard but reflected that even I had soon adapted to giving my own dalteparin injections.

In days gone by when I've had a patient with liver metastases, I've wondered how it must feel to think that there is a malign process growing in your liver and yet now that it had happened to me I hadn't stressed anything like as much as I would have imagined I would. And now to cap it all I had a bone metastasis. And I found I could accept it and get on with things in a relatively matter of fact way. Amazing. I never would have thought I would have been able to accept the thought so readily. Is it because I am an exceptionally strong, sanguine customer? Of course not. Is it because no matter what I've got it's not stage four inoperable stomach cancer with less than a year to live? I think it might be or that might at least go a long way towards explaining it. It was terrible having to contemplate in all probability dying in about nine months from stomach cancer, but what if the sequence of diagnoses had been reversed and I had been given initially a less serious diagnosis which was later changed to stomach cancer?

I'm sure the sense of partial reprieve I had made it easier to cope with all the vagaries of my situation. As I said earlier, any diagnosis that replaces one of stomach cancer feels like a blessing.

Maybe there is more to the whole business than can be explained on a human level. Maybe I'm getting more than just human support.

Chapter 25

Failing to Make Sense of Things

During the two-month gap between the first and second PRRT treatments, I had fortnightly blood tests at my GP's surgery to ensure that the treatment hadn't done any harm to the kidneys and bone marrow. It was very interesting attending the surgery and seeing how a practice worked from the patient's perspective. I have, I confess, always assumed that the services at the practice I worked at were better than other local surgeries but the staff at my GP's surgery, from receptionists to phlebotomists to practice nurses, were something of a revelation, proving to be really helpful and accommodating. In short, they were every bit as good as at my work surgery and I've actually had the heretical thought that they might be even better. This was despite my GP's surgery being very cramped. He and his partners had made strenuous efforts over many years to procure better premises – all to no avail. A casualty of NHS underfunding, but a great example of how hard people work in the NHS to deliver a good service for their patients even in adverse circumstances.

Some people are surprised that I am not a patient at my own practice. However, GPs are strongly discouraged from treating their partners as it can be very difficult to be totally impartial and objective if you do. For example, if your partner came to talk to you about his alcoholism would you have to stop him working for the safety of his patients even if he didn't want to stop? None of my partners have had a drink problem I hasten to say. (Well not as far as I know....!)

We booked another short holiday in Wales this time in the stunning Gower Peninsula in a beautiful boutique hotel. A friend had advised us to visit the art gallery in Rhossili where seemingly you could get a decent coffee as well. None of the pictures for sale that day inspired us, and the coffee shop had gone, but it sold jewellery and was run by a family who had moved from the jewellery quarter of Birmingham. Jane had been keen to buy me a wedding ring for years but had been even keener since the cancer diagnosis. I had eschewed one in 1976, as many men did in those far-off days, but to our great surprise and delight we found that the Rhossili jewellers were terrific and got them to make one for me. Not what I'd expected when we went into the place.

I had a pretty routine check-up appointment with Michael before going in for the second dose of PRRT. This time it seemed much easier and more straightforward with everything being much as before even down to the TV still not working properly. I think I was even still trying to read the same rather turgid book. The following morning, I had the octreotide scan to check that the PRRT had been taken up well by the liver together with a CT scan to look particularly at the pelvis where the metastasis was. At a brief chat in his clinic after the scan, Michael pronounced himself very satisfied that the liver had again taken up the PRRT well on the scan and said that if anything the liver looked a little improved. Most encouragingly, as he had predicted might be the case, he could no longer see the 'hot spot' that had betrayed the presence of the metastasis in the pelvis after the first PRRT treatment.

'Did this mean that the previous 'hot spot' had been spurious?' I ventured.

'No – it means that it's been so effectively treated by the PRRT that there is no longer anything in the pelvis to take up treatment. It's been zapped'

Not only did the liver evidently look a bit better but the hot spot was gone. That was brilliant news.

When the news was good like this, consultations were very brief and no doubt much easier for Michael. He qualified his comments about the scan by saying that we should really wait for the formal or official scan report from the radiologists, but as he must have looked at thousands of scans, I was confident it would confirm the good news. Michael didn't have the CT scan to hand to look at but would ask his secretary to forward me the CT and octreotide scan report when it was available, and we left on a high.

A few days later I duly received the formal scan report:

'There is similar pattern good metastatic uptake throughout the liver with approximately 50% hepatic replacement by metastatic disease'.

There was more on the report, but I didn't see anything beyond '50% hepatic replacement by metastatic disease'. Fifty percent. Half the actual liver had been replaced by metastases. I only had half a liver left.

It was truly shocking, because the basis for how long I could hope to live was determined by how quickly my particular liver metastases grew and caused the liver to fail.

If the liver metastases had more than doubled in size between the second scan in January and this one in May, then presumably at that rate the whole liver could be replaced within another three to six months which would, not to put too fine a point on it, be curtains for me.

Jane was equally shocked and distraught. She had been present at every consultation, so how could we both have got the wrong end of the stick and thought that the scans hadn't changed much at all from the original twenty per cent involvement we'd seen in a letter? I had recorded all the consultations, so I checked them but there was no hint of this sort of liver involvement.

The report must be wrong so we arranged to see Michael who we knew would sort it out.

But he didn't.

He confirmed that the report was correct.

He explained that he had always personally thought the liver was more involved than the official reports said, but he emphasised that estimating the volume of the liver affected was far from being a precise science. The reports were of different types of scans, reported in different ways by different radiologists, some of whom didn't give any figure for the amount of liver involved. He was sorry we were so shocked but stressed that the percentage figures didn't change anything, and in particular, the disease hadn't got worse between the PRRT treatments. The bone metastasis improvement demonstrated that the disease was responsive to the PRRT so the liver should, in time, also be helped. It really didn't matter that fifty per cent of the liver was involved as you can manage perfectly well with just ten per cent of your liver working. As it wasn't going to change the treatment in any way, and as he wasn't personally to blame for the way the scans were reported, I think he felt a bit unlucky to have two very upset people in front of him trying to make sense out of something that seemed to make no sense at all.

I felt a bit sorry for him so in the spirit of conciliation commented that I would rather the liver be fifty per cent involved and responding to the treatment than be only twenty per cent involved but not responding. The point being that if the liver disease improved after the PRRT, that would be better than a smaller amount of liver disease that got inexorably worse.

We did agree that one thing that might make communication better would be if I had copies of all my past and future scans.

The realisation that half my liver was shot to pieces was very distressing. Michael had however emphasised that you only need ten per cent of your liver to be working to manage perfectly adequately which I had been vaguely aware of anyway. Why is the liver so big then you might ask? I have no idea and don't care – I'm just glad that it is.

It had been extremely disappointing to think that despite all the lengths I had gone to, to try to make sure I assimilated all the medical information about myself as completely and correctly as possible, we had still been so unprepared for, and so shocked by, this blind-siding news.

Maybe sometimes patients don't get the right impression of their situation and it's not really anybody's direct fault. With so many links in the chain of care, it is a wonder that the chain doesn't break or get twisted more often. In my own work there would have been fewer people involved in the chain of care so less risk of major mis-communications – hopefully. Doctors have to tread a fine line between explanation and not either terrifying or misleadingly comforting their patients and are always up against the enemy of time.

In any event there was nothing we could do about it and it didn't seem possible, given that three different radiologists were involved, to get to the bottom of why the reports were so inconsistent.

Life was too short, and was certainly now too short, to bang my head against that particular brick wall.

We would just have to hope that the response to the PRRT would be good.

Chapter 26

The Verdict

So, the moment had arrived when I would find out if the PRRT liver treatment had worked. Possibly the most important moment of my life.

Really? What about the moment Jane accepted my marriage proposal or Laura's birth, or later Patrick or Duncan's birth for that matter? What about the moment Laura got her amazing GCSE results, which left me speechless, or when Patrick got his First from University, or when Duncan qualified as a doctor and 'joined the club', or the first time I met our grandson Theo? Or the moment I learnt I had stage 4 stomach cancer and the moment when I learnt I didn't? Or when I learnt my Dad had had a terrible stroke from a brain aneurysm or when I came around from a general anaesthetic to be told that the attempt to make my brain artery aneurysm safe by inserting a coil had failed? Or what about the death of my Mum, who we had looked after in our house at the end of her life and who I had been very close to? They were big moments too. So, no, I didn't think this moment was really the most important moment of my life, but it definitely was up there and may well be the most important moment in the remainder of my life, but who knows what's around the corner?

If the PRRT had worked there would be a possibility of me surviving maybe a year or two or even three, five or who knows how long? Michael had on several occasions mentioned that he had patients with NET disease like mine with extensive liver metastases, who had lived five or ten years. It was possible. It was a lot to ask for, but I'd been doing a lot of asking – praying as well – lately as had quite a few other people on my behalf. Which was a comfort.

If it hadn't worked, the next step would be to try chemotherapy. Whilst not exactly second best, chemotherapy is not a specifically-targeted treatment like PRRT, and generally doctors use their best treatments first – so-called 'first line' – so it would be a blow – a major blow – if the first line treatment had failed. It would also mean, of course, that there is one less weapon in the armoury to try when things later got worse. I had to admit chemotherapy remained a very scary thought.

I'd been told that there were three possible outcomes: One, that the metastases would have decreased in size. Two, that they would be the same size so would have been 'stabilised' by the treatment rather than getting worse which would still be a positive outcome. The third possibility was that the metastases would be worse. Michael had said that there was 'only' a small risk of them being worse but in my mind, it was a one in three chance and because it was a terrifying one, it therefore felt the most likely one.

My mind slipped into a circular, endlessly repetitive, fretting mode, going over minor details here and there and trying to read too much into them. The CT scan had been two weeks earlier, but my MRI just two days ago because of a glitch over the fact that I had a metal clip over the aneurysm in my brain which could be moved by the strong magnetic field in an MRI scan. Two weeks had seemed a long time to have to wait for the CT scan result. Surely Michael could have let me know if it was good, I reasoned?

But then he might have wanted the MRI first? No, he only had a CT to compare it with so the CT would be enough to tell if it was better or worse. If the verdict was bad, he'd hardly have rung me or emailed me to say so, but he might have if it had been good.

So that's that then, it's bad.

On the other hand, everything goes through the Multidisciplinary team which meet on Tuesdays – yesterday – so he'd have had to wait for that wouldn't he?

No, he's currently the only consultant oncologist at the MDT as the professor had retired and not been replaced yet, his view will surely hold sway in this situation, so he doesn't really need to wait for the MDT rubber stamp.

But hang on! I'm not the only patient he's got, am I, and as the only other NET oncologist has just retired he's probably up to his neck in work trying to cover his own patients as well as his own. He obviously works very hard already without having extra patients to manage. And he doesn't just deal with NET patients either.

And so it went on, frantically looking for clues about the outcome where there were no real clues.

The worry about the verdict had been building and building. This was a big deal. Had all the treatment been worthwhile or a waste of precious time? It felt like it did back in October when I had had the endoscopy and was waiting for the biopsy and scan results which turned out to be disastrous. I didn't feel optimistic then and I certainly didn't now.

Jane had been feeling the pressure as much, if not more, than me. Talking about our fears and sharing each other's anxieties just made matters worse and racked up the stress. We both desperately wanted to have hope of a few more years together.

Duncan had rushed to Oxford after work to be present at the 'Verdict' consultation, which was great and very supportive, but it was disconcerting to see that he was obviously nervous and feeling the strain as well.

We were about thirty minutes early for the appointment so stayed in the car in the underground car park for as long as possible before going to the waiting area. It was very busy as several clinics were on the go. A consultant I'd known for many years came into the waiting area to have a drink of water, but I didn't speak to him as I didn't want to have to explain about the NET and he wouldn't have had time to listen properly anyway. It wasn't a moment to exchange pleasantries.

The waiting area held bad memories for me. It was where I had waited prior to being told I would die within a year from stomach cancer. On the other hand, when I'd seen Michael on two occasions before at that clinic the news had been a lot better than I'd been expecting. I knew he'd have to tell me bad news at some stage and assumed this would be the moment. In my mind I'd rehearsed repeatedly how he would be when he explained that the liver was worse. He'd remind us that there had never been any guarantees that the PRRT would work and that we always knew that this could be the outcome. He'd say that chemotherapy could be successful when PRRT therapy had failed so we'd just have to get on with it and then see. He'd be sympathetic but keep a professional distance. I knew what I'd say in response and that would be that.

Then he came out to call us in.

He wasn't smiling so that was not good. Then again, he hadn't smiled before when calling us through to clinics even when the news had been good. Did he look a bit strained? Yes, but having to see extra patients after a long day at the NHS hospital would make anyone look a bit strained and I was doubtless not the easiest of his patients with my medical background, insistence on recording everything and tendency never to use one word when a hundred would do.

He got straight into it: 'The scan shows that the liver metastases have reduced in size, the largest one, which was six centimetres [in diameter] has now gone to three centimetres and they have all reduced in size – that's the only measurement the radiologists have given me but it's great news. It's very early days yet [meaning to have visible changes of shrinkage, as such changes may take rather longer than three months to be apparent on a scan] so that's very good. We'll scan you again in three months and see how things are.'

At numerous teaching sessions as a student and later as a GP, and in numerous articles about 'Breaking Bad News', the message had been very clear that, when given bad news, most patients will not remember what was said next. Various strategies to overcome that would be discussed, such as waiting for some time before speaking again, checking and re-checking that the patient had understood, and writing things down. No-one had ever discussed how good news should be discussed. In some ways it felt just as shocking, just as disorientating as hearing bad news and I'm not sure I took everything in after hearing that the metastases had shrunk. Could I really have heard him say that the scan was 'great news'? Exactly how good was 'great'? Did it mean I might live for years now? If it did, how many was the most I might live for, or was there no limit? What precisely did this mean for Jane and my future together? Might we resume our brilliant holidays in India and other far flung parts of the world? Would it be fine to build the house that we'd spent so long planning now?

All important questions, but I was too stunned to ask any of them, as the verdict had been much better than I had really allowed myself to hope for.

'Oh, that's great' I weakly offered in response. 'Well done. Forgive me for not jumping up and down but I'd been preparing for bad news'.

Jane was composed enough to ask about the pelvic metastasis.

'That looks better too – that looks more sclerotic which is like a healing process – which is better. Bone changes tend to stay so the chances are it will be with you even if it's completely healed. So that's really good – again a positive thing.'

'And there were no other bone …?' she continued

'No, none at all'

'Are you rushed off your feet now the other NET oncologist in Oxford has retired?' I asked.

'Yes!'

A few minutes later and we were back in the car after easily the shortest consultation we'd had, still trying to take things in and wondering, at least in my case, if I'd really heard things correctly and trying to think through the implications of what we had heard. Again, and again, I asked myself what were the implications? Again, and again, that thought, that question that I had hardly dared to contemplate, kept going around and round. Did this mean that I might live for years now? Could the nightmare of the last nine months be starting to finish? Could the normal proper order of things be starting to be restored? Could the status quo of me being a healthy, fit person be restored to its proper place? Could my life be back on its proper track with me destined to live to a ripe old age as I had more or less felt entitled to less than a year before?

No. Obviously not. Don't be ridiculous, but maybe, just maybe, the response to the treatment at this stage meant I had at least a realistic chance of another year or two with Jane and the family which I would very, very readily have settled for back in October when the initial diagnosis of widespread inoperable stomach cancer had been made. So, don't get ahead of yourself, I told myself. The situation is so much better than in October, just be thankful and hope that the next scan doesn't show a relapse.

The immediate implication of the news was clear – we had to go out for a celebratory dinner. It was quite a subdued celebration though. It had been too stressful getting to this point and we just felt very, very thankful that our prayers had been answered. We rang Laura and Patrick, my sisters and close friends. Letting the rest of the outside world know could wait. It felt risky – almost like tempting providence – to say too much too soon about our good fortune. Besides the situation was far from being clear-cut. I was to have scans at regular intervals – so called 'interval scans' and if the liver metastases were inactive nothing other than the regular monthly injections I had started after the PRRT would be needed. At some point, the metastases would start growing again and at that point further aggressive treatment would be required. But when would that point be? That was the imponderable. The intervals between scans could get longer if I was very lucky. We had let a lot of people know about the various stages of the illness but I suspected that quite a few would conclude that all was well if I just sent out an email recounting the situation.

The build-up to the consultation and getting the news had been so draining that, although we kept saying how great the moment was, no-one felt like shouting from the rooftops. I imagine anyone escaping a war zone who has reached a temporary safe haven from the violence they have been fleeing, would feel like we did. Safe, at least for a while, but still a long and unpredictable journey ahead.

Chapter 27

A Life Between Scans

Michael had explained, many consultations earlier, that the best way of predicting prognosis was to observe the behaviour of the NET over time and its response to treatment. Many NET tumours are slow growing or 'indolent' so if I was lucky, as some of his patients had been, I might not need any more treatment for several years. He had patients with similar, or even more extensive disease than mine, who had lived for over ten years and were still going strong. He just scanned these patients regularly, and, if the scans were unchanged or little changed, he didn't need to do anything more. When the disease got going again – or relapsed – which it was bound to do at some point, then he would give them some more treatment which in my case would probably be more PRRT.

What he hadn't said, and what I hadn't asked either, was what proportion of his patients who had disease like mine lived for over ten years. Doubtless this seems an elementary omission for any patient to ask, perhaps particularly a medical one, but maybe I was scared of the answer. My situation struck me as a simple binary one – either I did well or I didn't, and I had to just hope for the former and deal with the latter if that was going to be the case. The initial response to the PRRT certainly encouraged me to think that I stood a good chance of doing well.

The plan was to have scans at intervals of three or four months to see if the disease remained quiescent or had started up again. Many, many patients with cancer and their relatives will be all too familiar with the sense of dread that builds as you get nearer and nearer to your scans and their results and then, if the scans are good, experience a truly wonderful sense of dizzying relief and exhaustion. The tension melts away and you can get on with life again, but there remains a sense of disbelief. Jane even admitted that she had difficulty discussing the result with other people for fear it may not be right or even break the spell. The alternative if the result is bad is a resurgence of fear anxiety and a dread of what is to come.

My close friend, Doug, described it as living life in periods between scans. He had been having chemotherapy for a couple of years with bearable side effects and been remarkably calm and stoical throughout. We had gone together with his wife Sue, as a foursome on fourteen holidays all over the world, mostly cycling and shared innumerable meals. He had been diagnosed with his problem a year before me. When later I was given my diagnosis, we had an unusual shared 'interest' and talked a great deal about treatment and life in general. This gave us a particularly close bond and understanding of how we each felt and we were able to support each other, in what I think must be quite a rare way. It was a bonus for each of us to have someone who really knew how the other was feeling. When my turn came to have chemotherapy, I hoped I would tolerate it with as much dignity as Doug did.

I think recent events had also toughened me up or maybe just forced me to adjust to the uncertainty of life. Jane commented that everyone's life is full of uncertainties, the only certainty being that one will die, the major uncertainty being when. 'All' that had happened was that I was actually more certain about when my end would be than most. By looking at it that way, it helped her cope with the fact that everything in our lives had been turned upside down and everything had changed for us. Everything was seen through the lens of not having stomach cancer, so every day felt like a bonus.

I knew that one day I might need chemotherapy. I was slowly becoming a bit more measured in thinking about it – I'd evaded it for over a year and now just felt that when it came it came. I'd just have to deal with it – simple as that.

So, perhaps inevitably, I'd changed. I was living with a pernicious tumour that would shorten my life – a so called 'life-limiting' condition – which at any moment might be expanding again in my liver. Only a scan could tell me that. But I wasn't stressing about it nearly as much as I'd imagined I would and was getting on with life – except for the periods around the scans.

For the vast majority of the time I felt really well and was enjoying my only-slightly-brought-forward retirement. To Jane's dismay I'd 'plumped up' a bit, which meant the lean and mean Cassius look had softened a bit. I believed the many people who told me I looked really well, though I supposed relatively few people would be brutal enough to tell me if I looked really unwell. If someone asked me how I was I replied 'Fine' or 'Fair to muddling' which sometimes occasioned the cheery comment:

'Oh well you look well and if you feel well you must be well'

Sadly, that adage is simply wrong – at least in my case. Only a scan can say that the disease hasn't recurred which is what I mean by being well. I've given up trying to explain that concept to other than people close to me, as I think quite a lot of people, cling to the adage. They probably only really want to hear reassuringly good news, not least because it's much more difficult to know how to react to bad news.

I was nowhere near as fit as I was a few years ago – after all, my joints were ageing like everyone's do in their sixties, but I still ran a bit, though an attempt at running a 10K run in London ended rather ignominiously, at the halfway stage, with me having to catch the tube back because of a pulled calf muscle.

The highlight of my week, sad B***** that I am, was the Tuesday morning golf. The group I play with are all pretty much retired, ageing ex-proper sportsmen with high levels of self-delusion about their golfing abilities. Annoyingly the handicap system betrays the fact that I am actually one of the worst golfers in the group though in reality I feel if I just played a bit more.... Everyone has, rather like in Tarantino's 'Reservoir of Dogs', adopted a sobriquet. Mine is 'Genghis' after the gent whose motto was 'Winning is not enough – all others must die.' In the context of my golf it errs heavily on the side of irony. Others include 'The Old Warhorse', a retired GP who also went to St George's Medical school a year or two before me and 'The Assassin', so called because twice he has hit one of the others on the head with his driver. Accidentally. Allegedly. Then there's 'The Big Easy', 'Jesse James', 'The Terminator' who was a PT instructor in the RAF and bears an uncanny resemblance to Arnie, and 'Slit-Wrist' – the latter because of repeated threats to self-harm after playing badly, and one who because he is from Merseyside, rejoices under the nickname 'The Defendant'. Which is a bit outrageous but ...The latest addition is a retired policeman who is rather proud of his new name 'The Truncheon'. Over lunch we don't put the world to rights as we don't have time after we dissect exactly what the club management or committee have got wrong in the last week and proffer to each other, but obviously not the relevant authority, precisely what the correct course of action should or should not have been. You might wonder why someone like me, who was a respectable enough sportsman in my day, persists in playing a game I have manifestly failed to master despite trying for well over half a century and why I submit myself to the weekly punishment or humiliation that is my lot when playing golf. In truth, I only do it for the craic and the schadenfreude of seeing grown men, particularly 'Slit-wrist' disintegrate into torpors of misery each week.

My former partners, like all GPs, seem to be increasingly pressured and stressed by the unrelenting increase in the work and expectation the NHS has of them. I was always being asked if I'd fully stopped work or how did I feel about being retired. Now that I was off the treadmill of work and had a bit of perspective on the job of General Practice, I marveled that I 'got away with it' for so long – yes that old Impostor Syndrome still reared its head. I hardly missed work at all which really surprised me, as other than for my family, it largely defined who I was. I'd assumed that without that badge of office I would feel diminished somehow, but I didn't. It was far more a feeling of relief, especially as the job has changed so very much in recent years – it had to – but I preferred the older style work and it preferred me.

The only treatment I now had to have were the monthly injections. They induced a bit of tension firstly awaiting the special delivery of them, then ensuring the fridge door was properly shut, because, as each injection cost about a thousand pounds, we couldn't allow it to go off like an out-of-date lettuce. Jane expertly administered the injection but hated doing it partly because it was such a reminder that there was something amiss in the Coffey household and partly because, at that price, she didn't dare mess it up.

How long could the situation remain like that? It felt like the 'phoney war' of 1939 must have. There was really no telling. I might be lucky as I had been of late, with the far more successful than anticipated surgery and the very good response to the PRRT on the first scan.

The philosopher and Clint Eastwood alter ego, Dirty Harry put it well:

The question you've gotta ask yourself is 'Am I feeling lucky?'

Chapter 28

In Trouble Again

My first three scans after the PRRT had been very good, so things seemed to be going my way. About a year after finishing the PRRT I was scanned again, and the usual sense of dread and impending gloom descended on me prior to hearing the result from Michael. Jane was much more optimistic – she was convinced I would be another of his patients that lived for over ten years. 'Mr' Duncan Coffey accompanied us to the appointment to hear the scan results. He had recently passed his MRCS – Membership of the Royal College of Surgeons exam – so was now, like proper surgeons are, a Mister man.

Michael got straight to the point, speaking quietly:

'The scans, unfortunately, show some new disease in the liver; the previous metastases are virtually the same, but you have five new metastases in the liver. So, we ought to think about giving you some more treatment to try to get control of them. What I'd like to offer you is re-treating them with PRRT again – exactly the same as last time with two treatments about two months apart'.

He went on to explain that I had already got about twenty-five metastases in the liver, but those ones were stable. The largest of the new metastases was 3.6 centimetres. The hope would be that, since the previous metastases had responded to the PRRT these would as well. If nothing was done the metastases would of course get bigger. The fact that the PRRT worked for a year, he felt, made it well worth trying it again rather than using chemotherapy. If I didn't get a good response to this next course of PRRT, he would start thinking of other treatments such as chemotherapy, which would be likely to have more side effects so would be better avoided if possible. If more lesions appeared in a year, provided my bone marrow was OK after the second PRRT, I could then have a third course.

The moment we had dreaded had come much, much earlier than we had expected and hoped for. It literally felt like a thump to my stomach, a physical blow, to learn that the disease was active again so soon, not after five or ten years, but after just one.

There was, Michael explained, a backlog of about five weeks before I could have the first dose of PRRT. Before I could have the second dose however, the rooms where the PRRT was administered were having to be closed for six weeks because the drains had collapsed and needed repair work. Again.

'But 3.6 centimetres is quite large [for a liver metastasis] – how do we know it won't double in five weeks?' I asked.

'We don't. The bottom line is you've got this problem, we know what it is, we know what we need to do about it and we just need to get on with it. Talking about doubling times isn't going to change what we recommend' he emphasised.

It was a hammer blow to be told that the disease had recurred but to hear that the proposed treatment was going to be delayed yet again by a drains problem which sounded worse than before was surreal. It seemed like a badly written scene in a soap opera. It seemed ludicrous.

I ventured to Michael that all this made me wonder whether I should look into seeing if I could get treatment more speedily elsewhere.

'If you want to, that's fine but they will need to review your scans which will take some time.'

I came back to the thought, that was growing in my mind, that I really needed to try to do something to reduce the delay and the uncertainty.

'Is there any merit in getting a second opinion on all of this?' I asked, 'do people in this situation sometimes get one?'

'Yes, lots of people do – it's a very personal thing. If you want to, that's absolutely fine.'

'You wouldn't feel affronted?' I checked.

'Not at all, I want you to be happy that we're doing the right thing' he reassured me.

'And if I did, to whom should I go?'

'I'd go to Richard at The Royal Free Hospital – he's very good'.

He added that he was going to be away for two weeks in a couple of days so if I wanted a referral, I would have to decide quickly.

This was easily the worst consultation I'd had for well over a year. The fragile bubble of hope that I might still get away with a decently long existence had burst. I was well and truly up against it.

A part of me had thought that, as I'd felt so well for so many months, that my life was going too well and that I was bound to have a crash. So many people had commented on how really well I looked that maybe it was their fault for tempting providence. Both thoughts were a little crazy I knew – fatalistic nonsense but didn't someone or something have to be responsible for the situation?

Jane was shocked and visibly upset and Duncan looked distressed at the news we'd all heard. I experienced a bit of the feeling I'd had when I was told I had extensive stomach cancer. I felt pretty calm and was aware that the paper with the scan report on it didn't shake at all as I held it and that my voice was even and that I asked fairly measured questions. I suppose I was just more practised at receiving really devastating news.

Michael hoped that the PRRT might work for longer than the first course had, and if it did then survival for ten years just might still be possible. Common sense told me that it probably wouldn't and if it didn't, Michael had said that chemotherapy could be tried. 'Tried' didn't sound too encouraging a word. It didn't inspire a great deal of confidence.

Michael told us to check the admission details with Catherine, who was in charge of the waiting list for PRRT. When we did, she confirmed that the first PRRT admission would actually be six weeks after the appointment with Michael and she was quite certain that the second admission for treatment would be delayed by at least five weeks by the rooms being closed. When the second treatment would definitely be done would be dependent on the building repairs going to schedule. If they didn't, my second treatment would be delayed even longer. She went on to explain that because of the drain problems and a change in NHS funding for PRRT in Oxford, some NHS patients were having to wait four or five months for their treatment to start which made my wait of six weeks seem small in comparison.

In comparison that is, to what seemed to me, to be an altogether unacceptable wait.

So, my second dose of PRRT treatment would be delayed by at least eleven weeks overall and even that would depend on building repairs going to schedule. Hmmm. They had seemingly underestimated the problem last year so that the repair proved to be only a temporary one. What guarantee could I have that they would get it right this time? Absolutely none of course. Over the thirty-four years we've lived in our house, we've had lots of building work done by excellent builders, but no work has ever gone to schedule. That sealed the decision in my mind. I had to explore the option of having treatment elsewhere. It would be just too stressful if my treatment would be even further delayed by the building repair works falling behind schedule.

I phoned Michael early the next day and explained that, in the light of all the delays and uncertainty, I felt I had to, at the very least, find out what options I had regarding getting treatment sooner. He agreed to refer me to London and reassured me that I wasn't burning my boats with Oxford. I would remain on the waiting list for the PRRT at The Churchill and could decide after seeing Richard whether I wanted to have the treatment in Oxford or London.

It felt good that I'd been assertive and honest enough to seek a second opinion and that Michael had been so open to it.

We had been too taken aback by the news that the disease was active again to ask what this meant in terms of my overall prognosis. Michael hadn't gone into detail about the implications as that might have seemed unnecessarily hard for us to deal with at that point. Instead he had concentrated on the practicalities of what now had to happen, which seemed anything but straightforward because of the wretched drain problem. I'd been taught that you only discussed prognosis with a patient if he or she wanted you to. If they didn't ask specifically you might gently explore whether they wanted to talk about a prognosis, but you should let the patient decide and respect his or her wishes in that regard. I hadn't asked and Michael hadn't asked me if I wanted to talk about prognosis. I'd been focused on seeing if I could get earlier treatment outside Oxford. I hadn't consciously decided to avoid the subject but, perhaps subconsciously, it would have felt too much to process at the time.

After a few days I started to really consider the implications. As usual, my imagination and instinctive pessimism raced ahead, so I decided I had to get some proper advice on the subject and with Michael away, the obvious person to talk to was Phil, the specialist NET nurse. He explained, somewhat sombrely, that essentially the scan meant that the tumour was not indolent or slow growing but instead it was moderately active, meaning moderately aggressive, and likely to recur and spread elsewhere. I said I'd hoped that more PRRT could, if I was lucky, buy me lots more years but that in my heart of hearts I doubted it would.

Phil said that my heart of hearts was probably right but that the data on survival is always changing so it wasn't absolutely definite. He explained that I certainly had adverse risk factors in that I was a grade two tumour [where grade one is better] and I had quite a large volume of liver metastases at diagnosis. On the positive side, I was clinically well, and my bloods were normal. Ten years was now less realistic but was not impossible and one would need to see how things went over the next few years. He couldn't be drawn on how long the next few years might be, but said he thought that I should get on with any important projects I had planned, over the next year and then re-evaluate things.

Hearing it put like that, even though, as always, Phil was sensitive and considerate in his manner, was crushing. Clearly the situation was a lot worse than I'd assumed or wanted to believe. Prior to the last scan things had seemed so good, life was so good and I'd felt so well that I'd almost been able to say to myself that, even if I wouldn't make old bones, at least I'd get to my seventies, which in the greater scheme of things would not be too bad. Especially considering the initial prognosis was for less than a year. But now Phil was encouraging me to get important things done in the next year because time might be a lot shorter. How much shorter was far from clear but it was very clear that it would be a lot less than had seemed likely a mere week earlier.

I started to feel anxious and stressed as I had when I'd first been told I had cancer. Slightly breathless at times with a feeling that the sands of time were running out far too quickly. What important projects did I need to deal with? What was really important? It wasn't a 'what' it was a 'who'. Jane. Jane and the family, but mainly Jane. The guilt and sadness about leaving her prematurely re-surfaced. It was and remains my greatest regret about getting cancer. She would be left alone in a largish old house at far too young an age.

The last consultation's news had removed any lingering thoughts about building a new house in the garden. Now the task was to get the existing house into the best possible condition so that pretty well everything that could be, was done, to make it easier for Jane to enjoy. The driving force for me to get all these things done was so that when I'd gone Jane wouldn't have the stress of having to struggle on her own with such large projects. That was the least I could do for her. If at some point she decided to move to London, where all the children live, it would also make the house easier to sell. All this helped lessen the guilt feelings I had about abandoning her. We tried to look at the house through the eyes of potential new owners. What would they alter? The garden generally needed changing to make it easier to manage and particularly to reduce the hours of mowing required, sometimes twice a week. The end of the kitchen was in a poor state of repair and we decided to replace it with an oak-framed extension which would improve the layout as well. We'd planned to redecorate and re-configure the dining room. The list went on and on.

What other projects did I have to get on with in the next year? The Book. This book. As I'd relaxed more with the good scan results, I'd neglected writing for longer and longer periods allowing myself the luxury of waiting for any drops of inspiration to percolate through. Maybe now there wouldn't be time to finish it. Maybe I should just hurriedly get it to some sort of end and self-publish it. I'd allowed myself to hope that the book might just be good enough, if I put enough time and energy into it, to be published by a commercial publisher. I'd been on a writing course a few months earlier that had taught me a lot about writing and encouraged my ambition somewhat and I was planning to get it professionally edited to give it the best possible chance. But would there be time now? Would it remain on my computer unread? Had I already wasted too much time on the book? Was the book going to be good enough for people to want to read it anyway?

Matters at this time were made considerably worse by the fact that Doug, the very close friend who had coped so well with his cancer and chemotherapy, had deteriorated very quickly and died. We were terribly upset to have lost such a great friend and were determined to support Sue, his wife, as much as we possibly could. I felt privileged to be asked to say a few words about him at his funeral and rehearsed and rehearsed what I would say, determined to do one last task for my friend as well as I could. The service came and went and was very moving. It must have been particularly difficult for Jane, as she would project to the time in the future when she would be in Sue's place. Of course, I projected too, wondering what my funeral would be like. I thought I would like all my children to speak, as Doug's children had spoken so movingly and amusingly at his funeral. But I didn't tell my children – it felt too maudlin.

Having opened up the subject of my prognosis with Phil, I felt I needed to hear what Michael, who knew my situation better than anyone, and who has long experience of managing patients like myself, felt.

On his return from holiday, I rang early in the morning when he always started work and asked him, having monitored my disease for eighteen months, what he felt my prognosis was.

He spoke gently: 'Obviously the response to PRRT was not as long as I would have liked. Clearly your cancer is behaving in a more aggressive way than hoped for, but, as you had extensive disease on presentation, maybe that's not so surprising.'

I wanted him to be specific 'You mentioned patients with extensive liver disease like mine living ten years before' I ventured.

'Bit less realistic for you. Likely to be less Paul. The best I would expect with the PRRT would be another year before there is progression. Possibly you could have a third [PRRT] after that. Five years possibly may be optimistic, but it would depend on the response to the treatment. What tends to happen with PRRT, and chemotherapy, is that you get the best remission/response with the first treatment and subsequent ones become less effective as the first treatments kill off the less aggressive cells and the more aggressive cells remain. You may not therefore get a year's response from the PRRT this time. To be honest, because of the disease burden in the liver and the extent of the original tumour in the abdomen I wasn't initially expecting things to be like this after a year.'

'You didn't expect me to survive a year?' I said, somewhat taken aback.

'Yes, I did, but I wasn't expecting Alistair to be able to resect the disease. You did well with the PRRT but it's a shame the response didn't last longer as sometimes it lasts several years.'

We touched on other possible subsequent treatments he might recommend if the PRRT was ineffective and I finished by asking, in view of him knowing me and my case so well, if I could talk to him again after I'd had my London consultation to help me make up my mind on whether to stick with Oxford or go to The Royal Free for treatment.

'Of course, you can,' he reassured me.

So that was that. Five years was possibly optimistic. So maybe two or three years? My desperate hope that a second PRRT might be a lot more successful than the first one was exactly that. A desperate hope. It was almost certain to be less effective than the first PRRT which would probably mean that a third PRRT would not be sensible to try so then it would be chemotherapy. He'd said much the same as Phil but had explained why things were likely to be the way they were.

I felt to some extent cheated or at the very least very unlucky. There had seemed to have been a reasonable chance of ten years but evidently, with the benefit of hindsight, it had probably always been a slim chance given how advanced the disease was when it was diagnosed. I'd held onto his mantra that 'NET tumours haven't read the cancer rule book' meaning that they could behave differently to many cancers and could be very slow growing. I felt a bit sorry for myself and very sorry for Jane. I saw myself all too quickly in the same place that our very good friend Doug had been in so recently and frankly dreaded it. The end for him and his family had not been easy. He had assumed, when it came, that his decline would be slow, but it had come with a rush. Would I have sufficient time to get everything organised and more importantly be able to say the things I wanted to Jane and the children? On the other hand, I'd had a really good twelve months after the treatment had finished which had seemed impossible at the start of my cancer experience, and I was pretty hopeful of having at least another year or two and maybe longer so in total I would have had way more than I could originally have dared to hope for. The old thoughts about what you should do when time is very limited re-surfaced, but I wasn't able to shake off the feeling of despondency and throw myself into anything with much enthusiasm.

At this time England were playing their first match of The World Cup 2018 against 'the minnows' of Tunisia. Naturally I had to watch it and initially it seemed that England had finally shaken off their usual world cup inhibitions and were playing brilliantly. Then, inevitably, it all went wrong. Ruefully, I reflected that I would never see England win the World Cup again. I felt the cancer had even cheated me of that. Oddly enough, England managed a win at the very end of the match but the damage to my psyche had been done.

Watching the England football team under normal circumstances can be difficult but when your spirits were low to begin with it can be quite an ordeal.

Chapter 29

The Dilemma

I felt that the Oxford NET Unit had done me proud in many ways, the standout one being Alistair's surgery which seemed to have been little short of miraculous. I'd also had very good care from my anaesthetist and all the ward staff after the operation. The PRRT treatment, albeit after a longer than ideal wait, had been expertly and compassionately administered by Michael, Catherine and her colleagues and had been successful, although only for a year. Phil, the specialist NET oncology nurse was always very helpful and supportive.

All those were very good, very positive aspects of my Oxford treatment.

As is pretty well inevitable with any long, very complex treatment, there had been some communication difficulties and other problems. I knew that things frequently didn't go exactly as they should - indeed probably couldn't realistically be expected to – and I had, after all, made every mistake in the book myself and some that weren't even in 'the book' when treating patients:

Terry was a nice old boy – the salt of the earth and a typical Oxford countryman. He'd smoked a bit too much and, in his seventies, he was paying the price in terms of coughing and wheezing.

One afternoon in the late eighties he came to see me with a fungal infection of his big toenail. I always checked any prescription I did in a book called 'Mims' but on this occasion couldn't because I was consulting in a different room which to my surprise and dismay didn't have one. I prescribed the drug required – Livial – and got on with the other patients.

At home that night, a bolt of lightning hit me between the eyes. Livial was a hormone replacement tablet – for women only. I had meant to prescribe 'Lamisil' which sounds very like Livial. There was probably no need to panic as the patient might not have gone to the chemist for his drug and anyway if he had, the pharmacist would surely have realised my mistake and referred him back to me the following morning. I rang him straight away. Terry confirmed that he had indeed collected his pills and had taken the first one already. With great embarrassment I confessed my mistake and apologised. Terry didn't miss a beat and collected the correct pills the next day. He wouldn't have been harmed by taking one pill but that isn't the point. Of course.

Nowadays one checks prescriptions on the computer and if one didn't the computer would ask if I really meant to prescribe hormone replacement treatment to a man!

What my younger self would have said about a GP prescribing female hormone replacement tablets for a fungal toenail I can only imagine.

Knowing the near inevitability of mistakes occurring, I felt that I had to keep up with everything that was, or should be, happening to me. The price I paid for that was coming face to face with issues that other patients might have remained blissfully unaware of. It was part of the difficulty of being a doctor turned patient, seeing things from the 'other side' of the consultation desk. I was now 'the patient' and hoping for possibly an unachievable or unrealistic standard of care.

Ironically self-funding had contributed to communication difficulties as the private hospital where I had my clinic consultations wasn't connected to the NHS computers, so results of scans done in the NHS Churchill hospital couldn't be called up at the appointments whereas they would have been, if I'd been seen in the Churchill.

So, some things had at times been disappointing and at times stressful. I reasoned that just too much work was being expected of everyone. The hospital trust had delayed advertising for a replacement for the NET oncology professor, as trusts often do when someone retires, as it saves a significant amount of money. It put additional pressures on everyone in the NET unit, and, it seemed to me, an unreasonable amount on Michael, who took on all the extra consultant work himself to enable the unit to continue to function fully. He started work very early and finished late, so I surmised now had to be even more efficient in his use of time. It didn't matter to him I think whether I was self-funding or not as I'm sure he had a consistent approach to all of his patients. With the additional workload he didn't have as much time as he did initially, so the consultations couldn't be as long as they had been at the start of my treatment. I knew exactly what it was like to do surgeries when you were pressurised by there not being enough doctors around to share the workload. You felt very exposed and uneasy because you knew that, when having to work too quickly, you were much more likely to make a mistake to your patient's detriment and potentially your own, if it led to a serious complaint.

Still, Oxford was the devil I knew, and I had backed off getting a second opinion before because I had been so happy with the care I'd received.

Now, through no fault of any of the NET team, I had to look elsewhere but it turned out that going to London would create a terrible dilemma that I could never have envisaged.

Michael had been confident that the Royal Free team in London would also recommend PRRT treatment, but there was a complication. He was proposing to use radioactive Yytrium again whereas I knew that The Royal Free used a different, newer form of radioactivity called Lutetium. Yytrium theoretically might be better for larger metastases like mine but was more likely to be harmful to the kidneys and bone marrow than Lutetium, though my kidneys hadn't been harmed by it before. If I had treatment in London, might I be shooting myself in the foot by not having the tried and tested Yytrium which I'd had experience of before and which had seemed to work well, at least initially? Who knew whether the Lutetium would be as effective? Alternatively, if I stayed with The Churchill, might I simply be setting myself up for the risk of the second treatment being terribly delayed by the drain repairs with the attendant appalling stress of feeling your treatment and literally your life, was being compromised by building works that you could do nothing about?

Our plan was to mull things over for a few days after the London appointment, then, as agreed, discuss the overall situation with Michael and reach a decision on whether to stick with Oxford or switch to having my treatment in London. To make things more difficult, I was due to have a scan in London after my Friday appointment, so Richard, the Royal Free consultant would probably not want to make a recommendation till he'd seen that scan.

A few days before our London appointment, Catherine, of the nuclear medicine department at The Churchill, rang explaining she really needed to know as soon as I'd had my appointment in London, whether I was definitely going to come in for the PRRT in the Churchill or switch to London. I explained that I was due to have a scan three days after that appointment which might affect the treatment recommendation. She explained that because of the time it took to order the PRRT – which required a different dose for every patient – she couldn't wait till I'd had the result of the scan a day or two after it had been performed, if she was going to be able to get someone else into my slot. In that case I asked, would it be possible for me to have my scheduled date to come in for the PRRT put back by say a few days or a week to enable the Royal Free scan to be taken into consideration? No, she explained firmly, if I missed my arranged slot the next slot she could offer for the first PRRT would be thirteen weeks later.

So that was that. There could be no flexibility. Waiting thirteen weeks was out of the question. Catherine had been put in the very unenviable position of having to offer patients long waits for a treatment she wanted to give them quickly. In her time in charge this was the worst situation she'd ever experienced. It was awful for her and awful for all the patients waiting for their treatments. It would be unforgivable of me to say I would keep my Oxford PRRT slot and then pull out later, as it would waste a very precious treatment slot and delay another patient from starting their PRRT and I suppose, everyone else on the long waiting list would be delayed by at least a week longer than necessary. I couldn't have that on my conscience. I would have to decide, before the Royal Free consultant had all the information he needed, whether to keep my slot in Oxford or not. It would obviously make Catherine's life and the life of one of her waiting patients a little easier, if I opted for treatment in London, but would I be compromising my treatment by going to London and not having Yytrium? How ironic it would be if having the means to pay for private health insurance meant I inadvertently procured a less effective treatment?

And what if the Royal Free consultant didn't recommend PRRT but something else like chemotherapy? I would be back in the situation I'd been in a year before, when, faced with that possibility, I'd backed away from getting a second opinion and not gone to see him. Worst of all, if he only came to that conclusion a few days after the scan and I wanted to stay in Oxford and stick with the PRRT I would have to wait thirteen weeks before starting it rather than six.

But when I shied away from getting a second opinion before, things were different. Now the situation was terribly unpredictable in Oxford, with the Churchill treatment in a degree of chaos over the drains. I felt a second opinion was a good idea now, so I would keep the appointment and then decide. I promised Catherine I would let her know in plenty of time for her to get someone else into my slot, even if it meant telling her before a definite recommendation about the treatment had been made in London.

I knew I was fortunate to have private health insurance, but it didn't feel fortunate to be forced to make a decision like this in case I got it wrong. It felt impossibly hard and surreal. Almost as if the fates were punishing me for having the effrontery to have a choice and were tempting me, almost encouraging me, to make the wrong decision. It was bad enough that my cancer had become active again so much sooner than we'd expected but this felt incredibly tough to have to deal with on top of everything else.

Never in a million years, despite a life-time of working in the NHS, could I have envisaged having to wrestle with a dilemma like this.

Chapter 30

London

A couple of days after the disheartening telephone conversation with Michael about my prognosis, we headed off to our London appointment. I was very apprehensive and still despondent from the realisation that I was not going to be one of his patients who had relatively slow growing or indolent disease that could be managed for many years with just occasional treatment. I was pleased to be seeing Richard because he had spoken impressively at several lectures on NETs that I had attended and really seemed to be at the cutting edge of NET research and management. I'd met him briefly and he had seemed thoughtful and considerate. A recently retired gastroenterologist friend of mine, when enquiring how I was, had confirmed that he was definitely the 'go-to man' for NETs. Duncan joined us for the consultation. Richard had received a letter from Michael about me and an email with dozens of copies of letters, scan reports and the like from me. He had reviewed my case twice at his MDT. He had more than done his homework on me.

He started by asking me to recap the whole history from when my symptoms started to the present and tell him how I was in myself. This was followed by a thorough examination then a summary of how he saw things. Encouragingly, he commented that he didn't feel the volume of liver disease was particularly bad. Over the next hour or so, methodically and in an unhurried manner, he went through a wide range of treatment options – nine in total – that could be considered. He was quite clear that he wouldn't recommend Yytrium in my case because of its greater toxicity to the kidneys and bone marrow and because, if anything, he felt Lutetium might be slightly more effective anyway, especially as Yytrium hadn't worked for very long before in my case. That was a huge relief to hear, as it meant that I didn't need to agonise further about having treatment in Oxford – I could let my place on the PRRT waiting list there go to someone else. I began to relax.

His conclusion was that, unless the gallium PET scan that was scheduled – a cutting edge type of scan that hadn't been available in Oxford – showed a lot more bone metastases, he would probably not use PRRT at this stage but would favour using either Everolimus or Sunitimib, so called 'molecular targeted drug therapies' or else recommend chemotherapy. The Royal Free had stopped using the chemotherapy Oxford used, about two years ago feeling that a different combination was better. He explained what the average benefit from each treatment might be and that the benefits were additive i.e. you used one till it stopped working then started a different treatment.

'Even though you have progressive disease, I'd still be expecting you live for some years depending on the response to the first treatment. Hopefully given the options open to us, we will be looking at three, five or maybe ten years ahead. My aim would be a minimum of three to five years, but my hope would be that we should be considering potentially more. And good quality of life and treatment benefit for at least three years and hopefully five. We would be re-assessing all the time because the biology can change [meaning that the tumour could become more aggressive than originally was the case] in some people and if you didn't respond well, we might need to get a liver biopsy to see what was happening. Everyone at the Multidisciplinary Team meeting felt you ought to switch from PRRT to Molecular targeted treatment or CAPTEM chemotherapy and keep PRRT in reserve.'

He felt it would help us decide on which treatment to go for if we spoke to a medical oncologist colleague of his regarding the different types of drugs and, there and then, rang him, discussed my case and arranged an appointment to see him. He also gave us an appointment with himself to later put all the information together and make a definitive plan. He said he was generally optimistic about my situation but if things did not go well, he assured us that he would be quite frank with me about it.

The whole appointment had taken perhaps an hour and a quarter, and he had anticipated and discussed pretty well all the issues I'd wanted to discuss so comprehensively that, unusually for me in a consultation, I hadn't had to ask many questions. This had been precisely the sort of consultation I had hoped for – in fact it had exceeded my expectations.

We left feeling much happier than we'd felt going in. Richard had been very impressive and helpful; he'd seemed engaged, interested in my particular situation and very optimistic that he could arrange effective treatment and good quality life whilst having it. We were elated and hugely relieved to have him in our corner.

Duncan said that Richard had reminded him of the most impressive consultant that he'd ever worked for – at the cutting edge of research and with a positive, optimistic manner. What he'd said about my prognosis was, in reality, not all that different to what I'd heard in Oxford, but it felt much better and the fact that he was clearly prepared to try so many different approaches was very encouraging. He'd imbued us with a lot of that most precious of commodities – hope. He put me in mind of Arthur, the very supportive oncologist I'd contacted back at the start of my cancer odyssey.

Duncan, almost thinking out loud about my experiences, said how tough it had been for me. 'You were given what felt like a reprieve after what seemed like the grimmest of prognoses when the diagnosis was changed from stomach cancer and now this feels like another kind of reprieve after hearing about the progressive disease'. There was no doubt in any of our minds – it was the right thing to have further treatment in London. There might come a time when we needed to revert back to the Oxford NET Unit for practical reasons, but for now, we would cut the umbilical cord.

The terrible dilemma we had contemplated had disappeared.

A few days after seeing Richard, I attended for the gallium PET scan. A week or so later I was rung by Richard.

The gallium PET Scan was a game changer, as because it is much more sensitive than MRI or CT scans, it showed quite a few other metastases. One in a vertebra a third of the way down my spine and possibly one at the bottom of the spine, a small one in the right lung and lymph gland metastases in the abdomen and pelvis as well as of course the liver metastases. It wasn't possible to be certain whether these were new metastases or old ones that just hadn't been visible on the other scans. Richard felt that because bone metastases usually respond well to PRRT, that would, after all, be the best approach to take and he would arrange it as soon as possible in the NET Unit at The Wellington Hospital in North London. I'd hoped that the gallium PET scan wouldn't have shown any more mischief so it felt very dispiriting, but he said it didn't change my prognosis and was essentially what he thought he might find. I should keep my appointment with him in London in a week or so to discuss final arrangements.

The second consultation with Richard was straightforward and a few days later Jane and I checked in at The Wellington reception. For the week before, we'd both been feeling tense about the admission. Jane because she hated seeing me go through the ringer – me less so because of that, as the treatment hadn't been that tough a year earlier – but just because so much was at stake and it was a hospital I hadn't been to before.

The Wellington is the largest independent hospital in the UK and has patients from all over the world. The reception area is smart enough but in a 1970s style and much smaller and far less impressive than the huge reception area of The Churchill Hospital. It felt like going to a plush but slightly dated London hotel. I'd been sent a brochure from the hospital like a hotel welcome pack and was pleased to see that it had extensive TV channels on a large flat screen in every room. This was of crucial importance to me because The British Golf Open was going to be on Sky TV, so I had banked on that distracting me from the boredom and side effects of the treatment.

A very helpful porter took us up to the ward and proudly showed me the room, the phone numbers, how to summon help and then, with a flourish, the pièce de résistance, the impressively large, modern flat screen telly. Could he put it on Sky Sports please? Of course he could. But he couldn't – the Sky channel didn't work.

The ward or 'WellNet Unit' consisted of just three patient rooms, two of which were generally used for PRRT once a week. One was out of commission because of a toilet problem – what is it about foul drainage and NETS? – so I was the only patient in the Unit. There was an experienced staff nurse who was training a health care assistant that day looking after just me. The room was larger and airier than the 'cell' in the Oxford ward I'd been into before, and best of all had windows with views of Lords Cricket ground.

The health care assistant came to take some blood but was clearly a bit nervous as it was her first day on the ward and couldn't get any blood. She was terribly apologetic and flustered, as if she had let me down terribly, but all I could do was reassure her it wasn't a problem as my mind went back to all the times as a student, then as a young inexperienced ward doctor, that I had repeatedly tried to get blood from a patient and failed. I remembered with shame, repeatedly trying – irrespective of any discomfort I must have been causing my patient – to get a drip into someone during the wee small hours – and failing. It crossed my mind to encourage her to try the other arm, but she left it to the staff nurse who easily got the blood.

An hour or two later, the oncology registrar came to check me over and to put an intravenous drip needle into each of my arms. She was doing research into some aspects of cancer immunotherapy for her PhD, which she would need if she were to get a consultant job in London. She ruefully explained that, out of a group of sixteen contemporaries, nine had left the UK to work in Australia, for the far better terms and conditions and work life balance there, which made her wonder about the wisdom of her decision to stick with the NHS as she, and our son Duncan had done. It said so much about how young doctors are treated in the NHS.

In the afternoon, a charming nuclear medicine consultant introduced himself and explained exactly how he and a colleague would administer the Lutetium PRRT treatment. He explained that I would feel nauseous for the first ten minutes of the procedure during which he would therefore talk a lot to distract me! He would arrange that I had my scan the next morning early, because I was a colleague and he felt it very important to give colleagues every consideration. It didn't really make any great difference to me, but it was lovely to feel the warmth of a colleague anxious to do all he could for another. Exactly as he had warned, I did feel quite nauseous at the start of the PRRT infusion but knowing it wouldn't last long made it easy to bear and when his flow of conversation slowed the nausea had gone. Jane had been required to leave to keep away from any harmful radiation, so I found myself on my own for the rest of the time. She rang in the evening to say that the wife of a former patient of mine had rung seeking some advice and information about her husband who had been admitted to hospital. She had pointed out that I was in hospital myself. My ex-patient's wife was thus very surprised when I rang her and chatted for thirty minutes. It made a change to watching the TV and hopefully was a bit more useful. To my slight embarrassment I was taken down in a wheelchair for the scan the next morning then, at midday or so, Jane arrived, and we were free to go. I walked the mile and a half to the railway station and selected a seat well away from Jane and any other passengers to ensure no-one had any untoward radiation exposure.

The Wellington Hospital had been my first in-patient experience of a private hospital. How did it compare with the NHS hospital? Well it was definitely much more pleasant, perhaps like a four-star hotel compared to a two-star one and the treatment was far more personal. I was the only patient on the Wellington Unit so got pretty well instant attention on the few occasions I buzzed for it and always from the same person. Essentially the sort of frills which made a somewhat daunting experience a bit easier compared to the no-frills NHS hospital.

Frills are nice but the bottom line was that the TV in neither hospital was working properly.

Chapter 31

Being a GP and a Patient

The word 'patient' is derived from the French word which means 'to endure without complaint.'

I have endured personally but not without complaint.....

When I worked I tried to run to time but it's pretty difficult when you have only ten or twelve minutes per consultation and sometimes problems are very complex or patients save up several problems to deal with 'to save taking up another appointment'. The vast majority of patients are long suffering and tolerate waiting, sometimes for quite a while, with good grace realising the constraints of the service we work under, particularly if we have the good manners to apologise.

A few years ago, we bought the drinks for my son Patrick's wedding. There were two barrels of beer, a quarter full, left over which I took home and which needed to be drunk quickly before the beer went off. I rounded up village friends, three nights in a row, to help us with this challenging task and needless to say a very good time was had by all. The day after the beer ran out the first patient for my afternoon surgery turned up ten minutes before her time. Keen to run to time for as long as possible, I saw her straight away so had twenty minutes to wait before the second patient was due. I seized the opportunity to do some admin work – looking at results of investigations and hospital letters.....and was very startled to wake up an hour later! Appalled, I hastily called the next patient in and apologised profusely for keeping him waiting so long.

'That's OK Dr – I realise how busy you chaps are.'

'Yes, well of course...' I let my voice trail away and worked my way through the rest of my surgery.

No one had noticed. No one complained. The receptionists assumed I was busy on something.

A postcard said, 'There's no such thing as normal people – just people you don't know well.' The same holds true for doctors and most definitely patients, who, let's face it, wouldn't be patients in the first place if everything about them was 'normal'. They are 'ill' or 'unwell' in some way or another, although in my case most of the time I feel fine. If this book has succeeded in letting you 'wear my shoes' as Atticus Finch put it, you will know that I'm not even a 'typical patient' as I am, or at least was, a doctor, which makes me a tricky-to-deal-with, challenging sort of patient. Or probably just a royal pain in the ….

A million times at work and social occasions someone has said to me 'I couldn't possibly do your job' and meant it. Being a GP is a difficult, exacting job but I was trained to do it and had a lot of practice at it, so I felt comfortable most of the time that I practised. Being a patient, I have found a great deal tougher.

People ask if it's harder or easier being a patient when you are a doctor. In the past, I'd assumed it was easier because having medical knowledge should enable one to better understand what was happening regarding investigations and treatment.

Now I think it's a distinct disadvantage.

Being a GP makes you a bit of a Jeremiah. You're trained to consider the worst diagnosis possible when you see a patient lest you miss something very serious. Having a high index of suspicion of the possibility of a serious condition makes you do tests to check something out 'just in case', often causing great anxiety for your patient. Unfortunately, it not infrequently turns out that the diagnosis is indeed the worst one possible. To make matters even more difficult you get a very distorted view of conditions, as you generally don't see much of the milder end of the spectrum of any given disease but instead see the bad, complicated ones that actually need treating.

Inevitably because I'm medical and know a bit more (or at least should do) about medical matters than lay people, I ask some questions that most patients wouldn't know to ask about and seek more detail in the answers, which obviously makes it harder for the doctor or nurse consulting to run to time. This is compounded by the need I feel to double check everything. I know that if I had a patient with whom consultations always overran, a part of me would be determinedly concentrated on trying to limit the 'damage' that patient would do to my other patients' appointment times, so it wouldn't have been a relaxed easy consultation. I suspect that may be partly why quite a few of my consultations as a patient haven't felt as comfortable as they might have been, especially given the time-pressures people are under. Recording, as I do, all my consultations, doubtless could make the person seeing me more guarded than normal. Listening to the consultations, as I've done again for the book, frequently makes me cringe, as I'm sometimes ponderous, waffle and repeat myself and my questions, because I'm anxious about what I might hear or have heard or because of occasional inconsistencies in what I've heard. It's not helped either by being naturally garrulous.

I'm also used to handing out treatments rather than being on the receiving end of them.

So, take pity on my poor doctors and bear all this in mind when you read a lot of what follows.

What have I learnt by being a patient? Everything I guess about how important a job I used to do and how much better I should have done it. Every small act of kindness is greatly appreciated and there are an awful lot of kind acts to appreciate. The receptionist keen to help with an appointment, the health care assistants taking blood cheerfully and expertly, the eagerness of ward nurses to help make your admission as bearable as possible, being just a few examples, to say nothing of similar actions from doctors and all the other professions that help in the course of your treatment. The converse is also true: every encounter with someone who is a bit inconsiderate or overly hurried is more upsetting than it should be, as you are vulnerable and less resilient than you would normally be.

In the real world, as opposed to the fictional one, some NHS personnel are wonderfully thoughtful, kind and considerate pretty well all the time, most are good most of the time but fall short of the ideal on occasions, especially when they are very short of time, and some are average most of the time but occasionally very good. All of my medical attendants were clearly competent and some superbly so. I suspect that generally far too much is being expected of people in the limited time that is available because of the pressure everyone is constantly under. The imperative is to get the vital work done, so that although everyone knows of the importance of, and would like to practise, holistic care, it's often a casualty of time pressures.

It's hard to begin to describe how difficult it is hearing that you have a condition that, in all likelihood, will cause your death within a year, especially when you didn't feel particularly unwell. I know from personal experience that it's not easy telling a patient this sort of news either. When you have been told something like that – even if it's been done with great sensitivity and empathy – you don't come away from the consultation thinking how well the caregiver performed because you're simply devastated by the actual news. One might come away thinking how badly the news had been imparted because one is angry and upset. There is an element of wanting to shoot the messenger because the news is so grim or because the information has not actually been handled with sensitivity. With my delusional mindset, I would, of course, always have done it with great empathy, insight, patience and kindness!

I've been surprised by what felt like a lack of empathy in some consultations. Jane had felt the same and as a result been quite upset and even angry at times. The pastoral care has not been quite what I was expecting. Though what should I have expected? I mentioned a friend who had had an even bigger operation than me – she had found exactly the same. Sometimes she felt clinicians could be pretty insensitive. Whether being a colleague makes it more difficult for doctors to put a metaphorical arm round to comfort you or not I don't know. Perhaps if colleagues suspected you needed that arm it would force them to recognise the vulnerability and fallibility that even doctors, those God-like, super-resilient, tougher-than-average individuals, suffer from. Perhaps it would feel like crossing a line or breaking a secret code?

In The 'C' Word and in When Breath Becomes Air the authors seemed to have had great relationships with the professionals they encountered. I've experienced that with several of my consultants who gave me great confidence that they were really on my side and involved with me as a person and not just as a patient. After every interaction with them I took some encouragement.

Jane says I have reacted to bad news during consultations with amazing stoicism and without showing much emotion – about the worst I've said is 'That's very disappointing'. The old boarding school stiff upper lip. Jane gets very emotional and thinks I keep my composure for her sake. There is undoubtedly something in that. She wonders if that is perhaps why my caregivers don't hold my hand, figuratively speaking, or ask how I feel about some information that's just been imparted assuming, that because I appear to be composed, I must be OK and therefore don't need empathy. The job I did does instil in you an ability not to panic or flap about when someone is really ill but to almost slow down the thought processes to make sure you stay calm and get them right. That same process kicks in with me when I hear bad news. It's an outer protection for the world. Of course, I feel great sadness and at times panic about the fact that I won't be around for many years to come and will be leaving my family at a relatively early age, but it's no different for me than for anyone else.

When I saw patients, I generally tried to put myself in their shoes and tried to interact with them the way I would have wanted for myself. At least I hope I did. Of course, I must have failed many times to do that and not spent enough time discussing how my patients felt about being told bad news and exploring how I could have made it easier for them. I heard John McEnroe say that the longer it gets since he was playing tennis competitively, the better he feels his standard of tennis was, and I've no doubt I'm the same about my practice of medicine. Unrealistic.

There are some other interesting, odd, good and bad, funny and sad, uplifting and depressing things about being a patient – especially one with a doctor's mindset.

It's endlessly fascinating being on the other side of the consultation observing the processes going on and seeing how well or otherwise your colleague is doing and reflecting on how you think you would have done it. I spent a lot of time trying to improve my 'consultation skills' so that I could help my patients more effectively, sometimes going away for days at a time on residential courses. Some doctors seem to be just naturally effective consulters but most of us have to study videos of ourselves consulting to learn how to do it well, so that it becomes almost second nature. The principles are the same for hospital consultations – in theory – but in practice at least they often felt very different. Sometimes it was only after the consultation that I realised just how skilfully conducted the consultation had actually been done.

Being a patient is very strange particularly if people realise you are one and even more so if you have forgotten or at least stopped thinking of yourself as one. My experience in the Spa Hotel in Wales was salutary. Patient? Cancer? Don't touch him.

One of the tougher things to appreciate is that the world is no longer your oyster – at least not if you want to have holiday insurance, which generally I would suggest is wise. Jane manfully took on the task of organising holiday cover and found it profoundly depressing when we first tried to get cover for a week's holiday in France. The first company that was prepared to cover me wanted over £600 for just the week in France. Don't even think about going to America or areas nearby that send patients to America. Luckily, I don't particularly want to go to America. Jane had particularly loved the three trips we'd had to the Indian sub-continent but whether we will get back there because of insurance issues is another matter.

What is interesting is how quickly you adapt to the new status quo. Without a spleen I am more vulnerable to certain infections. I've observed patients adapt to adversity so often and marvelled at how they've done such things as cope with colostomy bags, having to inject themselves several times a day if diabetic. However, when I had to have blood thinning injections, I took to it far more readily than I'd ever have imagined I would. If there's no alternative, you do it.

In days gone by, when I've had a patient with liver metastases, I've shuddered to think how it must feel to know that there is a malign process growing in your liver whose purpose, if that is the right word, is to do you ever increasing harm. Now I have liver and bone metastases, a lung one and lymph glands affected, and I'm surprised to find that I've accommodated to the situation and most of the time just got on with things in a relative matter of fact sort of way. Maybe it helps to have seen so many patients in this situation before me and noting how they just have had to get on with things as best they can – hopefully perhaps with a bit of support from their GP.

As I've said before you can learn a lot from your patients.

Chapter 32

The Bungee Experience

I'd had the first London PRRT with very little incident and the second dose was even easier with the bonus of being able to watch from my window the MCC cricket team thrash some unfortunates on the Lords nursery ground during the admission. In between the first and second PRRT doses, there were, as before, blood tests every fortnight and then after a couple of months I had my repeat gallium Scan. I also had a neck MRI because I'd been having quite a bit of discomfort, stiffness and 'clicking' in my neck. Pretty well all patients with a history of cancer worry that any symptom they develop could be related to their cancer and I'm no different. In my case, I was wondering if I had developed a metastasis in my neck. Although I'd had a stiff neck for decades and episodes of neck pain, this was the longest and worst episode I'd ever had. I knew I couldn't really see a physio unless the neck had been checked out as well, as mobilising a neck with metastases could be very harmful. The neck scan was fitted in with just a few days' notice by a very helpful radiographer and was pretty grim as I had to lie completely flat and wear a 'Silence of The Lambs' type of mask with a camera in it. I was certain I wouldn't be able to cope with the pain but after a while, miraculously it went.

So back to see Richard a few days later, after the now all-too-familiar build-up of stress and dread. It was becoming a little easier to bear with practice but was still pretty awful. He got straight to the point explaining in a measured, calm way – as if what he was about to tell me was entirely to be expected – that I'd had a very good response to the PRRT and so he'd do another scan in four months' time. The neck scan showed just wear and tear of the neck vertebrae – as I'd hoped for and expected really. He said that I could have more PRRT down the line but that it was quite likely I'd get a sustained response with the treatment I'd had, so, if I needed some more, say in two years' time he could do that. He also reminded us that there were lots of other treatment options as well. He seemed so relaxed, confident and comfortable, exuding the message that this is just routine business, that I felt emboldened to ask the question that I had avoided asking, but was always at the back of my mind. Hesitatingly and apologetically – because it felt like a very needy, non-doctor sort of question – I ventured:

'Do you expect to be seeing me in your clinic in five years time?'

'Yes I'd be looking for longer than that, certainly that's my expectation with the treatments we have coming through.' Hearing Richard state that in such a matter of fact way made our spirits soar and we felt very thankful. It felt immeasurably more hopeful than when Phil had advised me that I should get anything important done in the next twelve months or the last conversation I'd had with Michael when he'd spoken in a rather sombre, sorrowful way about my prognosis. It felt wonderful, particularly compared to just over two years earlier when I'd heard that I might have as little as six months to live. This would be more than twelve times as long. What an amazing turnaround from those terribly dark days. If Richard was right. My spirits had been up and down so often that the cautious part of me was a bit wary but overall it felt great. If the glass wasn't quite half full there was certainly enough in it now to really savor. Getting ahead of myself – try as you may it's hard not to – I calculated that I'd be almost seventy-two then and not all that many years ago that would have seemed a decent age to get to. The Hebrew greeting 'May you live a long life' encapsulates what most of us, I guess, hope for, which is to live a decent length of time, at least the average expected time and ideally more, so that we get our 'fair share'. Some people see it slightly differently. Many years ago, I had to tell a patient, who was about to retire, that he had terminal lung cancer and his first reaction was to express how annoyed he felt that he'd miss out on the pension he'd worked so hard for and would see so little of. I could understand that myself as the longer I lived for, the longer it would be before Jane received only half of my pension. That mattered to me but not to her.

So back to the routine of having scans at regular intervals to check on any sign of the disease becoming active again. Richard had indicated that the average time before this would happen in cases like mine was about eighteen months so I could reasonably hope for a further year without needing new treatment if my disease was average. The first post-Lutetium PRRT treatment scan had seemingly been very encouraging which led us to think we had a good chance of at least being average and of course we hoped that I'd do rather better than average and might get a further eighteen months before needing any more PRRT. We were buoyed up with hope for the future.

We didn't really dwell on the thought that for every person that does better than average there is one that does less well than average.

The second post PRRT scan was duly booked in for the beginning of April 2019 and feeling just a bit more relaxed than usual, we waited outside Richard's clinic a week later to hear the result. I'd been feeling a bit overly full after meals and mildly nauseous again for a couple of months and had experienced a slight change in my bowel pattern, which I'd emailed Richard about but he hadn't felt the symptoms were likely to indicate anything of great importance. I assumed the nausea and fullness were a legacy from having major stomach surgery and that the bowel symptoms were due to the monthly injections which were well known to cause precisely those sorts of symptoms. After enquiring about those symptoms Richard told us the result of the scan:

'There's been some increase in size of the liver metastases and there are also some new metastases in the liver, small but new ones which would suggest that it's growing again. We need to get an up-to-date gallium scan but also an FDG scan to look at the biology of the tumours, just to see if they have changed from being low grade to becoming more active. [FDG scans will reflect how active or aggressive a tumour is] If they remain largely low grade lesions, we could consider either more PRRT, or PRRT with capecitabine [a chemotherapy drug] or the oral chemotherapy combination of capecitabine with temozolomide [otherwise known as 'Captem'] which is well tolerated.'

He went on to say that he would do an endoscopy to check out my stomach symptoms.

He was confident that he should be able to get the disease under control but that it was important from a survival perspective to do it quickly before the liver lesions enlarged too much.

'Once it was under control' I pressed, 'would five years still be possible?'

'I'm an optimist by nature and with all the other options available, particularly if we can get things under control in the next few months, which we would hope to do. I'd still be optimistic that five years should be achievable and would be my aim.'

Richard described the situation as needing an 'escalation of therapy' Bringing the heavier guns into play in other words. It sounded like escalation probably meant chemotherapy.

Innumerable times the cancer experience is described as being a 'rollercoaster of emotions' precisely because, cliché or not, it is. But on a real rollercoaster you know when the ride will finish. A better metaphor I read was that it was 'emotional bungee jumping. Blindfolded. Without knowing how long the bungee cord is, nor what it's made of, nor, precisely, just where you're jumping from or towards. Or when the damned jump is finally going to stop.' To which I'd add 'Or whether the rope will even hold you at all.'

The news that my PRRT hadn't held the line for anything near to average and in fact had only been effective for a mere six months or so was like the bungee rope being let out further so that my head was closer, perilously so, to the ground. Just when I'd thought we'd have a period of respite from the wild fluctuations of emotions occasioned by hearing life threateningly bad news, the cycle was starting again. Richard had been fairly measured during the consultation, but I had had to press fairly hard to ring a five year prognosis out of him and even then it had been qualified by an 'if' and he hadn't sounded anything like as confident as he had been at the preceding consultation. The preceding consultation. What a contrast! Euphoria after that one. Despair after this one. My disease was revealing itself to be more and more malevolent. It had shaken the first PRRT in Oxford off after only a year and the London second course in half the time. I didn't really have any confidence in PRRT working now. Maybe it might be OK if given with capecitabine but on its own it seemed to be outgunned by my disease. What was to happen next would depend on what the two scans showed. If the FDG was strongly positive I was in real trouble as it would indicate that the disease was really aggressive and so would be very hard to stop in its tracks. I didn't think a 'well differentiated grade two NET' like mine was supposed to be like this. 'Well differentiated' to my mind was supposed to be almost synonymous with 'well behaved' but this was aggressive, bad behaviour. But then again, it 'hadn't read the cancer rulebook.' Whilst many or maybe most, didn't behave like mine, obviously some did. It was the 'luck' of the draw. Back to the feeling that I hadn't had much luck in the last two and a half years. Except for the surgery. Of course, I'd been lucky that Alistair had the skill to remove so much of the cancer. Very lucky.

Back also to the fear of abandoning Jane rather sooner than had appeared likely. What had happened was very much what Michael had predicted, so when I remembered that I was less shocked and more resigned to the situation. And what of Jane? It was as though throughout the bungee jump she was tied to my back or I to hers – like doing a tandem jump – only there was no experienced instructor to ensure all went well – just me, as bewildered and powerless to control the situation as she was. She went through every emotion I went through and probably even more. I was desperate to raise her spirits and my own as we left the hospital. Sometimes le mot juste comes at just the right time.

'It's not a disaster' I said firmly, as much to bolster my spirits as hers, 'it's a setback. It just means that we have to ditch the PRRT approach sooner than we'd expected and go on to the next therapy.' I repeated this several times and it definitely helped raise my spirits a millimeter or two. Maybe, after my rapidly accumulating experience of unwanted health news, I was becoming better at not catastrophising. A hard way to learn one of life's lessons. It also helped to use 'setback' when later explaining things to family and friends.

The two scans were duly done on consecutive mornings and, as planned, I attended for an endoscopy a week after them. Richard had said he wanted to make sure there were no varices or problems with the sutures in my stomach. When I came around from the endoscopy, he came to the cubicle and said that the endoscopy was good. The motility or movements of the stomach were a little bit slow as a result of the surgery and this was probably the cause of the mild nausea, but it wasn't important in the greater scheme of things. He suggested taking an anti-nausea pill called metoclopramide which would increase the motility of the stomach and speed up the emptying of the stomach. The gallium PET scan showed that the previous boney metastases had actually improved and were negative for FDG which was definitely encouraging. Three of the new liver metastases were positive on the FDG scan indicating they were a little bit more aggressive than the other lesions and the same held true for a couple of the lymph nodes in the abdomen. It would have been a lot worse if most of the metastases were FDG positive. He would take my case to the MDT meeting to seek a consensus on the best way forward, but he felt the Captem chemotherapy was the most likely to be recommended. In thirty per cent of patients who took Captem, he informed us, the metastases shrink down by more than twenty-five per cent and fifty per cent of patients got stabilisation of the disease so that overall eighty per cent benefitted from the treatment. The length of time that Captem worked for those patients varied from nine months to two years. Though not explicitly mentioned, this meant that twenty per cent of patients got no benefit. He felt that it would be wise to cancel our cycling holiday in Italy which was booked for a few weeks' time. He would ring me in a few days with the results of the routine biopsies he had taken, and at the same time tell me what treatment the MDT meeting recommended.

Listening to the recording, I see I asked the same question three times, my usual slowness to grasp a subject being exaggerated by the brain dulling effect of the sedative drug injected before the endoscopy to put me asleep. Essentially, I was just dopier than normal.

A few days later Richard rang. The stomach biopsies, as expected, were normal. He told me that one of the blood tests which is used as a screening test for bowel cancer was slightly raised which evidently could be caused by a NET but he had also looked again at the CT scan with a radiologist, which had shown some possible bowel thickening, so he felt that it was important to do a colonoscopy to, hopefully, exclude bowel cancer.

The MDT confirmed that the recommendation for treatment was the oral chemotherapy Captem and if it was needed later for the boney metastases PRRT could be added. He had already liaised with Mathew, one of the oncologists on the NET team who would send me an appointment.

So not just one old nemesis – two. Chemotherapy and another colonoscopy – the procedure I'd really struggled with before. I couldn't have bowel cancer as well as a badly behaving NET?

Obviously, I could.

But I didn't. The colonoscopy was fine.

That left me with 'just' the chemotherapy. The treatment I had dreaded so much two and a half years earlier and had been delighted to avoid when the surgery turned out to be so successful.

Chapter 33

Facing My Chemotherapy Nemesis

Preparing to have palliative chemotherapy for my suspected stomach cancer was an experience I didn't ever want to have to go through again. Later, when things had seemed to be going my way with the NET, I allowed myself the luxury of thinking I might manage to avoid chemotherapy altogether but as the bungee experience worsened, I knew I'd have to confront my nemesis one day. That day had arrived.

Jane and I duly went to see Mathew the oncologist who we had met once before. Naturally, beforehand I had tried to get a 'feel' for Captem from the internet. The most helpful information was from a metanalysis, a review of lots of trials, which showed that side effects bad enough to require stopping of the treatment were uncommon. The most common reason for having to stop the Captem was because of the drug's effects on the bone marrow, which could put a patient at risk of bleeding and make him or her susceptible to infections and also could cause severe anaemia, which might require a blood transfusion. Other occasional causes for having to stop seemingly were fatigue, nausea, diarrhoea and mucositis, the latter being painful inflammation and ulceration anywhere along the lining of the gastro-intestinal tract from the mouth onwards. Trial information only listed severe side effects and not what usually happened to patients, so I didn't really get a feel for what common side effects occurred which weren't so severe as to have to stop the medication. That information I'd need to get from Mathew.

Mathew started the consultation by explaining that, of the choices available, he felt chemotherapy had the best chance of getting the disease under control and the combination he felt would be best was indeed Captem - the combination of the two chemotherapy drugs, capecitabine and temozolomide, that Richard had mentioned. If that didn't work, he would switch to 'platinum based' chemotherapy which had to be given intravenously and had more side effects.

Captem was given over a four-week cycle so that I would take fourteen days of capecitabine tablets and for the last five days of the capecitabine I should add in the temozolomide tablets and then have 14 days off tablets before starting the cycle again. After three cycles he would scan me to see if the Captem had worked and if it had, continue the four week cycles for as long as Captem continued to work – as shown by three monthly scans. There would be blood tests prior to each treatment to ensure that it was safe to carry on. The commonest side effects, he explained, were fatigue, mouth ulcers and soreness of the hands and feet and diarrhoea. Nausea and vomiting could be controlled very effectively with anti-sickness drugs. As I was already on metoclopramide, he suggested continuing that. The majority of his Captem patients were able to continue with their working lives particularly if their bone marrow hadn't had to cope with other chemotherapy or PRRT. He seemed very relaxed and was very reassuring about the possibility of getting much in the way of side effects, to the point that I wondered if he was downplaying them a bit as I'd got a somewhat worse impression from what I had read about Captem. I felt I needed as precise an estimate of side effects as possible. My big concern was the likelihood of getting nausea and vomiting – was it maybe one in ten I asked?

'If that' was the reply.

'Would I lose my hair?'

'Captem usually doesn't cause hair loss.

Most people, he said, felt a bit tired while on the chemotherapy but that resolved during the two weeks off medication. Only about 5% got difficult symptoms of diarrhoea and when I collected my medication there would be some loperamide – an anti-diarrhoea pill included to take if needed. He didn't feel that my splenectomy was likely to make me more susceptible to infections which had been a concern of mine. He needed to check the level of an enzyme called 'DPD' which helped the body get rid of the capecitabine because a small proportion of people had a major deficiency of it and so capecitabine levels could build up in the body and cause those patients to become unwell. If the DPD level was very low he wouldn't risk giving me capecitabine. In some patients it was a bit low in which case one could have a reduced dose. I felt it important to explain that my experience as a GP had made me very wary of chemotherapy as the only patients I ever saw, were those having a grim time with side effects or else ones I had to admit to hospital as an emergency with an infection. He said that although it was still possible, it was uncommon to have to admit patients to hospital with Captem or even with most of the stronger chemotherapy drugs these days. Things had improved a lot in that respect. He suggested starting the Captem a day or two after the colonoscopy.

Richard had also said that Captem was usually well tolerated so little by little and with some reluctance, my mind was beginning to take on board the possibility that this chemotherapy might not be the end of the world after all. Just to absolutely confirm this, as I was leaving, I asked:

'With your knowledge and experience of Captem, if you were me, you wouldn't be too fazed about taking Captem?'

'No, particularly once we've checked for DPD deficiency. The people who get really sick from Capecitabine are the ones who are DPD deficient.'

I subsequently had the DPD blood test.

The next step was an appointment at the chemotherapy unit with a specialist chemotherapy nurse a few days later to go through the details of taking the pills and go over the side effects in more detail. I'd read the patient information sheets on capecitabine and temozolomide, which again gave me the impression that I was more likely to get side effects than Mathew had indicated. The nurse patiently went through everything about the drugs for some time and then I asked the question that was uppermost in my mind.

'Was my DPD level OK in the blood test?'

'No – you have a deficiency.'

'Oh no!' I exclaimed unable to disguise my bitter disappointment. The last thing Mathew had said was 'The people who get really sick from capecitabine are the ones who are DPD deficient.'

That's it then I'm done for, I thought. I can't expect to be able to tolerate this Captem treatment at all. I couldn't believe I could be so unlucky: only a very small proportion of people were DPD deficient. At every turn, things seemed to be stacked against me. Why did the outcome of my tests always have to be bad? I would have to go to the 'Platinum based' chemotherapy which had to be given intravenously and usually had more side effects than Captem. And what then? There was one less treatment available now and it was even worse than that, as certain other chemotherapy drugs couldn't be given if you were DPD deficient. The NET seemed to be closing in on me. I listened to the rest of her talk in a desultory way. It hardly seemed worth it.

Realising how despondent I was she said, 'I'll get the oncology registrar to go through this with you when he's free' and went looking for him.

He appeared and explained it was nowhere near as black as I'd assumed. Yes, I did have a deficiency but the type I had probably only required a smaller dose of capecitabine than normal. He showed me the report '...the evidence for the association of this with severe toxicity to capecitabine is contradictory.[!] Consider a 20% dose reduction and if tolerant after the first cycle, dose increment to the normal dose.'

What this meant was that it was far from certain whether my DPD test mattered but to be on the safe side the dose needed to be reduced a bit initially at least. If there were no significant problems, I could take the full dose after that. Phew! Not a disaster then. Not a catastrophe. I calmed down though I was uneasy about it in case my impression was incorrect and so emailed Mathew the following evening and we spoke the next morning. He confirmed the above and said he didn't expect it would cause a problem.

A day later I was to start.

And the next day the sun rose in the morning and set in the evening. Life went on.

Symbolically it felt massive, but it boiled down to just taking two tablets in the morning and two twelve hours later. I had to take my usual anti-emetic, metoclopramide, half an hour before breakfast and drink a glass of water straight after the pills but that was actually all there was to it. I carefully recorded the precise time

I took the pills each day. I had a blood test after a week and the registrar I'd met rang me to ensure I hadn't had a problem with my blood which I hadn't. After nine days I was supposed to take temozolomide tablets as well in the evening two hours after any food. As I was on metoclopramide the registrar advised not taking the more powerful anti-emetic granisetron because pretty well everyone got constipated from it and I might not need it. That made sense. At 10pm I duly took the four pills of temozolomide and remained fine. Until I woke up four hours later and began an hour of heaving and retching.

Usually after vomiting you feel a bit easier for a while but not with this. I took a granisetron tablet and miraculously went off to sleep for several hours and then felt fine. The next night I took the granisetron before the temozolomide and remained fine so did this on the following three nights of temozolomide. What was less than fine was the constipation but that was a whole lot better than nausea and retching. At times I did feel tired whilst taking the pills and for maybe three or four days after they had stopped. It was not so debilitating and after a few more days I went for the first run on the treadmill.

I had 'survived' my first cycle pretty well intact. Elation is perhaps too strong a word, but I was certainly mightily relieved and thankful that it had been relatively gentle with me. The DPD deficiency hadn't, as predicted, caused an issue. It was only one cycle and of course I knew that it didn't mean I'd never get side effects, but it was a better start than I'd expected.

I'd confronted my nemesis and, just as Mathew and Richard had predicted, it really hadn't been all that much of a penance. It was dawning on me that probably my hang-up about chemotherapy was just that – a hang-up. Had I been wrong to demonise chemotherapy? In general, perhaps yes, though later I asked one of my former partners and she had exactly the same impression about chemotherapy that I'd had. So, given my work background perhaps it was inevitable that I was wary of chemotherapy. It was definitely an instance where being a doctor had been unhelpful.

Chapter 34

The End of the Book....That is....Not Me

My life now feels very different to how it was before October 2016 and in a way that my younger self could hardly have imagined. Then, I took it for granted that I'd live a long life and didn't really spend much time thinking about how long I'd live for. Now, I can't really take anything for granted and I think a lot about how long I may have. My situation is that I have what is termed a 'life limiting condition' which means the NET will get me sooner or later, but I'm fully committed, with the help of my medical advisors, to trying to put that day off for as long as possible. Obviously.

There are various treatments that have been shown to halt the progression – or 'get control of the disease' as the doctors put it – of NETs like mine. They work for a period of time in some people but not everyone. The plan therefore is to try a treatment and if it works to keep using it until it stops working and then try another and another, and as many other treatments as is practical. Not all the treatments are equally effective and it's important, in order to maximise my prognosis, to get control of the NET as quickly as possible. Currently the advice is that the treatment most likely to get control, without too much in the way of side effects, is the Captem chemotherapy. Research shows that most people don't benefit for more than a year or two. If I was lucky enough to be one of the people that did respond, I would probably still need to change to another treatment in time. This would lead to more side effects and/or be less effective. Some patients don't get any response to the Captem of course, and some for less than the average time. If I have a poor outcome to Captem my situation will become increasingly precarious as I will be moving through the better options for treatment alarmingly fast. Even if the first scan after three cycles of Captem does show a response, I've no way of knowing whether that response will, like with the PRRT, be short-lived or give me a year or even more before we have to try something else. I daren't really entertain any serious expectation that the line will hold for much more than a year or eighteen months at best, although Mathew has patients that have been benefitting from Captem for over two years. I've even read of a patient who responded for eight years to Captem which would be the dream, but long responses like that seemed to have more common with PRRT and once bitten...

So, in effect, I just have to keep taking the pills and hope I don't get any major side effects and hope they work for longer than average. I have to hope I can be in the 'long tail' that Arthur, the research consultant in Oxford talked about. Some people have to make up the long tail, so why not me? It entails a lot of hoping for me my family and friends and quite a bit of praying also.

At one level my situation may seem a pretty unenviable - one with so much uncertainty and only one unpalatable certainty. A million times I've read or heard someone in a tight corner say 'I never thought it could happen to me'. I can't say that because my job sometimes entailed trying to help someone in very difficult straits and always, I would find myself trying to imagine what it must be like to be in that situation and wonder how I would cope in his or her place, especially if they were younger than me. Except I never really believed it would happen to me. Not really deep down. Until it did. Once it happened, I guess my work did help me come to terms relatively quickly with what I was up against. Or at least some sort of terms. As I type this just after running over a mile and a half and then doing a bunch of exercises, I can't really believe that I've got cancer throughout numerous parts of my body and have taken chemotherapy tablets just a few hours earlier. I'm too well for that. Surely?

'There's always someone worse off than you.' Bizarrely that is sort of a help. I've had patients with pretty terrible diseases of the lung, heart and relentless neurological diseases as well as very aggressive cancers – far more so than mine – which makes me, if not exactly appreciative of my particular form of cancer at least appreciate that it could have been far, far worse. Indeed, for a couple of weeks I truly believed I had stage four cancer of the stomach, after which a NET seemed like a blessing. That colours everything and helps compensate for the bungee line being abruptly let out from time to time.

Additionally, I feel I am fortunate to be in the position I'm in where I have had excellent medical advice and treatment both in Oxford and London. It's not the BUPA insurance that makes me feel fortunate – it's being born in the UK where there is cutting edge treatment and great expertise available which sadly is denied to many NET patients in other parts of the world.

There is a heightened sense of appreciation of 'the moment' because of the feeling of being given a partial reprieve. In my best moments, I've wondered if knowing that the length of one's life was going to be shortened might in some ways even be a good thing. I've always tended to put things off and leave them to the last minute with the inevitable result that all too often they don't ever get done. Now, knowing that the 'last minute' may not be all that far away, I'm more focused and better at actually getting things done. If you assumed you'd live forever, the temptation would be to endlessly put things off and never actually do anything. 'Manana' in other words.

Ironically, in the past the 'C' word was not mentioned in the media much at all – now it seems to me – although I know I'm hyper-sensitive to the subject – that the media are trying to make redress and appear determined to mention it whenever they can. It's always an unwelcome reminder when I've managed to put my cancer to the back of my mind. Minor symptoms, common for someone in his mid-sixties, worry me a lot more than they should in case they are the harbingers of new disease. I try to dismiss them from my mind, then worry in case I'm foolishly neglecting something important. I guess I'm really getting insight into the lives of my former, apparently hypochondriacal, patients.

There are very few restrictions on me at present – I have to pop a minimum of four pills a day which goes up to a maximum of ten at times in the cycle. 'Sans' spleen and on chemotherapy, I get nervous about being coughed over or being in proximity of people with some bug or other as I'm at increased risk of developing infections and even life-threatening sepsis. Travel insurance for some parts of the world is horribly expensive but I can go to most of the places I want to go to. I just need a bit of courage to go to far-off places as the infection vulnerability makes me wary of some countries where bugs are said to abound and where there might not be very good medical facilities and hospitals.

The very best moments for Jane and me over the recent past have been sharing in the joy of seeing Theo grow from a baby to a toddler and having a part in looking after him. I've been really surprised by how extraordinary it feels having a grandchild – I know, another cliché – and how really special the times are when he's come to stay and been looked after by us. I had, at one stage, been a bit wary of getting too close to him lest I disappear very quickly but those feelings have been put aside and replaced with enthusiasm for having more grandchildren. Naturally, I want to see Laura, Patrick and Duncan, and their partners, develop and really enjoy their personal lives and careers and through Duncan I will keep a vicarious foothold in the medical world. There now even seems a chance that I could still see England win the World cup in 2022. I'd like to become a much better golfer but that may be only marginally less likely than a World Cup win.

I don't have a [before I kick the] 'bucket list' or any other unfulfilled ambitions other than to avoid the Grim Reaper for as long as possible so that I can grow at least a bit older with Jane. She has done everything she can for me, been to all the hospital appointments and given me the monthly injections. She got me through the operation and the period afterwards so well that I can hardly imagine how anyone could cope on their own. Resilience is needed for life and work – particularly in demanding stressful jobs like medicine. Having a resilient team around you as a patient undergoing the sort of experiences cancer patients have, makes it far easier to cope with the bungee experience.

Research shows that married men do in fact live longer than men on their own in my situation precisely because of 'the love of a good woman'.

My work has given me great satisfaction and I've met and treated some amazing people. One of the most remarkable was Gerald:

Gerald was a patient of one of my partners. He was a lovely man, very sociable and had been very successful in his career in business. He was 'a wise old Bird' and with his kindly disposition was always willing to give people the benefit of his experience if they sought his advice. His joie de vivre was such that people several decades younger than him sought out his company, inviting him to parties and social gatherings. He was very enterprising and smart, and when his wife became very frail and infirm, despite his age, he looked after her magnificently. Eventually Gerald became unwell and needed quite frequent visits. When my partner was unavailable, I deputised for him so visited Gerald quite a lot. Gerald was very stoical in his last weeks and retained his good humour right to the end. A few days later the surgery received 'a letter from heaven' written by Gerald.

'I expect you may all be a bit surprised to be reading a letter from beyond the grave but I did just want to thank you all one last time for the care you gave my wife and me.'

Everyone was delighted to read the letter which was typical of Gerald. Thoughtful, kind and appreciative – he had been well enough organised to write it, put a stamp on it and to ask one of his relatives to post it a couple of days after his burial. Remarkable.

Regarding the question as to whether it's harder or easier being a patient if you are medical: overall, I think it's harder but the experience of being a doctor, or a GP at any rate, taught me so much about life and death that I feel I am better prepared than I would have been if I had indeed become a travel agent.

I started the book by writing about the effect my patient Peter's wonderfully simple insight and description of the real purpose of life has had on me.

He lived another ten years before succumbing to a different form of cancer and lived his last days with all the dignity and integrity you'd have imagined he would.

He remains someone for me to try to emulate.

Chapter 35

The Last Chapter

Paul died on a beautiful sunny day, at home, on the afternoon of 29th April 2021. Patrick, Duncan and I were holding his hand.

Paul never wanted to talk about dying, other than to tell us he wanted to be at home, so we did everything we could to fulfil his wish. He was pain free and comfortable. When we realised the end of his life was imminent our job was to stay close, to talk softly and just be with him. We put on the soundtrack from the *Last of the Mohicans*, a favourite film and music that he had listened to as he trained for the marathon nine years earlier. As we watched his breathing slowing we prayed for him and told him how much we loved him. Tears streamed uncontrollably. As his life faded, we told him how he was loved so dearly and we toasted his life.

I felt as though my life ended with his that day.

Paul died in the way he had dealt with his diagnosis some four and a half years earlier. With quiet dignity, serenity and acceptance. He never complained about his condition. Remarkably he never talked of unfairness about his diagnosis. Never 'why me' only 'why not me'.

The last eleven days of Paul's life were surreal. The family were together, sitting with him, providing all the care he needed, playing music, watching a film whilst he was beside us. All of us in the sitting room, Paul on the hospital bed, several of us sitting on our bed that had been brought downstairs when he had become frail, some on the sofa, the two grandchildren coming and going.

After the palliative care teams visited him at home to tell him the results of the latest scans he said very little. But the love in the room was phenomenal. Our family came together in the most amazing way. We provided the care he needed. He was comfortable at home surrounded by the family he loved so much.

It helped that between us we had the skills and knowledge to be in that privileged position. We were there 24 hours a day. The care we gave him kept us with him, and him with us.

From the moment we were told the awful news it was like the world was happy to provide everything we needed to keep him at home for his final days. The palliative care team organised all the equipment we could possibly need and got it all delivered within a day. The nurses put up an infusion to give continuous pain relief. The GP visited and provided support and advice.

Our priest came and gave Paul the last rites. Two days later a school friend who is now a priest came to see him to say goodbye and again gave him the last rites. I know this would have provided comfort to Paul. Towards the end of his visit, Duncan asked if he would give him and Sarah, his fiancée, a blessing. He explained the pandemic had meant they had to postpone their wedding in May. Furthermore, because they had wanted Paul to be there a plan had been made to have a smaller wedding in our garden in November. That too had to be cancelled because of lockdown. The priest was so kind and accommodating. He agreed to let them make their vows explaining that they would not be legally married but Paul would be able to hear. Sarah ran upstairs and managed to change into a pretty dress and contact her mother and brother on Facetime so they too could be present. It was amazing. Duncan and Sarah knelt beside Paul and the three of us held his hand. Laura held the phones to keep those on Facetime in the picture, whilst taking photographs. Patrick had driven to his home earlier, before any of this had been dreamt of, to get his wife Lucia and children so they could say goodbye to Paul. Sadly, they only saw snatches on WhatsApp as he drove. Paul's nephew and his wife recorded the whole thing. Paul was quiet throughout. That was on the Thursday. He had hardly spoken since Monday but at the end of the blessing he quietly said 'Open the champagne Jane.' He had heard everything and I know he would have been thrilled.

So moving, so amazing, so, so wonderful.

Sadness and despair intermittently gave way to other exquisite moments. The time Patrick and Lucia brought our grandchildren Theo and Willow to Paul's bedside. Paul had only seen them three times in the last year and only at a distance because of the pandemic. His face lit up. The whole family witnessed that smile. Heart-wrenching and heart-warming.

There were days when Paul quietly let us know he wanted to join us all at the breakfast table. We managed to get him into a wheelchair and then transfer him to his favourite recliner brought from another room to make him comfortable. He didn't speak, he closed his eyes but he was with us and content. Another afternoon – the April weather had been particularly kind – he indicated he wanted to join us outside. Laura put a hat on his head to protect him from the sun and we took him out onto the patio to sit in the bright spring sunshine with all the family.

My most treasured memory of that time was when, after wheeling him to the bathroom we stopped for a while before getting him back to bed. He reached for me and just held me. So, so tenderly. Just him and me. He caressed my head and kissed me. He might not have spoken very much during these last days but he said goodbye and showed his love more than any words could. I told him I understood. The most powerful outpouring of love and leaving from my wonderful husband.

We were not alone, behind us all the children had noticed and stood with us.

Laura acted as the communications spokesperson and wrote some of the most moving emails I have ever read. So many people have told me how wonderful they were. She had returned from abroad and sat and held his hand and was with him, often reading kind words friends sent or passages from a book or gently talking to him. A few days after she returned she excitedly told us that her article 'Walking around Menorca: My lockdown project is never staying still' had been published in the Guardian. She told Paul who I know would have been over the moon. He had been gently encouraging her to write about her lockdown adventures.

All of the children helped me to provide the care he needed. Sarah, Duncan's fiancée was incredible, cooking and co-ordinating. Lucia, Patrick's wife, looked after the two small children and helped with everything. Friends brought in food, words of comfort and support. Marie Curie nurses, or angels, as we called them, came for three nights to allow us to sleep. We did sleep but all in the same room with Paul and ready to help or respond.

Those days were surreal. Exhausting and heart-breaking but possibly the most worthwhile of my life.

Paul wrote this book from 2017 until his chemotherapy treatment in 2019. He finished writing then, when he was feeling fairly well. He was hopeful, as he wrote earlier in the book, that he would see the 2022 World Cup. Sadly, that was not to be. Good times became peppered with less good times. Even on the bad days he was stoic and bravely accepting.

On the good days his usual sense of humour was prominent, he loved the funny side of life.

2020 was not a good year for many more reasons than the pandemic which, of course, limited his social contact and therefore support from friends and family who could no longer just pop in. He was immunocompromised, he was on chemotherapy, steroids and had no spleen making him more susceptible than most to any kind of infection let alone Coronavirus. Sadly, he died just as the lockdown was lifting.

During the pandemic he was quietly accepting of the lockdown and frequently said that he was happy just being at home. Us against the combined threat. Coronavirus had made managing the cancer worse in many ways and surprisingly better in others. Chemotherapy treatment was given at home, consultations were done via the telephone negating the rush to travel to London when Paul was really not well. Being confined to home meant that life was simpler. Just the two of us plus Zoom meetings, telephone calls and supermarket deliveries.

To return to where Paul left the reader.

Paul completed the six cycles of chemotherapy in 2019 with relatively few unwanted effects. Scans showed a partial response. On the whole life was good. He had his personal trainer, walked, cycled, played golf, saw family and friends. He did ordinary things and felt well.

Unfortunately, by January 2020 the disease process had increased again. Two of the liver metastases had grown significantly. Treatment was changed to a different chemotherapy.

In February, a transarterial embolisation of the rogue metastases was to be carried out. This procedure would hopefully cut off the blood supply to the two metastases thus causing them to shrink. The radiologist explained the procedure in great detail. Evidence showed that there were very few side effects and that Paul would be able to go home the following day. There will always be exceptions to evidence and Paul was sadly the exception. He was in a great deal of pain that night after the procedure and he went on to develop post-embolisation syndrome. This affected his heart causing pericarditis, his abdomen, causing pain and his general health. Later the scan showed that the embolisation had not provided as good a result as we had hoped.

In March 2020, immediately before lockdown, Paul was admitted to hospital. He had a great deal of pain following the pericarditis. He was also nauseated and had a temperature. During this admission I was able to visit each day which raised his spirits. As earlier, when he was in hospital he found having me there with him immensely reassuring. A week later no visitors were allowed in hospitals as the lockdown took hold.

In light of the lack of response of the rogue metastases from the embolisation and the change in chemotherapy, treatment was changed again.

This time Paul was prescribed the first type of chemotherapy but combined with the targeted treatment of PRRT this time intra-arterially. This was done in July 2020 and October 2020. The scans taken in December sadly showed further progression of the metastases despite the intervention.

By now we knew there was only one more throw of the dice. Six cycles on another chemotherapy (the last in the 'toolbox' of possible treatments for neuroendocrine cancer). This was administered at home every three weeks. Soon after the start of this intervention he developed sepsis. The paramedics were called and he was admitted to hospital for assessment. This admission was frightening for both of us. I could not accompany him into hospital because of the pandemic. Paul was unwell and weak and I knew he would have valued my presence. Luckily that admission was short.

Paul was just so determined to stay with me and the family as long as he could. He was brave, stoic and focused on getting well, optimistic that this might 'hold the line'. Three cycles in and he was becoming frail and tired. He continued his mantra – 'Jane we have just got to get through this'. His oncologist suggested an earlier scan to see if there was any response but Paul wanted to complete the six cycles.

Living with cancer is tough. When the pain kicked in he would hold my hand and say that he just had to get through it. No crying out, no anger, just he had to get through it. Together we managed the bad days. Sometimes just a hot bath would take the edge off the pain. Sometimes it didn't. Sometimes the morphine took such a long time to take hold of the pain and then I would massage his hand hoping the distraction would help. Sometimes he tried kneeling to take pressure off his abdomen. Usually we chatted or watched the television for the added distraction all the time waiting for the medication to take effect. Never, ever did he say anything negative. The stiff upper lip he had developed in his early life perhaps stood him in good stead to face this ultimate challenge.

The scan was carried out in London following the last treatment cycle. Paul, by this time was so frail I had to ask to stay with him (we were still in lockdown). The following day he had a blood transfusion in London. I saw a significant deterioration over those two days.

On return home I now knew I needed to contact the palliative care team at the hospice.

I didn't need to be told the result of the scans. I knew.

On Monday 19th April 2021 Paul too was told the results. I think he knew too but we had been bolstering each other with any possible positive signs…. until then. He lived another eleven days in a room filled with all the love in the world. The pain of saying goodbye was and is unbearable. He was my world.

The family were amazing. They all helped to care for Paul. They supported me and each other. I am incredibly proud of them all

Paul started this book with the story of Peter whose simple insight and description of the purpose of life he admired and tried to emulate. Paul lived his last days with all the dignity and integrity in the way that he had described Peter's end of life. Paul lived a successful life and he is missed so very much by me, his family and his friends. My husband was the best he could ever have been. He was, as one friend put it, a real 'one off'.

Appendix One: Effective Patient-ing

It's very difficult being a patient and you don't get training to become one, so I hope that a few tips or observations gleaned from my experiences as both a doctor and a patient may be useful.

The NHS is an amazing organisation and for the last seventy years has provided fantastic care for so many of us regardless of who we are or what we do. All my working life was spent in the NHS and I am very proud to have been a tiny part of it and have seen lots of extraordinary work done by incredibly dedicated and talented people. However, it is underfunded for what we expect of it and the gap between what can be done and what the government judges the taxpayer is willing to contribute to it, is ever widening.

So, what should you expect from the NHS as a patient?

You should and can expect the NHS and the people who work in it to do their very best on your behalf and to arrange to see and treat you as quickly as possible. Most patients declare themselves pretty satisfied with the service they get from it. You should not expect better care than the NHS can provide for everyone else so if there is a wait for something, however unpalatable that may be, you will usually have to wait. The government sets targets for waiting times for certain conditions, like being seen within a maximum of two weeks after a referral for suspected cancers, but these may only get you as far as your first appointment. Thereafter you can experience a frustratingly long hiatus before you get actual treatment because the waiting targets may not apply after your first specialist appointment. Usually delays in your treatment are not due to errors but just due to a lack of resources and it is dispiriting, to say the least, to be informed that the wait will be so long.

GPs can't control a lot of what happens even in their own practices and have even less power to control what happens in hospitals so don't assume your GP can just pick up the phone or write to your consultant to get you seen earlier, as used to happen in my early career. Your GP may be able to help, if the seriousness of the condition clearly demands an earlier appointment than you have been given, or if your condition significantly deteriorates while you are waiting to be seen, but otherwise she or he can rarely get you seen faster.

What if the delay seems wholly unacceptable and you cannot get around it? Should you complain or threaten to complain? Back in the day, the merest hint of a possible complaint could work wonders. Nobody wanted the rare experience of being the subject of a complaint. I occasionally wrote to the consultant and said 'I fear this patient may complain unless ...' fairly confident that it would lead to the desired outcome of an earlier treatment or clinic appointment for my patient. Nowadays doctors will not allow themselves to be driven by a complaint, let alone the threat of one. Indeed, the mindset might almost be 'bring it on... it's not my fault, it's the system, so if you do complain it may help us argue the case for more resources'.

Can your MP help? Almost certainly not. When I chaired a rationing appeals committee, we often had letters from a local MP checking that the correct procedures had been followed for their constituent, which invariably they had, so the MPs were rarely able to make any difference.

The official service for helping patients navigate the NHS, get advice and make complaints is called 'PALS' Patient Advice and Liaison service. It is certainly worth a try, although the feedback I got about PALS from patients was mixed.

So, given that you may have to wait longer than you expected to, it is vital that once you get into the system you get the very best you can from it and what follows are some suggestions as to how to do that.

The most important principle of your care is that ultimately you are in charge of it. No one else will, or indeed could, have as much invested in it as you. Your doctors cannot as they have to keep a professional distance and must treat everyone fairly and of course, they have lots of other patients – you just have you.

It can also make you feel better if you take some control of your own 'pathway.' You must be prepared and willing, to get actively involved at every point of your care. You will usually be sent a copy of the letters from the hospital that your GP receives. You will need to read these and keep them filed. If you don't receive a copy, ask the consultant's secretary for one and to be copied in with all future letters.

You need to be really well organised and aware of what is supposed to be happening so that you know if it hasn't occurred. Don't assume that your care is bound to happen smoothly and efficiently and be ready and willing to ring, write or email persistently, appointment departments, secretaries and your hospital doctors and GPs, if things are not happening the way they should be.

Mark was a patient of mine who probably taught me more about how to be a patient than anyone else. There was never any question of who was in charge of his treatment – he was. He had had a very successful career before getting stuck with cancer and he brought all his know-how and organisational skills into managing and monitoring his condition. He had an office at home devoted to the job in hand and assiduously checked all his blood results himself, having learnt what he needed to know about them and communicated quite frequently by email to his consultant oncologist and myself but always in a positive constructive way. He was very self-reliant and rarely came to the surgery – so much so that, even though he lived alone, before he died, I had only done one visit to his home. He knew what he wanted from life and right to the very end of it he ensured he was in charge. I have tried to emulate his approach but haven't got his sureness of touch, nor have I been as successful as him in knowing what's going on.

You can also ask your partner, family or a friend to help you with this work. The key is that someone needs to keep on top of it and it can be a fair amount of work. Hospital secretaries, in my experience, are pretty committed to what they do and are keen to help. They, however, are frequently so snowed under with work that if they answered their phones rather than put the answerphone on, they would never get any letters done. They sometimes resort to coming in really early so that they can have a good run at work before the phone starts ringing insistently and incessantly. In my experience it pays to try their numbers at eight o'clock in the morning, or even earlier.

It follows that whenever you are told what will happen next you need to ask the question of how long the wait will be and to ask your doctor to let you know if he or she doesn't have the information to hand.

Effective Communication is absolutely key to making the most of any service you use, and this is never truer than when you use the NHS. If you are attending a hospital clinic you are pretty well bound to be feeling stressed which greatly impairs your ability to take information on board and ask pertinent questions. It's well established that even in the best situations a patient will only recall a fraction of what he or she has been told in any given consultation. In the worst situations – when you have just been informed you have a very serious condition – your mind may go into shock and barely hear anything after that. Doctors know this and try to allow extra time to adjust for it and to write things down and check that you have understood things correctly, but still a lot of information will be lost. Depending on the diagnosis, the information imparted will naturally vary from consultation to consultation and sometimes may be brief but many times, when I asked what was said at a clinic, my patient said 'nothing' which is just not credible and suggests that they just didn't take on board what was said.

As a minimum, I'd suggest you need to understand what your diagnosis is or the options for what it might be if the doctor is not yet sure. You also need to know what treatment and next steps or 'investigations' are planned and how long they will take and, if surgery is recommended, what the operation entails and how long you should expect to wait.

In the midst of a stressful consultation how do you remember everything you need to have answers to? It comes back to the principle of being well organised. You need to prepare, quite carefully, for your consultation.

You should aim to have a list of a few key questions you need the answers to. Keep referring to that list during the consultation until all the questions have been addressed. Check that you have got the answers correct as well. If a friend or relative is able to come with you and write the answers down that can be very helpful. You can also ask all doctors that you have consultations with to explain again and help you understand some of the jargon.

When I first had my brain aneurysm diagnosed, Jane and I consulted a very experienced surgeon, who was a great authority on the condition, to get a feel about the whole issue. We took notes of what he said but a couple of months later we needed to see him again to talk about him operating on me. We looked at our notes but to our dismay couldn't make much sense of them! So, when we went back to see him, I asked for permission to record the consultation which was quite long and complex. Subsequently, I listened to the recording several times and really got a grasp of the situation. A recording of what was actually said can help enormously. I am a very strong advocate of recording consultations and have advised patients, friends and relatives to do this for quite a few years now. With smartphones, iPads and the like, it's very easy as they come with recording software, and this enables you to listen and re-listen to ensure you've captured all the information in the consultation. Trying to write stuff down in a consultation and really listen at the same time is far from easy and much less accurate than a recording. I record all my consultations because I know, from my own experience and that of my patients, and from research evidence, that only a small proportion of information at a consultation is recalled accurately by patients and I am anxious not to miss anything important. I know many people are reluctant to record consultations feeling it may be intrusive, but I believe it is well worth any initial awkwardness asking to do so may entail. You can also share it with trusted members of your family particularly if you don't fully understand what has been said. I wondered myself if it was disconcerting for my doctors and once asked my consultant, Michael if it was – he said absolutely not and mentioned that when he had first started in oncology patients were lent recorders so that they could make a tape of what had been said. He wasn't sure why the practice had stopped. Recording consultations doesn't guarantee that misunderstandings won't still occur, but they will be less frequent.

Not all doctors are as enlightened or confident as Michael, so some might feel a bit threatened in case they said something that was incorrect. I suppose this could lead to them adopting a cautious approach to a recorded consultation.

All doctors and all patients in all hospitals bemoan the lack of sufficient car parking so when you have an appointment, allow vastly more time for parking than you'd expect to need or get someone to drop you off. Better still, if your condition allows it, take a bus or taxi in. Don't assume that you will be seen on time as you might expect to for a solicitor's appointment – the NHS is not a properly-funded commercial business – so don't plan something else that matters soon after your appointment time or you will just add extra stress.

Rather like flights, many clinics are often overbooked to allow for patients who don't turn up for the clinic. You should have a reasonably long appointment particularly if it is the first one at the clinic, but it may be foreshortened by an emergency or for any number of other reasons, so being well-prepared is essential to get the most out of the time available. Difficult as it may be, you need to try to ensure you still get enough time to get the answers you need.

When you see a doctor in a hospital clinic, the first thing to make a note of is their name and whether that doctor is a consultant, registrar or SHO (senior house officer). You need to know whose clinic you are attending, as a consultant's name will always be assigned to a clinic. If you subsequently need to find out something about your treatment that information will make it much easier to track it down. Knowing the names of your doctors, nurses or other health professionals, makes your relationship with them more human and reciprocal, which can only be a good thing for everyone

All GPs and consultants will be paid a reasonable salary and patients have every right to expect good and courteous treatment. Period. It goes without saying that courtesy works both ways. This obviously applies also to nurses and auxiliary staff, who will be caring for you in your most painful and vulnerable moments but are often assumed to be 'just doing their job'. A 'thank you' is a good idea in any walk of life as everyone wants to feel appreciated for their efforts. Giving presents is quite unnecessary and can even lead to problems:

Mary was very old school and had lived a considerable part of her long life before the NHS existed. Whenever her daughter brought her to see me for a check on her blood pressure and heart, she always ended the consultation by giving me a miniature bottle of whisky. I really dislike whisky, but I appreciated the gesture and after many fruitless attempts to stop her, accepted that it felt important to her to give me something. I always thanked her profusely then slipped the whisky into the bottom right hand drawer of my desk. Eventually there was a sizeable collection of bottles. One day a patient needed a relaxation tape which I kept in the same drawer. As I opened it I saw her eyes widen at the sight of all the bottles. I judged it better not to try to explain what she had seen as I felt pretty certain from her demeanour that she would feel 'he doth protest too much'. She never consulted me again having obviously concluded, that I was a whisky-drinking alcoholic. I gave the bottles away after that. Eventually Mary became too infirm to manage to come to the surgery, so I visited her at her home and at the end of each visit the mandatory whisky miniature was given to me as a token of thanks. This time however on the way down the stairs I gave it back to her daughter who re-cycled the one bottle on many occasions till Mary's death.

Appendix Two: All about Neuroendocrine Cancer

It has taken me a long time to get a 'feel' for what neuroendocrine cancers are about, partly because of their rarity and partly because there are such a wide range of different types affecting different parts of the body, some producing lots of symptoms and some none at all until they have grown really quite large, so there is a lot to get one's head around. I am still learning. This isn't a medical textbook so I will take a few shortcuts (or liberties depending on your point of view) to keep this section short. For a much fuller and better description of neuroendocrine cancer please visit www.neuroendocrinecancer.org.uk.

The first thing to say is that neuroendocrine tumours (NETs) and neuroendocrine carcinomas (NECs) are both cancers. NECs are just more aggressive than NETs. They are both neuroendocrine cancers. Normally 'cancer' and 'carcinoma' are used interchangeably to mean a malignant condition so this is a bit unfortunate but there it is. I will elaborate on this shortly.

NETs and NECs are cancers that affect neuroendocrine cells in the body. These cells produce hormones and other chemicals essential for the body to function when stimulated by nerves. They can be found in the brain, the skin, the breasts, liver, the adrenal glands, the thyroid, the lungs, the pancreas, the stomach, the small and large bowel, the appendix, ovaries, testes, prostate and rectum. NETs and NECs may occur in all those parts of the body. NETs in particular, may produce an excess of one particular type of hormone or another depending on the part of the body affected so, for example, if the pancreas is affected too much insulin may be produced causing the blood sugar level to be abnormally low, causing sweating, hunger, dizziness, confusion and irritability and if severe even loss of consciousness or a fit. There is a very wide range of other symptoms that can occur as a result of abnormal hormone production. In some patients no hormones are produced at all and the NET may just grow very slowly and undramatically so that a patient – like me – may be blissfully unaware anything is wrong until the tumour has grown quite large and spread far and wide. Indeed, with pancreatic NETs that don't produce excessive hormones, over half of patients already have spread or metastasised to the liver when they are first diagnosed.

How rare is rare? The neuroendocrine cancer UK website describes 6000 people a year or about 17 people a day being diagnosed with a NET or NEC in England. That compares with almost 40,000 men being diagnosed with prostate cancer every year (109 a day) in England and over 46,000 cases of breast cancer (126 people a day).

Put another way, that is just over nine new cases occur in the UK per 100,000 population. Although only a relatively small number of people are diagnosed with neuroendocrine cancer, because they may survive for longer than those diagnosed with other cancers the number of patients living with a NET or NEC at any one time is relatively high and there may be as many as 30,000 people in the UK currently diagnosed – a higher prevalence than gastric cancer, myeloma and Non-Hodgkin's Lymphoma.

NETs and NECs are being diagnosed far more frequently now than in the past with evidently almost eight times the number detected in 2015 as was the case in 1973. This is partly because ever more is being learnt about them and doctors are becoming more aware of them than hitherto and have more sophisticated tests for this varied form of cancer. Additionally, there is generally more screening and other scans being done leading to small, symptomless tumours being diagnosed by chance. Because neuroendocrine cancers, by individual type, are rare it follows that harnessing as much expertise as possible in a multidisciplinary team is particularly importance to get the best outcome for the patients.

The cause of neuroendocrine cancers in the vast majority of cases is simply not known. They can run in families, may be commoner in smokers and in families that tend to get cancer but, in most cases like mine, there is no clear reason.

Diagnosis can be difficult and not infrequently, particularly with bowel NETs, the diagnosis may not be made for several years after the first symptoms appear. This is because the standard tests doctors do for bowel symptoms may not reveal a definite cause so irritable bowel may be diagnosed and treated. Indeed, patients may have both as irritable bowel is common so there is bound to be some overlap.

I thought the fact that I had been initially diagnosed with something which later turned out not to be the case, would be really unusual and interesting for people to read about, particularly given that I was a doctor. However, talking to other neuroendocrine cancer patients, it became clear to me that it was quite common for patients to be given a diagnosis, which later, and sometimes a lot later than in my case, was changed to a NET or NEC.

It's a truism amongst doctors, that rare conditions often take a disproportionately long time to be diagnosed. There is, as yet, no useful or practical screening test available in the UK.

Grading of Neuroendocrine Cancers

In some of the commoner cancers like breast, prostate, bowel and lung cancers a large percentage of the cancer cells will be growing actively whereas as few as 1% of neuroendocrine cancer cells may be active, which is why the cancer may be present for a long time before it grows to a size that causes symptoms. Neuroendocrine cancers are 'graded' or given a mark, as it were, by the experts based on how many cells are actively dividing with grade 1 NETs having the least number of actively dividing calls and grade 3 NECs having the highest number and so are generally or usually at least, the worst ones to have. Michael memorably said to me that 'NETs haven't read the (cancer) rulebook' meaning that they don't necessarily behave in as predictable a way as other cancers do so that you can't altogether rely on the grade your tumour is. A grade 1 or 2 NET may behave more aggressively than expected, according to its grading – after all it hasn't read the rules, so doesn't necessarily behave as it's supposed to.

Differentiation of Neuroendocrine Cancers

This is a term that describes what the cancer cells look like under a microscope. Put simplistically – if the cancer cells don't look all that different to normal cells – they are said to be 'well differentiated.' If they look very different to normal cells they are described as 'poorly differentiated.'

It is better if the cancer cells are 'well differentiated' (I tend to remember this as being almost synonymous with 'well behaved' with poorly differentiated conversely being 'poorly or badly behaved).' Like all generalisations it has its limits and so called 'well differentiated NETs' can, like mine, be rather badly behaved.

It will hopefully be apparent that the more aggressive type of neuroendocrine cancer is a grade 3 one which is 'poorly differentiated' This combination is called a neuroendocrine carcinoma.

All other combinations are called neuroendocrine tumours.

Staging of Neuroendocrine Cancers

The stage a NET or NEC is at can also predict, to some extent, what a patient's prognosis may be. The stage basically describes whether the tumour has spread or 'metastasised' and if so, how far and wide and also gives an idea of size. Obviously, it is far better if it hasn't spread at all and is very small. Stages vary from stage 1: Where there is a single cancer that is less than 1 cm in size and hasn't spread anywhere, to stage 4: where the cancer has spread to distant parts of the body like the liver and to one or more lymph nodes.

So generally, the best prognosis would be to have a grade 1 stage 1 NET and conversely the worst would be a grade 3 stage 4 NEC.

I have a grade 2 stage 4 NET so by no means the worst but far from the best prognosis, though benchmarked against a stage 4 stomach cancer, which was thought initially to be my diagnosis, it's a far better position to be in.

There are other factors that affect prognosis but for the sake of brevity I'm not going to attempt to describe them all. Early in the course of my treatment Michael said that after monitoring how my particular NET behaved, he would get a 'feel', from his many years of experience of managing them, about my prognosis. What this meant in my case was, that because the disease recurred relatively quickly after the PRRT treatment, the prognosis was unlikely to be as good as in some of his patients who had the same stage and grade as me who had lived over ten years with their NETs.

One of the things that greatly troubled me for a long time was how could someone like me, a practising, very experienced doctor and someone who was into leading a healthy lifestyle, be so unaware of what was going on in his own body that by the time I went to see my GP I had a large tumour in my abdomen with extensive spread to my liver? Surely, I reproached myself, I must have had some symptoms that I'd overlooked? When initially told about my condition a lot of people obviously thought the same thing too. The simple truth was that I hadn't been aware of anything amiss until a few weeks before I was diagnosed. It was something of a cold comfort to find that the majority of patients with my type of NET also had metastases in the liver when they were diagnosed. The reason for this is that often the tumour grows slowly so that the body accommodates to it, giving it a chance to spread until it gets to a critical size that eventually causes some symptoms. In other words, you don't really get much of a chance. On the other hand, you could reasonably argue, that's better than having a rapidly growing cancer that causes symptoms early which will continue to grow rapidly once it's been diagnosed.

As Richard in Chapter 30 explained, there are lots of different treatment options in addition to the surgery, PRRT and injections I have had to date. A discussion of these is beyond the scope of this book, and definitely way beyond the knowledge of the author. For far better and more detailed information I suggest you go to the Neuroendocrine Cancer UK website www.neuroendocrinecancer.org.uk where there is more information which is well-written and from which I have unashamedly, but with permission, taken large chunks for this chapter.

Since diagnosis, I have struggled to get a feel for how serious neuroendocrine cancers are and specifically how serious my own one is. In hindsight, I guess it was because all my experience as a GP seemed to be saying that if you have a stage 4 cancer you are in terrible trouble, but the message I was getting was that with my NETs that isn't necessarily the case.

If you are reasonably lucky you could live for quite a few years with a NET but by no means everyone does. Although my own NET has unfortunately not been one of the slow growing ones there are lots of treatment options still available, which could hold things for a few and possibly even quite a few years to come. If I'm lucky.

Neuroendocrine cancer website

Living with this level of uncertainty is not easy, but there is help available. neuroendocrine cancer UK (www.neuroendocrinecancer.org.uk), as well as being an invaluable source of information, is a charity that supports neuroendocrine cancer (both NET and NEC patients) and their families and works to improve awareness of the conditions. The charity organises regular patient support meetings in different venues throughout the UK which they call 'NCUK Natters.' The Oxford NET unit, run regular 'Natters' meetings in Oxford.

Specialist Cancer Nurses and NET Natters (Support Groups)

The www.neuroendocrinecancer.org.uk website encouraged new patients in the Oxford area to contact Phil, the neuroendocrine specialist cancer nurse. Sam, the palliative care nurse who visited us had also recommended him to us. It appeared that Phil supported both the patients and the specialist medical team so was a key person in the unit. All roads seemed to lead to Phil, so I emailed him to see if I might come and see him to get a better feel for my somewhat bewildering NET, and he invited Jane and me to his office in Oxford. Jane knew him slightly from Oxford Brookes University. He was warm and friendly with the sort of good 'people skills' that all teachers and lecturers need to have. Over the space of about an hour we learnt more from him about my diagnosis than we had managed to find out for ourselves or gathered from consultations with the doctors or nurses who had treated me. He was extremely helpful and seemed really knowledgeable. Phil has subsequently been a great source of support.

He encouraged us to come along to the 'Natter' meetings which he organises. Although I've advised literally hundreds of patients to seek information and support about their illnesses from the relevant patient support group and given them contact information, I hadn't thought that sort of thing was really for me and nor had Jane been keen on the idea. I suppose I thought I would know enough from my work about any given condition or know where to get information about it without needing to go to a group. Additionally, the stiff-upper-lipped independent me thought I didn't need group support and would be uncomfortable in a group setting. So, it was with some misgivings that I thought I ought to at least give them a go and a few weeks later Jane and I attended the meeting which was held in the Maggie's Centre.

There were, I thought, a surprising number of people present for a rare cancer group, maybe thirty or forty, and after a welcome from Phil there was a talk from the professor who led the specialist team. He was a very down to earth, unassuming man and he talked about neuroendocrine cancers, specifically NETs often being a 'chronic condition' meaning something patients had for a long time. Over tea and cake after his talk, I checked that I had understood that concept properly. He confirmed that was often, but not by any means always, the case which was of course encouraging from where I stood. Neuroendocrine cancer patients are an eclectic lot because this group of cancers affect so many different areas of the body and cause so many different symptoms so that although it is enjoyable meeting people, I have yet to meet anyone with quite the same mix of elements as my disease. Going to the meeting had been well worthwhile and Jane and I subsequently now go to all the meetings we can.

Neuroendocrine Cancer Research

At another meeting the CEO of the www.neuroendocrinecancer.org.uk asked for a volunteer to go to a medical meeting in London as a patient representative. There weren't any other volunteers, so I got the 'gig' and have subsequently attended a few meetings of the National Cancer Research Institute's – NCRI – neuroendocrine cancer sub-committee, where leading experts in this field meet and discuss what research they are doing. I'm sometimes asked what I think about a particular research trial set-up from a patient perspective whether patients would be happy to enroll and that sort of thing. I can only really speak for what I would personally feel of course. As a former 'coal-face Doc' this is a world of medicine that I had very little involvement with and it's ironic that I'm much more involved with it as a patient than I ever was when working.

One of the common misconceptions is that because neuroendocrine cancers are rare, you assume very little research is being done on the condition. You might even wish that you had a far commoner cancer on which far more research is being done on the assumption that a 'cure', or at least significant improvement in treatment, may emerge soon enough for you to benefit. In fact, the NCRI meetings revealed that there is far more research being done in the UK than I'd imagined, which was heartening.

Outside of the UK there is a great deal more research being done and every year there is a very large meeting held in Barcelona, the European NETs conference or ENETS, at which world-wide knowledge and the latest research is shared and discussed. To my surprise, I was asked to speak briefly at that meeting as a patient representative, where I also got the opportunity to give a GP's perspective about this disease. It was also very heartening to realise that there are very strong patient support groups in many other parts of the world, and I met patient reps from Israel, America, Holland, Australia and the UK. The global picture that emerged showed some inequalities; for example, monthly injections like I had are not available to 80% of the population of Brazil and PRRT is even less freely available worldwide and the latest high powered most accurate gallium scans are not even available in all specialist centres of excellence in the UK. Neuroendocrine cancer specialist cancer nurses are rare in some parts of the world – amazingly there are only two in the whole of Australia, one of whom spoke very eloquently at the Barcelona meeting. The Royal Free NET lead spoke very impressively and showed their very well-worked-outpatient pathway and explained how they try to ensure patients get the information and services needed for optimal care. It was Richard. I came away from the conference feeling that although, as a still rare cancer, neuroendocrine cancers, NECs and NETs, get far less funding than required, nevertheless there is a determination among some very impressive people to raise standards of care throughout the world.

Printed in Great Britain
by Amazon

81990742R00144